ECLIPSE DISTILLED

eclipse
the eclipse series

SERIES EDITORS Erich Gamma ▪ Lee Nackman ▪ John Wiegand

Eclipse is a universal tool platform, an open extensible integrated development environment (IDE) for anything and nothing in particular. Eclipse represents one of the most exciting initiatives hatched from the world of application development in a long time, and it has the considerable support of the leading companies and organizations in the technology sector. Eclipse is gaining widespread acceptance in both the commercial and academic arenas.

The Eclipse Series from Addison-Wesley is the definitive series of books dedicated to the Eclipse platform. Books in the series promise to bring you the key technical information you need to analyze Eclipse, high-quality insight into this powerful technology, and the practical advice you need to build tools to support this evolutionary Open Source platform. Leading experts Erich Gamma, Lee Nackman, and John Wiegand are the series editors.

Titles in the Eclipse Series

John Arthorne and Chris Laffra, *Official Eclipse 3.0 FAQs*, 0-321-26838-5

Kent Beck and Erich Gamma, *Contributing to Eclipse: Principles, Patterns, and Plug-Ins*, 0-321-20575-8

Frank Budinsky, David Steinberg, Ed Merks, Ray Ellersick, and Timothy J. Grose, *Eclipse Modeling Framework*, 0-131-42542-0

Eric Clayberg and Dan Rubel, *Eclipse: Building Commercial-Quality Plug-Ins*, 0-321-22847-2

Steve Northover and Mike Wilson, *SWT: The Standard Widget Toolkit, Volume 1*, 0-321-25663-8

ECLIPSE DISTILLED

David Carlson

↭Addison-Wesley

*Upper Saddle River, NJ • Boston • Indianapolis • San Francisco
New York • Toronto • Montreal • London • Munich • Paris • Madrid
Capetown • Sydney • Tokyo • Singapore • Mexico City*

The publisher offers excellent discounts on this book when ordered in quantity for bulk purchases or special sales, which may include electronic versions and/or custom covers and content particular to your business, training goals, marketing focus, and branding interests. For more information, please contact:

> U. S. Corporate and Government Sales
> (800) 382-3419
> corpsales@pearsontechgroup.com

For sales outside the U. S., please contact:

> International Sales
> international@pearsoned.com

Visit us on the Web: www.awprofessional.com

Library of Congress Number: 2004115820

ISBN 0-32-128815-7
Text printed in the United States on recycled paper at Phoenix Book Tech.
First printing, February 2005

Contents

About the Author

David Carlson has a Ph.D. in Information Systems from the University of Arizona (1991), specializing in knowledge-based systems and object-oriented technology. He has more than 20 years of experience in systems design, programming, and business analysis and was an Assistant Professor of Information Systems at the University of Colorado in Boulder prior to returning to the consulting profession in 1994. Dave is currently a self-employed consultant working in Boulder, Colorado.

David Carlson is also the author of *Modeling XML Applications with UML: Practical e-Business Applications* (Addison-Wesley, 2001). He designed and implemented an Eclipse plug-in called *hyper*Model that implements the design concepts from his previous book.

Foreword

Every artisan in every craft employs tools that extend and amplify the craftsman and through which their creativity is made manifest. For the code warrior, the integrated development environment (IDE) is typically home, the place in which and with which all work is carried out. The IDE is therefore at the center of the developer experience in building, deploying, and evolving quality software-intensive systems.

Over the past several decades, resources for the developer have evolved from command-line tools to disparate desktop tools to the integrated experience we take for granted today. Eclipse is perhaps the most important realization of that experience: not only is the Eclipse platform a powerful foundation for development, but as an open source application it is also a broadly supported and extensible home for developers of all domains working in a variety of languages.

Eclipse is indeed a rich platform, but as such it may appear far too rich for those developers who simply want to carry out the essential tasks of development. In this book, Dave does an excellent job presenting the most important and most common-use cases for Eclipse: installation, programming and refactoring, debugging, testing, configuring, and releasing. It is all too easy for this genre of book to be little more than extended product documentation, but Dave does far more by offering a conceptual model of Eclipse as well as very detailed and visually approachable scenarios for using the platform in an agile context by individuals as well as by teams. Dave also addresses the creature comforts and daily hygiene provided by Eclipse, through which the developer experience may be customized to the particular needs of the individual.

For the novice, you'll find this book to be a gentle yet firm guide to the essentials of Eclipse. For the experienced user—well, I've been using Eclipse myself for some time, and I discovered a number of useful things that have shaved a few rough edges in my use of the IDE.

Grady Booch
IBM Fellow

Preface

This is the book I wanted to read when I started using Eclipse three years ago. The book didn't exist—until now. It's different from other books that assume you know nothing, but it does not leave you hanging if subjects such as JUnit or CVS are unfamiliar. If you are experienced in Java development or are already working with Eclipse, you'll still benefit from a clear description and examples that can turn you into a power user. This book distills the extensive features and preference settings so that Eclipse becomes the indispensable tool it has become for me.

The topics presented in *Eclipse Distilled* are essential knowledge for anyone using Eclipse to develop Java applications, whether you are creating new plug-ins that extend Eclipse or building and testing enterprise applications. Other books have been written about developing new plug-in contributions for Eclipse (see references at the end of Chapter 1). This book is about *using* Eclipse. In it, we work on an order management and product catalog application while learning Eclipse.

Many project teams are striving to become more agile by following an iterative development process and accommodating new or changing requirements throughout the lifecycle. Your team may be following a specific methodology, such as Extreme Programming (XP), or customizing a set of agile development practices suited to your organization's culture and project requirements. Successful agile development requires a combination of management practices and software development practices. This book describes specific capabilities that are designed into Eclipse to support agile development while writing, building, and testing your code.

This book is based on my personal experiences and those of others around me while using Eclipse to build production code. I've monitored the Eclipse newsgroups for three years, and I've included answers to common questions and misunderstandings in this book. While distilling these topics I tried to convey a deeper insight into how Eclipse works and how you can use it in the most productive way.

You will benefit from *Eclipse Distilled* if

- ○ You are developing any kind of Java application and are either new to Java or already an expert. You'll step through wizards while creating and running your first Java project and use the advanced capabilities while debugging, unit testing, and more.

- ○ You are creating new plug-ins for Eclipse and need a deeper understanding about how Eclipse works and how it is used for professional development. The most successful plug-ins fit seamlessly into the natural flow of activities performed by Eclipse users.

- ○ You are applying agile development practices or would like to do so. Even if you are part of a traditional, non-agile project team, you can still benefit from applying unit testing, refactoring, and continuous integration to your deliverables.

- ○ You really don't care about methodology but want expertise in Eclipse that only comes from a deeper understanding of how it was intended to be used.

- ○ You are a college student using Eclipse for a class project. Having access to an open source development tool with these capabilities allows more complete, realistic assignments and team projects, and it prepares you for quick transition into your first job.

Roadmap for this Book

Eclipse Distilled is organized into two parts to help you find answers quickly, whether you are new to Eclipse or an experienced user looking for deeper insight. This book is written so that the chapters can be read in sequence, but you can also jump ahead to specialized topics in Part 2 and return to any chapter for future reference.

Part 1: Getting Started

These first seven chapters give you a solid understanding of how the Eclipse IDE is organized and how it works. The explanation is not simply a series of screen images; we methodically step through the details of organizing your workspaces and projects, customizing your perspectives and views, and leveraging the Java editor for rapid development and code navigation. You will learn how to debug local and remote Java applications by stepping through multi-threaded execution, displaying and changing variable values, exploring object structures, and evaluating code snippets in the context of a suspended thread.

New users should study Part 1 carefully to understand how the Eclipse IDE is organized and how to configure Java projects and gain optimal use of the editor's features. Eclipse often has several ways to accomplish a task. The choice among these alternatives is sometimes based on personal work preferences, and at other times it is guided by the structure and complexity of your projects. I don't attempt to list all possible alternatives, but instead I present an approach based on common practice in Eclipse and describe alternatives in some cases.

Experienced Eclipse users may still find useful insight within Part 1, or they may proceed directly to Part 2.

Part 2: Getting Agile

Eclipse itself was created using an agile development process and includes features that add agility to any development effort. The rest of us benefit from the fact that creators of Eclipse have added tools to make their own lives easier and more productive.

Chapter 8 introduces the principals of agile development and its use of iterative development cycles. Each remaining chapter in this section focuses on one aspect of agile development and how to accomplish it within the Eclipse IDE. You could read these chapters in any order or jump straight into one of these chapters before finishing Part 1. For example, if you are joining an established project team, you may not create your own Java project from scratch. Instead, you'll check out projects from a repository such as CVS. In that case, you should read through Chapter 13 earlier in your study. Other chapters in Part 2 cover continuous testing with JUnit, refactoring, continuous integration with Ant, and coding standards.

Chapter 9 explains how to enhance the Eclipse workbench with new or updated plug-ins. The integrated Update Manager allows you to search local or remote sites for compatible plug-ins, schedule automatic updates, and manage your workbench configuration. Several hundred plug-in contributions are available, and the rate of new plug-in creation is accelerating.

The Road Ahead

In February 2004 the Eclipse community was reorganized into a not-for-profit corporation named the Eclipse Foundation. The initial open source contribution came from IBM in November 2001. Its future is now governed by an independent body whose charter is to advance the creation, evolution, promotion, and support of the Eclipse Platform and to cultivate both an open source community and an ecosystem of complementary products, capabilities, and services. All technology and source code provided to this fast-growing ecosystem will remain openly available and royalty-free.

Eclipse continues to grow in breadth and depth, moving faster than most people expected for an open source community project. Many open source contributions are under development, as are many commercial products that build on the foundation provided by this platform. It's getting harder to answer the question, "What is Eclipse?" But there's no doubt that the road ahead will be fast and exciting.

Conventions Used in this Book

The following formatting conventions are used throughout the book:

Bold—Used for the names of UI elements such as menus, buttons, field labels, tabs, and window titles.

Italic—Used for emphasizing new terms and web URLs.

`Courier`—Used for code examples, references to class and method names, and filenames.

`Courier Bold`—Used to emphasize code elements.

"Quoted text"—Used for text to be entered by the user.

Acknowedgments

Special thanks to Simon Archer, who went beyond the call of duty to provide very helpful, detailed comments on every chapter. Also thanks for review and comments by Luc Bourlier, Jared Burns, Kevin Geminiuc, Prashant Rane, Darin Swanson, and John Wiegand.

Thanks to Rally Software Development for their valuable input on agile development processes and best practices for iterative development. Text and diagrams from their white paper are used in Chapter 8.

Thanks to John Neidhart, Gina Kanouse, Ben Lawson, and Michael Thurston at Pearson Technology Group for making this book a reality.

PART I

Getting Started

These chapters give you a solid understanding of how the Eclipse IDE is organized and how it works. We methodically step through the details of organizing your workspaces and projects, customizing your perspectives and views, leveraging the Java editor for rapid development and code navigation, configuring Java projects, and using the debugger.

CHAPTER 1

A Java IDE and So Much More!

Looking at Eclipse is similar to looking at a well-cut diamond. What you see depends on the angle of your view and on how deeply you gaze into the interior. To some viewers Eclipse is a Java IDE with the usual features one expects from such an environment: editor, debugger, and project builder with a wide array of preference customizations. To others Eclipse is a generic framework for tool integration providing an extensive, flexible plug-in API. The *www.eclipse.org* home page declares that "Eclipse is a kind of universal tool platform—an open extensible IDE for anything and nothing in particular."

Both perspectives are valid interpretations. As the Eclipse community continues its rapid expansion, other users will see it as a modeling tool, a business rules management application, a business process designer, a development environment for embedded systems written in C++, or an HTML authoring and document management environment. Using the Rich Client Platform (RCP) configuration, Eclipse is the basis for any end-user client application.

Many books have been and will be written to describe each facet of the Eclipse diamond. This book focuses on Eclipse as an integrated development environment for building Java applications. Those applications may be other open source utilities, large enterprise systems, or new plug-ins for Eclipse. This book is equally applicable to each of those project teams and individuals.

Eclipse is developed by and for teams using a modern, agile development process. Eclipse is developed using Eclipse in a large, distributed team and with an iterative approach that rebuilds and tests the entire project every night. As a result, Eclipse is well suited to any project using these methods. This book describes several best practices common to agile development teams and explains in detail how Eclipse assists you in those tasks.

In this chapter, we'll view these facets of Eclipse:

○ Building blocks of the Eclipse platform architecture.

○ Development components provided by other Eclipse projects.

○ Alignment of Eclipse with the principles of agile development.

1.1 Eclipse Platform Architecture

Given the wide-ranging interpretations of Eclipse, it is difficult to present a quick summary of its architecture. The most general description is an abstract view of the development and runtime environment for creating and deploying plug-in contributions. Alternatively, we can take a functional view that describes Eclipse as a flexible, extensible integrated development environment (IDE). We'll take the latter viewpoint and focus our attention on how Eclipse provides an unparalleled opportunity to improve productivity of software development work.

The Eclipse IDE is as follows:

○ **Multi-platform.** The target operating systems of Eclipse 3.0 are Windows, Linux (motif and GTK), Solaris, AIX, HP-UX, and Mac OSX.

○ **Multi-language.** Eclipse is developed using the Java language, but it supports writing applications in Java, C/C++, and Cobol; additional language support is being developed for Python, Perl, PHP, and others. Plug-in contributions to Eclipse must be written in Java.

○ **Multi-role.** In addition to programming activities, Eclipse supports modeling, testing, Web authoring, and many other roles.

The functional building blocks of the Eclipse IDE are illustrated in Figure 1-1. Each block added to the structure builds on the foundation of those below it. It's this modular nature of the Eclipse platform that has led to its unprecedented growth. The entire platform is open source and royalty-free for other open source or commercial products that add new building blocks.

The shaded blocks represent this book's focus. However, along the way we'll review other contributed plug-ins that enhance the platform's capabilities for specialized tasks. Examples are unit-testing frameworks for Web-based applications, static code analysis tools, and a style checker that ensures consistent use of coding standards.

The next several sections introduce each of the building blocks shown in Figure 1-1.

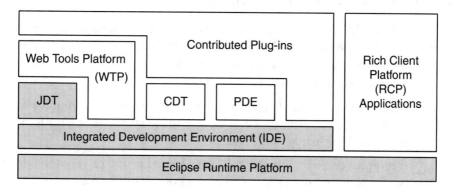

Figure 1-1   Functional building blocks of the Eclipse development environment.

1.1.1 Eclipse Runtime Platform

The core runtime platform provides the most basic level of services:

- ○ **Plug-in registry.** Loading plug-ins and managing a registry of available plug-ins.

- ○ **Resources.** Managing a platform-independent view of operating system files and folders, including linked resource locations.

- ○ **UI components.** The Eclipse user interface components are based on SWT and JFace libraries.

- ○ **Update facility.** Eclipse applications have built-in support for installing and updating plug-ins from URL addressable locations, including remote Internet sites.

- ○ **Help facility.** A common help facility is shared by all plug-ins.

The Eclipse model for platform-independent resources is an important foundation for representing projects, folders, and files in an IDE; we review this in Chapter 3, "Managing Your Projects." The update facility assists you in customizing your IDE with new plug-in contributions; we review it in Chapter 9, "Updating the Eclipse IDE."

All of these basic services are implemented as plug-ins on a very small kernel. The Eclipse design makes everything a plug-in. The intent was to treat all developers (and all plug-ins) the same. This ensures that the facilities are both sufficient for the platform itself and for any clients.

1.1.2 Integrated Development Environment

The Eclipse IDE provides a common user experience across multi-language and multi-role development activities. Other contributed plug-ins that build on this IDE foundation don't need to reinvent the wheel.

The most significant IDE features are as follows:

- **Shared views.** Many Eclipse features share the use of common views for displaying and editing properties, for listing syntax problems found in the code, and for listing work tasks.

- **Perspectives.** A perspective collects a related group of views in a layout suited to particular tasks, such as Java development, debugging, and version control.

- **Preferences.** A centralized dialog gathers preference setting pages for all plug-ins installed in the workbench.

- **Search engine.** The platform search engine provides general capabilities for searching resources and presenting results. This facility can be extended with resource-specific search criteria, e.g., for Java, C++, or UML model resources.

- **Debugging.** Defines a language-independent debug model and UI classes for building debuggers and launchers.

- **Ant project build files.** Ant provides general-purpose, flexible build services that can be extended with specialized tasks. The IDE includes an Ant editor and runtime configuration.

- **Team-oriented.** Eclipse provides a generic API for integration with version control repositories. Complete support for CVS is included, and plug-ins are available for other vendors' repositories.

In Chapter 4, "Customizing Your Workbench," we'll study the use of Eclipse perspectives, views, and preferences. The debugger is covered in Chapter 7, "Debugging Your Code," and Ant build files are used in Chapter 12, "Continuous Integration with Ant." The team-oriented capabilities are covered in Chapter 13, "Team Ownership with CVS."

There are additional Eclipse IDE features that are not provided in a generic way by the platform, but users have learned to expect the following capabilities in editors:

- **Synchronized editor and outline.** An outline displays a hierarchical list of constructs in the file being edited. Select an outline item to position the editor at the corresponding location.

○ **Content Assist.** The editor suggests appropriate content to be inserted at the cursor location when the **Ctrl+Space** key combination is pressed.

○ **Templates.** Code or other text patterns (such as a Java `for` loop or an HTML `table`) are defined in templates that are inserted into a file as part of Content Assist.

○ **Formatter.** Syntactic formatting rules are defined and customized in preference settings and are applied to editor selections or entire files.

○ **Problems identified on-the-fly.** Errors or warnings are identified while typing in the editor and are highlighted by icons and messages in the ruler at the editor left margin.

We'll use these features while studying the Java editor in Chapter 5, "Rapid Development," and then we'll see them again while using the Ant build file editor in Chapter 12.

1.1.2.1 Java Development Tools

Java Development Tools (JDT) are the only programming language plug-ins included with the Eclipse SDK. However, other language tools are available or under development by Eclipse subprojects and plug-in contributors. The Eclipse Java development perspective is shown in Figure 1-2.

Fundamental capabilities provided by the Java tools include the following:

○ **Editor, outline, Content Assist, templates, and formatting.** These general editor features are provided for Java source files.

○ **Java views.** Several views are provided for navigating and managing Java projects. The Package Explorer view is the cornerstone of the Java perspective, and a specialized Java Browsing perspective assists developers in understanding and navigating large, multi-project applications.

○ **Project Configuration.** Extensive support is included for configuring Java project classpaths, dependencies, libraries, compiler options, and many other characteristics.

○ **Debugger.** A rich debugging environment is provided by the Java tools. You can set breakpoints, step through execution, inspect and set variable values, and change method code during debugging.

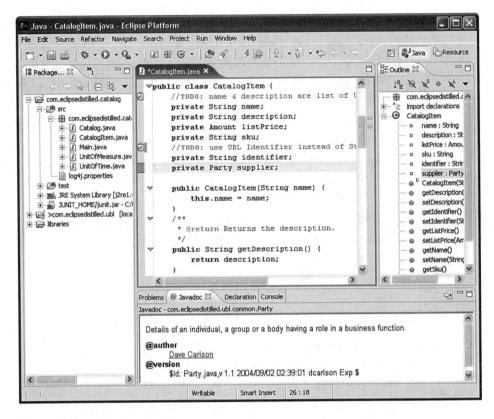

Figure 1-2   Eclipse Java development perspective.

We cover Java project configuration in Chapter 6, "Java Project Configuration," and debugging in Chapter 7. The Java tools devote special attention to supporting agile development techniques. Section 1.3, "Agile Development with Eclipse," introduces this topic with more detail, and Part 2 of this book, "Getting Agile," is dedicated to studying agile development in Eclipse.

1.1.2.2 C/C++ Development Tools

The C/C++ Development Tools (CDT) project is creating a fully functional C and C++ IDE for the Eclipse platform. The current focus is on developing and deploying on Linux, but this project's leaders are interested in participation from contributors who would like to extend the work in other directions. For example, targeting Windows, Unix, or embedded platforms and providing wizards that assist development with particular library, database, or messaging APIs.

The CDT 2.0 release includes the following:

○ **C/C++ editor.** The generic platform text editor is specialized with C/C++ syntax coloring, Content Assist, and formatting.

○ **C/C++ debugger.** A default debugger implementation is provided using GDB.

○ **C/C++ program launcher.** Similar to launching Java programs with optional debugging, CDT provides support for launching C/C++ programs.

○ **C/C++ parser and syntax API.** The parser is an essential foundation for other plug-in contributions that extend CDT.

○ **Search engine.** General platform search facilities are specialized with C/C++ syntax options that accurately locate code definitions and references.

○ **Makefile generator.** Similar to the use of Ant in Java development, makefiles are ubiquitous in development of C/C++ projects.

Details and downloads are available on the CDT Web site, *www.eclipse.org/cdt/*.

1.1.2.3 Plug-in Development Environment

The Plug-in Development Environment (PDE) supplies tools that automate the creation, manipulation, debugging, and deploying of plug-ins. The PDE is part of the Eclipse SDK and is not a separately launched tool. In line with the general Eclipse platform philosophy, the PDE provides a wide variety of platform contributions (e.g., views, editors, wizards, launchers, etc.) that blend transparently with the rest of the Eclipse workbench and assist the developer in every stage of plug-in development while working inside the Eclipse workbench.

○ **PDE perspective.** A specialized perspective includes views and shortcuts to commands used most frequently during plug-in development.

○ **Host Versus Runtime workbench.** The workbench that you are running as you develop your plug-in is the *host* workbench. After you are happy with your plug-in and want to test it, you can launch another workbench—the *runtime* workbench. This will utilize the same plug-ins as the host workbench, but it will also run the plug-ins you were working on in the host workbench.

○ **Debugging plug-ins.** The Java debugger enables complete control while testing plug-ins in the runtime workbench.

○ **Packaging plug-ins.** Tools for packaging plug-ins and features for distribution to users via an update site are provided.

This book does not address plug-in development specifically, but all Eclipse capabilities described here are applicable to the PDE. Other books in this series describe patterns for plug-in development (Gamma and Beck, 2004) and cover the details of building commercial-quality plug-ins (Clayberg and Rubel, 2004).

1.1.2.4 Web Tools Platform

The Web Tools Platform (WTP) project was formally approved by the Eclipse Board in June 2004 and received initial open source code contributions from IBM and Object Web. At the time this book was written, those contributions were being reviewed and assimilated into the first milestone integration build. This project is of great importance to the Eclipse community and is likely of interest to most readers of this book. It is still in a formative stage; nonetheless, here we review the project's charter and summarize its expected integration into the Eclipse IDE.

The mission of the Web Tools Platform project is to provide a generic, extensible, and standards-based tool platform that builds on the Eclipse platform and other core Eclipse technologies. The project will deliver a common foundation of frameworks and services upon which software providers can create specialized, differentiated offerings for J2EE and Web-centric application development. Key objectives are to enable product innovation with adherence to vendor-neutral standards and technologies while delivering practical solutions to real development concerns.

The WTP project is composed of two parts. The Web Standard Tools subproject will provide a common infrastructure targeting Web-enabled applications. This includes tools for developing three-tier applications (presentation, business, and data logic) and publishing the resulting system artifacts to servers.

Tools provided by this subproject will include the following:

○ **Standard languages.** Support will be provided for HTML/XHMTL, XML, XML Schema, Web Services, XQueries, SQL, and other languages used by Web-centric applications.

○ **Editors.** Editors will be provided for supported languages, including consistent features for outlines, Content Assist, templates, and formatting.

○ **Validators.** Languages based on XML will be validated against associated schemas and other semantics from the specifications.

○ **Server publication.** The workbench will provide commands and views for starting, stopping, publishing, and running applications on multiple target servers.

The J2EE Standard Tools subproject will provide common infrastructure for developing applications based on J2EE 1.4 specifications targeting J2EE-compliant application servers. Deliverables include generic J2EE tools for other Eclipse-based projects and products, and IDE workbench plug-ins that support developing, deploying, testing, and debugging J2EE applications on JCP-compliant servers. The J2EE workbench will support use cases such as developing a JSP page, enhancing the "Pet Store" blueprint application, and exposing an EJB session bean as a Web Service.

Tools provided by this subproject will include the following:

○ **J2EE artifacts.** Tools will support EJB, Servlet, JSP, JCA, JDBC, JTA, JMS, JMX, JNDI, and Web Services.

○ **JSP editor.** The editor will support mixed HTML and JSP tags, including JSP tag libraries, plus outline, Content Assist, templates, and formatting.

○ **JSP refactoring.** Java refactoring (e.g., renaming a class, method, or package) will find and refactor dependencies within JSP pages.

○ **Search facilities.** Search criteria are aware of syntax for JSP, XML, and other document types. For example, searching for a method name includes cases where that name is used as a method, but not when used in other text strings.

○ **Comparison of syntax.** Comparing two JSP or XML files considers syntax while identifying logical code constructs, such as when viewing differences between two versions of a JSP file in a repository.

Details and downloads are available on the Web Tools project Web site, *www.eclipse.org/webtools/*.

1.1.3 Rich Client Platform

The Eclipse Rich Client Platform (RCP) is more notable for what it *doesn't* have than for what it has. Although the Eclipse platform is designed to serve as an open tools platform, it is architected so that its components could be used to build just about any client application. The minimal set of plug-ins needed to build a rich client application is collectively known as the Rich Client Platform.

These rich applications are still based on a dynamic plug-in model, and the UI is built using the same toolkits and extension points. The layout and function of the workbench is under fine-grained control of the plug-in developer. When contributing to the IDE, plug-ins are built on the platform SDK workbench. Alternatively, in a rich client application, developers are responsible for defining the application's workbench presentation.

The same PDE tools are used when developing any Eclipse plug-in contributions, including RCP applications. See the PDE references previously in Section 1.1.2.3, "Plug-in Development Environment," for more information on this topic.

1.2 Other Eclipse Projects

We reviewed the Eclipse runtime platform and several projects that build on the IDE foundation, but there are others that contribute development frameworks and tools. Some of these projects are mature and already in widespread use, while others are just getting started. Additional Eclipse technology projects are not listed here, such as the aspect-oriented programming plug-ins called AspectJ. Although these topics are beyond the scope of this book, you may find additional tools that facilitate your work. Each project has a home page on the Eclipse Web site at *www.eclipse.org/projects*, or as a subproject within the Tools or Technology projects listed there.

These components can be used to create new Eclipse plug-ins, and many can also be run outside of the Eclipse workbench. For example, the Service Data Objects (SDO) contribute a framework for data exchange in Web Service applications. The Java IDE capabilities described in this book are used when building applications with these components. The components from each project are packaged as a set of Eclipse plug-ins that is added to your workbench using the Eclipse platform update facility.

Some of the components are illustrated as building blocks in Figure 1-3. The layers show dependencies where a component builds on one or more others. In particular, many components build on the capabilities of the Eclipse Modeling Framework (EMF). The dependencies between these components and others in the Eclipse family may be better represented as a graph of relationships instead of a layered architecture, but this figure offers a quick overview of the primary building blocks provided by these components.

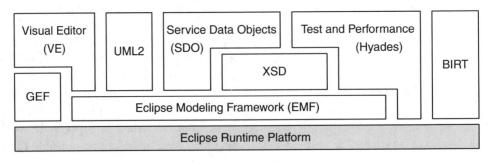

Figure 1-3   Other components built on the Eclipse platform.

Graphical Editor Framework (GEF). Allows developers to create a rich graphical editor from an existing application model. The developer can take advantage of many common operations provided in GEF and/or extend them for a specific domain. GEF employs an MVC (model-view-controller) architecture, which enables simple changes to be applied to the model from the view.

Eclipse Modeling Framework (EMF). A modeling framework and code generation facility for building tools and other applications based on a structured data model. Provides tools and runtime support to produce a set of Java classes for the model, a set of adapter classes that enable viewing and command-based editing of the model, and a basic editor.

Visual Editor (VE). A framework for creating GUI builders for Eclipse; includes reference implementations of Swing/JFC and SWT GUI builders. Intended to be useful for creating GUI builders for other languages such as C/C++ and alternate widget sets, including those that are not supported under Java.

Unified Modeling Language 2.0 (UML2). Provides an implementation of the UML 2.0 metamodel to support development of modeling tools, a common XML Schema to facilitate interchange of semantic models, test cases as a means of validating the specification, and validation rules as a means of defining and enforcing levels of compliance.

XML Schema Infoset (XSD). A reference library for use with any code that examines, creates, or modifies XML Schemas (standalone or as part of other artifacts, such as XForms or WSDL documents). XSD is a separate Technology subproject, but it is usually downloaded as part of EMF.

Service Data Objects (SDO). A framework that simplifies and unifies data application development in a service-oriented architecture (SOA). It supports and integrates XML and incorporates J2EE patterns and best practices. SDO is not a separate project; it is included in EMF as a general application of that framework.

Eclipse Test & Performance. Frameworks and services for test and performance tools that are used throughout the development lifecycle, such as testing, tracing/profiling, tuning, logging, monitoring, analysis, autonomics, and administration. The first component was delivered in the Hyades subproject.

Business Intelligence and Reporting Tools (BIRT). Infrastructure and tools for designing, deploying, generating, and viewing reports in an organization. Over time, additional subprojects may address Online Analytical Processing (OLAP), statistical analysis, Extract Transform and Load (ETL) tools, and others.

Other Eclipse projects use these components, and they are available for your development. For example, the Web Tools Platform uses the EMF, XSD, and GEF components. These frameworks are not described in this book; indeed, entire books will be written about some of the projects (Budinsky, et al, 2004).

1.3   Agile Development with Eclipse

Agile software development is a general name for a family of related methodologies, including Extreme Programming (XP), Scrum, Crystal Methodologies, Adaptive Software Development, and others. Its core principles emphasize empowering the programmer through small self-organizing teams, close collaboration with customers, use of iterative development cycles, and continuous unit testing by the developers.

Eclipse provides a development platform that supports and accelerates the iterative agile development cycle. Extreme Programming (XP), as a member of the agile development family, outlines a set of twelve practices for achieving successful results (Beck, 1999). We'll explore five of those practices that are especially relevant to programming activities:

- **Continuous testing with JUnit.** Programmers continually write unit tests, which must run flawlessly for development to continue.

- **Refactoring your code.** Programmers restructure the system without changing its behavior to remove duplication, improve communication, simplify program logic, or add flexibility.

- **Continuous integration with Ant.** Integrate and build the entire system many times a day, every time a task is completed. Integrating one set of changes at a time makes it easy to identify problems and prevents a surprise at the end of an iteration.

- **Team ownership.** This requires good tools that enable efficient code sharing and a team culture that encourages such behavior.

- **Coding standards.** In agile development processes, the code is of central importance in documenting system design and behavior, and this is possible only when consistent coding standards are used.

Part 2 of this book explains how Eclipse supports each of these agile development practices. Detailed examples are based on a sample application used throughout all chapters.

1.4   Sample Application

We'll use a consistent, practical example throughout this book. The example application is built in two iterations of an agile development process. The goal is to present a realistic situation that demonstrates the power of Eclipse without allowing the application's complexity to interfere with your understanding of Eclipse.

The development iterations will be used to build the following application features:

> **Product Catalog.** Create a domain model representing product catalog information with several kinds of catalog items, including products, services, and product bundles. Each catalog item includes pricing data and a reference to the supplier.

> **E-Commerce Components.** Create a reusable library of components for representing electronic commerce data. This Java library will be based on the XML Schemas and specifications published by the OASIS Universal Business Language (UBL) technical committee.

1.5   Distilled

- ❍ The functional architecture of the Eclipse platform is composed of building blocks that add new features to the core runtime platform. Several hundred Eclipse subprojects and independent open source or commercial products build on this platform.

- ❍ Generic IDE support is provided, which is then specialized for Java, C/C++, Web Tools, and other development activities. The generic IDE is a team-oriented workbench supporting multiple perspectives, views, search facilities, debugging, and more.

- ❍ Java Development Tools (JDT) adds specific support for configuring Java projects and a rich environment for editing and debugging.

- ❍ Other languages, such as C/C++, are supported with optional plug-in features available from the Eclipse Web site and other independent projects.

○ The Web Tools Platform (WTP) project is the newest addition to the Eclipse family and will provide an extensible, standards-based platform for J2EE and Web-centric applications development.

○ Eclipse provides a development platform that supports and accelerates the iterative agile development cycle. Specialized features are included for continuous testing, refactoring, continuous integration, collective ownership, and coding standards.

1.6 References

Beck, Kent, *Extreme Programming Explained: Embracing Change.* Boston, MA: Addison-Wesley, 1999.

Budinsky, Frank, et al., *Eclipse Modeling Framework.* Boston, MA: Addison-Wesley, 2004.

Clayberg, Eric, and Rubel, Dan, *Eclipse: Building Commercial-Quality Plug-ins.* Boston, MA: Addison-Wesley, 2004.

Gamma, Erich and Beck, Kent, *Contributing to Eclipse: Principles, Patterns, and Plug-ins.* Boston, MA: Addison-Wesley, 2004.

CHAPTER 2

Hello Eclipse

Eclipse was created to improve developer productivity and to get results quickly. So let's get started! There are many options for customizing your workbench and setting preferences that determine its default behavior. We start developing the product catalog application using only the installation defaults, and then the remaining chapters in Part 1 explain how to give Eclipse your personal touch and how to set up larger projects.

In this chapter, we'll see how to

- ○ Install and start the Eclipse workbench.
- ○ Create a new Java project.
- ○ Use the Java class wizard to create several classes.
- ○ Run your application within the workbench.

2.1 Installation and Startup

If you have not already done so, download the Eclipse SDK from *http://www.eclipse.org.*

Be sure to get the *Eclipse SDK* download; the alternative "platform runtime" download configuration includes only the base workbench and omits all Java development tools. In addition to the Eclipse SDK, you must have installed Java JDK 1.4 or later *before starting Eclipse.* You will find four categories of Eclipse downloads:

> **Latest Release.** Releases are builds that have been declared major releases by the development team—for example, "R3.0". Releases are the right builds for people who want to be on a stable, tested release and don't need the latest greatest features and improvements.

17

Stable Build. Stable builds are integration builds that have been found to be stable enough for most people to use. They are usually based on significant project milestones. The latest stable build is appropriate for people who want to stay up-to-date with what is going on in the latest development stream and don't mind putting up with a few problems in order to get the latest features and bug fixes.

Integration Build. Periodically, component teams will reach what they believe is a stable, consistent state, and they indicate that the next integration build should take this version of the component. Only advanced Eclipse users should work on these builds.

Nightly builds. Nightly builds are produced every night from whatever has been released into the HEAD stream of the CVS repository. They are completely untested and will almost always have major problems.

If you are new to Eclipse or are working on production development, then the latest release build is your best choice. This book is based on the Eclipse 3.0 release. The examples in this book were prepared using Windows XP; however, builds with identical capability are also available for Linux, Solaris, AIX, HP-UX, and Mac OSX.

Tip: You must have installed Java JDK 1.4.1 or later *before starting Eclipse*. JDK downloads are available from *java.sun.com/j2se/*. If you are unsure which JDK version you are running, open a command window and type "**java -version**."

Eclipse is not distributed with an automated installer that creates a desktop icon and program startup group. Instead, just unpack the ZIP archive. This will create an `eclipse` directory at your selected location, typically at `C:\eclipse` for Windows computers.

Within this folder, you will find an executable file named `eclipse.exe` on Windows. You can browse to this location and run the program here, but it's most convenient to create a desktop shortcut icon for starting Eclipse. Running this program should display the dialog shown in Figure 2-1.

You should avoid using this default location nested within the Eclipse installation directory. Instead, enter a workspace location such as the following:

```
C:\EclipseDistilled\workspace
```

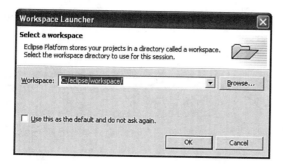

Figure 2-1   Select the current workspace when starting Eclipse.

You should increase the amount of heap memory allocated to Eclipse. This is not required, but it will speed up execution when developing and debugging large applications. To allocate 256MB, change your startup command (or target in your desktop icon) to read as follows:

```
C:\eclipse\eclipse.exe –vmargs –Xmx256M
```

You might have several versions of Java installed on your computer and need to specify which one is used to run Eclipse. If this is the case, add the –vm option on the Eclipse startup program and provide the JVM command path. Also add the -showlocation option to include the current workspace path on the workbench title. Your startup would now appear similar to this:

```
C:\eclipse\eclipse.exe -showlocation
     -vm c:\j2sdk1.4.2_02\bin\javaw.exe -vmargs –Xmx256M
```

> **Tip:** It's common to have several JVMs installed on your machine. You may have both Sun's Java SDK and IBM's J9 VM, or both version 1.3.1 and 1.4.2. Use the –vm option when starting Eclipse to specify which JVM is used to run the workbench. It is a good idea to always add this option to your startup command because many developers are surprised to find that the wrong JVM is being used by default.

2.2   Eclipse IDE Workbench

When you start Eclipse, you are greeted with a **Welcome** page that provides links to several tutorials and examples. We'll bypass the introductory tour and go straight to development, so click the arrow icon in the upper-right corner of the

Welcome screen, which will take you to the workbench as shown in Figure 2-2. This is called the **Resource** perspective.

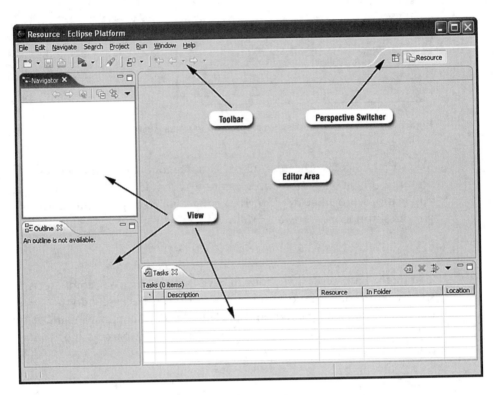

Figure 2-2 The Eclipse workbench resource perspective.

> **Tip:** You can get back to the Welcome tour at any time by selecting the menu
> **Help > Welcome**.

An Eclipse *perspective* defines a selection of *views* and their layout within the workbench window. Several perspectives are available, where each is configured for a particular task, such as Java development, debugging, or browsing CVS repositories. This initial resource perspective is the most generic and may be used to view and edit files in any kind of project.

2.3 Create a New Java Project

We are now ready to start the first iteration of our product catalog application. Our first goal is to get something running and learn how to work in Eclipse, so we'll start very simply. A class diagram for the first project is shown in Figure 2-3.

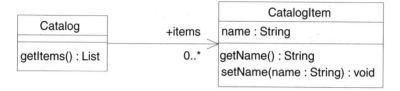

Figure 2-3 First iteration design for order processing application.

The following tasks are completed in this section:

❍ Switch to the Java perspective.

❍ Create a Java project.

❍ Customize code templates used by the Java class wizard.

❍ Create two Java classes that implement Figure 2-3.

❍ Create a class with a `main()` function to test our design.

2.3.1 Open the Java Perspective

We'll move through these first steps in quick succession. Most of your Java development work will be done in the **Java** perspective. Get there by selecting the menu **Window > Open Perspective > Java**. You will now see both the **Java** and **Resource** icons appear in the *perspective switcher* located in the upper-right corner of the workbench window. Depending on your screen resolution, one or more icons may be hidden, and you'll see a >> symbol on the right. If so, click on the left edge of the perspective switcher and drag it left until all perspective icons are showing.

There are several changes to the views that are available in the Java perspective—we'll get to those shortly. Look for three *wizard* icons in the center of the toolbar, as shown in Figure 2-4.

Figure 2-4   Three wizards for Java projects.

Wizards are used extensively in the Eclipse workbench to give guidance when performing multi-step activities. Some of these steps are invisible to you but are an essential part of configuring new resources or creating project files.

These three wizards perform the following tasks:

❍ Create a **New Java Project.**

❍ Create a **New Java Package.**

❍ Create a **New Java Class.**

2.3.2 Create a Java Project

We'll follow a common convention and use *qualified names* for projects in the Eclipse workspace that reflect the primary Java package contained in each project. Our product catalog project is thus named `com.eclipsedistilled.catalog`. The qualified name convention is useful to assure unique self-describing names of projects shared in a source control repository such as CVS. You can shorten the name to `catalog` or use other descriptive names such as `product-catalog` without affecting the way we write code within this project.

1. Click the **New Java Project** wizard to create a project that will contain Java code.

2. Enter the project name: `com.eclipsedistilled.catalog`

3. Check option: **Create separate source and output folders.**

4. Click **Finish** to create the project. There are additional pages in this wizard that allow you to configure project dependencies and libraries, but we will configure those options later.

The project wizard is shown in Figure 2-5. Be sure to check the layout option to **Create separate source and output folders.** This option creates an `src` folder to contain all source code and a separate `bin` folder to contain the compiled class files. Without this option, `.java` and `.class` files are co-mingled in the same folders.

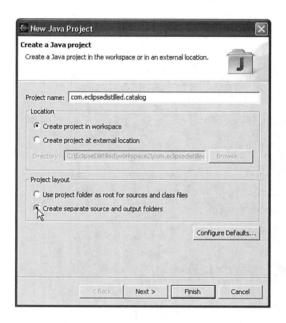

Figure 2-5   New Java Project wizard.

2.3.3 Create a Java Package

1. Select the project folder in the **Package Explorer** view. A Java project folder is indicated by an open folder icon with an overlaid "J."

2. Click the **New Java Package** wizard to create a new Java package.

3. Enter the package name: `com.eclipsedistilled.catalog`.

Your **Package Explorer** view will now look similar to Figure 2-6. Within the workspace directory on your file system, three nested directories are created inside the project folder, named `com`, `eclipsedistilled`, and `catalog`. The **Package Explorer** view shows these names concatenated into one package name similar to the way you see it in your Java source code.

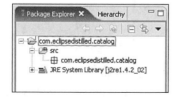

Figure 2-6   Java **Package Explorer** view with one empty package.

2.3.4 Create a Java Class

1. Select the `com.eclipsedistilled.catalog` package within the `src` folder in the **Package Explorer** view. A Java package is indicated by an icon resembling a box wrapped with string.

2. Click on the **New Java Class** wizard to create a new Java class.

3. Enter the class name: `Catalog`.

4. Click **Finish** to create the class.

The **New Java Class** wizard is shown in Figure 2-7. Other options are available for creating inner classes, specifying a superclass, implementing interfaces, and generating method stubs.

Figure 2-7   The **New Java Class** wizard.

Your Java perspective will now look similar to Figure 2-8. The Java file editor contains a new class that is created from a template and filled in with your selections from the wizard. Like most aspects of Eclipse, you can customize this template to modify the content of default comments. This is our next task.

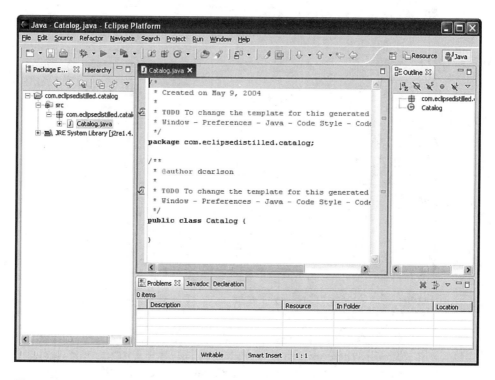

Figure 2-8   Java perspective with one project containing one class.

2.3.5 Customize Code Templates

Eclipse contains many code generation templates that you can customize, but two of these should be modified right at the beginning because they affect every new file. In Figure 2-8, you can see the default comment inserted at the top of every new Java file and also the comment inserted immediately before the class declaration. Both comments contain TODO notes suggesting that you modify them.

1. Select the menu **Window > Preferences,** and then in the resulting dialog select **Java > Code Style > Code Templates.**

2. Select **Code > New Java files,** as shown in Figure 2-9.

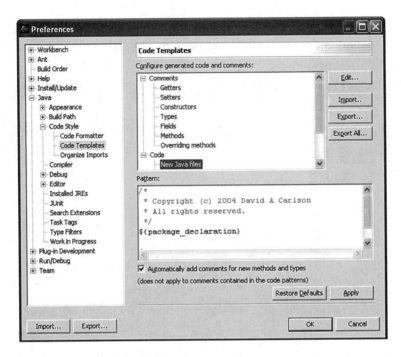

Figure 2-9   Code templates preferences.

3. Click the **Edit...** button, which opens the dialog shown in Figure 2-10. Modify the comment block, but at least for now, do not change the template parameters following the comment. Click **OK**.

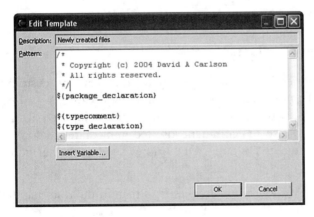

Figure 2-10   Edit the template for new Java files.

4. Select **Comments > Types**.

5. Click the **Edit...** button to modify the class declaration comment. You might want to include standard Javadoc tags such as `@author` and `@version`. Click **OK**.

6. Click **OK** to save the new preferences.

The quickest way to get these new comments into your first class file is to delete and re-create it. Select the `Catalog` class in the **Package Explorer** view and press delete. Then repeat the previous step to create this same class, where you will now see the new comments.

Our initial implementation also requires a second class:

1. Select the `com.eclipsedistilled.catalog` package in the **Package Explorer** view.

2. Click on the **New Java Class** wizard to create a new Java class.

3. Enter the class name: `CatalogItem`.

4. Click **Finish**.

2.3.6 Writing Methods

We'll keep these classes very simple for now and focus on getting this program running. Open the editor for `Catalog.java` and edit it as follows to add an `items` field and `getItems()` method.

com.eclipsedistilled.catalog/Catalog.java
```
package com.eclipsedistilled.catalog;
import java.util.List;
import java.util.Vector;

public class Catalog {
    private List items = new Vector();

    public List getItems() {
        return items;
    }
}
```

Open the `CatalogItem.java` file and add a `name` field with associated `getName()` and `setName()` methods.

com.eclipsedistilled.catalog/CatalogItem.java
```
package com.eclipsedistilled.catalog;
```

```
public class CatalogItem {
    /** The catalog item name */
    private String name;

    public CatalogItem(String name) {
        setName(name);
    }

    public String getName() {
        return name;
    }
    public void setName(String name) {
        this.name = name;
    }
}
```

When finished making changes in an editor, press **Ctrl+S**, press the **Save** icon on the toolbar, or select **File > Save** from the workbench menu. You may not realize it at this point, but your code is already compiled! The project is rebuilt automatically whenever a Java source file is saved. Switch back to the **Resource** perspective by clicking on its icon in the perspective switcher. In the **Navigator** view shown in Figure 2-11, expand the src and bin folders where you will see a compiled .class file for each .java file. We'll dig into this automated build capability in Chapter 6, "Java Project Configuration." Return to the **Java** perspective to prepare for the next task.

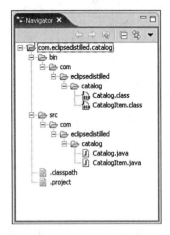

Figure 2-11 **Navigator** view showing compiled classes.

2.4   Run Your Application

The project represents the domain model for our product catalog, and we may or may not add an implementation for a user interface. When following an agile development methodology, we should write a JUnit test suite for this project. We'll take this approach in Part 2 of this book.

For now, create a new class named `Main` with a `main()` method. Our implementation includes a command-line prompt where you can add new items to the catalog and request a list of the current contents. Click the **New Java Class** wizard, enter the name `Main`, and check the option **public static void main(String[] args)**. Then use the editor to fill in the method as follows:

com.eclipsedistilled.catalog/Main.java

```java
package com.eclipsedistilled.catalog;
import java.io.BufferedReader;
import java.io.IOException;
import java.io.InputStreamReader;
import java.util.Iterator;

public class Main {

    public static void main(String[] args) {
        Catalog catalog = new Catalog();
        List items = catalog.getItems();

        while (true) {
            System.out.print("command? ");
            BufferedReader reader = new BufferedReader(
                    new InputStreamReader(System.in));
            String data = null;
            try {
                data = reader.readLine();
                if (data == null || data.length() == 0) {
                    System.out.println("done.");
                    return;
                }
            } catch (IOException e) {
                e.printStackTrace();
                System.out.println("exiting.");
                return;
            }

            if (data.startsWith("add ") && data.length() > 4) {
                String name = data.substring(4);
                CatalogItem item = new CatalogItem(name);
                catalog.getItems().add(item);

            } else if (data.startsWith("list")) {
                CatalogItem item;
                for (Iterator iterator = items.iterator();
                        iterator.hasNext();) {
```

```
                        item = (CatalogItem) iterator.next();
                        System.out.println("Product: "
                            + item.getName());
                }
            } else {
                System.out.println(
                    "usage: add <item name> || list");
            }
            System.out.println();
        }
    }
}
```

Now let's run it! Eclipse includes a **Console** view that displays output written to `System.out` and `System.err`. You can use it to run and test any Java application that would be executed from the command line outside of Eclipse.

1. Open the **Console** view by selecting **Window > Show View > Console**.

2. In the **Package Explorer** view, right-click on the `Main.java` class and select **Run > Java Application**.

3. The prompt `command?` will appear in the console.

4. Click in the **Console** view, type "add Digital Camera", and then press **Enter**. Repeat for other products.

5. Type "list" to display a list of all products in the catalog.

6. Press **Enter** without typing any command, and the program will terminate.

The **Console** view appears as in Figure 2-12 while the program is running. You can easily tell the difference between an application that has terminated and one that is running or suspended while waiting for input because the heading of the **Console** view changes to include `<terminated>` before the program name. If `<terminated>` does not appear, you can press the **Terminate** toolbar icon on the **Console** view.

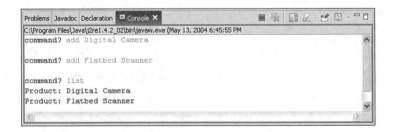

Figure 2-12 **Console** view showing input and output while running our application.

Eclipse also includes excellent capabilities for debugging programs. We'll look at the **Debug** perspective in Chapter 7, "Debugging Your Code."

2.5 Distilled

❍ Because Eclipse is an open source project, you have an inside view of the ongoing development. But most newcomers should not download the nightly or integration builds. Stay with the latest release or maybe a stable build.

❍ Eclipse starts in the default **Resource** perspective. Switch to the **Java** perspective for most development work.

❍ Use the **Java** perspective wizards to create new projects, new packages, and new class files.

❍ Customize the code generation templates that are used to insert code into a new Java file.

❍ Run your application within the Eclipse workbench and use the **Console** view for command-line input and output.

CHAPTER 3

Managing Your Projects

Now that you have a project started, let's take a step back and review the ways in which Eclipse helps you manage content and complexity as your projects grow. Each of your resource files (code, documentation, or anything else) is contained within a *project*, and each of your Eclipse projects is grouped within a *workspace*.

In the previous chapter, we created our first Java project for catalog management. The agile development process encourages us to get started as quickly as possible and to rely on testing and refactoring for adapting to evolving requirements.

In this chapter, you'll learn how to

- ○ Create multiple workspaces for independent work
- ○ Navigate and filter Java project views
- ○ Link project folders to directories outside the workspace
- ○ Plan the structure of your workspace and projects

3.1 Your Project Workspace

Each instance of Eclipse is associated with exactly one workspace, but you can select the workspace that will be used for the current session.

The workspace launcher dialog, shown previously in Figure 2-1, allows you to pick the current workspace when you start Eclipse. Alternatively, you can type a directory path into the dialog field to create a new workspace or browse to an existing directory. The location is completely up to you, although it's best not to accept the default location embedded within the Eclipse installation folder. When you upgrade to a new version of Eclipse, such as moving from 3.0.0 to 3.1.0, you will unpack a new distribution ZIP and either replace the `c:\eclipse` installation directory with a fresh copy or create a new installation directory, such as `c:\eclipse-3.1.0`. If your workspace is not embedded within the installation directory, then you can simply delete the old version of Eclipse.

If you look in the workspace folder using your operating system file explorer or command prompt, you will see a child folder named `.metadata`—don't mess with this unless you know what you are doing! Also be certain to back this up along with your other workspace project folders because it contains important data about your workbench state and preferences.

You can rename or move your workspace folder at any time without ill effect, as long as you always keep the child folders, including the `.metadata` folder, intact within a given workspace.

> **Tip:** If you encounter errors while running Eclipse, the first place to look for more information is the `.log` file located within the `.metadata` folder in your current workspace. If the `.log` for your workspace starts to get large, it can be safely deleted.

> **Tip:** You may receive an error when restarting if your operating system crashes or if Eclipse exits without proper shutdown. If this occurs, look for a `.lock` file in the `.metadata` folder and delete this file if it exists. Do *not* delete this file under normal circumstances. On Windows you will not be able to delete the `.lock` file until the Eclipse process has terminated.

3.1.1 Using Multiple Workspaces

If you create multiple workspace locations, then the project resources contained within each workspace should be independent of those in other workspaces. However, independent projects may be included in the same workspace. Some common reasons for multiple workspaces include the following:

- ❍ Independent work topics, possibly managed in different version control repositories (although projects within one workspace can be associated with any number of repositories).

- ❍ You are a consultant and need to maintain clear separation between client resources.

○ Two or more workspaces are used to distinguish concurrent work on maintenance branch versions in CVS.

To create a new workspace, simply start Eclipse and enter a new location in the Workspace Launcher dialog.

3.2 Eclipse Resources

An Eclipse workspace is mapped to the file system directly and contains *resources* that represent your projects and their contents. This logical view is platform-independent and identical in structure whether running on Windows, Linux, Macintosh, or other operating systems.

The resources are contained in a hierarchical structure with a singleton workspace as its root. The primary resource types are shown in Figure 3-1.

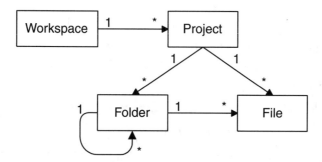

Figure 3-1   Eclipse platform resource types.

You can modify a resource on the file system directly or from within Eclipse. If you create or modify a resource from within Eclipse, then its counterpart is created immediately in the file system. If you create, delete, or modify a file system resource within a folder that is managed by Eclipse, then the Eclipse workspace must be *refreshed* to synchronize its state with that of the actual files.

Resources may be refreshed manually or automatically by a periodic background thread in Eclipse. If you are working on very large projects with thousands of files, automatic refreshing can become an excessive processing burden; otherwise it's very helpful. You can enable automatic refresh by checking the option for **Refresh workspace automatically** in the preferences dialog opened via the menu **Window > Preferences > Workbench.**

Manual refresh is invoked for projects, folders, or individual files via the context menu in either the **Navigator** view or the Java **Package Explorer** view, as shown in Figure 3-2.

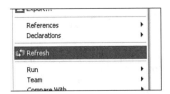

Figure 3-2 Synchronize Eclipse resources with the file system.

3.2.1 Projects

Projects are special entities in your workspace. They carry metadata about project characteristics and contribute automatic behavior when their resources are modified. A project is a container that groups resources into buildable, reusable units.

Features of projects include the following:

- A project collects together a set of files and folders.
- A project's location controls where the project's resources are stored in the local file system.
- A project's build spec controls how its resources are built.
- A project can carry session and persistent properties.
- A project can be open or closed; a closed project is passive and has a minimal in-memory footprint.
- A project can refer to other projects.
- A project can have one or more project natures.

The type of project is determined by its *project natures* (there can be more than one), which are assigned by a wizard when a project is created. Unless you are developing new plug-ins for Eclipse, you can generally ignore the details of how natures are assigned. If you have created a new Java project, you will see a J on top of the project folder icon in the **Navigator** or **Package Explorer** views.

What are the unique characteristics of Java projects? They record their build path in a `.classpath` file and add the Java incremental project builder to the project's build spec. In all other respects, they are just regular projects and can be configured with other natures and other incremental builders. Java project configuration is described in more detail in Chapter 6, "Java Project Configuration."

If you are working with a large number of projects or a large number of fold-ers within a project, you can narrow your current scope to a subset of workspace content. There are two ways to control your view content.

In either the **Navigator** view or the **Package Explorer** view, pick any project or package folder and select the **Go Into** context menu item, as shown in Figure 3-3. You can then use the Back, Forward, or Up toolbar icons on that view to move between a series of sub-folder focus areas. This creates a Web browser-like navigation through a series of project and folder contents. You navigate backwards and forwards through visited workspace "pages" or go "home" to the workspace root.

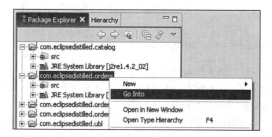

Figure 3-3   Drill into workspace focus areas using **Go Into**.

Alternatively, in the **Package Explorer** view, right-click on a project folder and select **Close Project**. Then filter your view as shown in Figure 3-4 to hide all closed projects (click the down-arrow icon on the view toolbar to get the view menu). This approach has an additional benefit of reducing Eclipse resource con-sumption by not caching or evaluating build state information for closed Java projects.

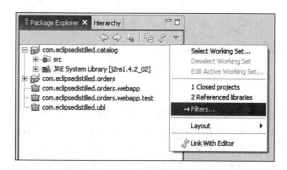

Figure 3-4   Filter content of the **Package Explorer** view (click down-arrow icon on the view toolbar to get the view menu).

3.2.2 Linked Resource Locations

By default your workspace hierarchy is identical to the corresponding file system directory and file structure. You can, however, map parts of the Eclipse workspace hierarchy onto disjoint locations in the file system. Some reasons for doing this are as follows:

- ○ Including configuration or class file directories that are stored outside of the project, e.g., in a Tomcat or JBoss server installation
- ○ Accommodating inflexible file location requirements of other tools used in combination with Eclipse
- ○ Referencing shared network drive locations containing source or library files
- ○ Referencing other product installations on your file system

Linked folders and files appear as an integral part of your Eclipse project, but they must be located directly within a project, not nested within a subfolder.

Right-click on the project where you want to create a linked resource and select **New > Folder** or **New > File**. As shown in Figure 3-5, specify the name of the folder as it will appear in the workbench and browse to the linked folder. The Eclipse folder name can be different from the name of the folder in the file system.

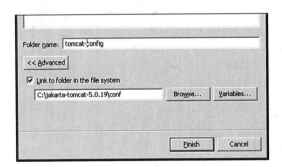

Figure 3-5   Create a linked folder for an external product library.

Linked resource locations can be specified relative to a *path variable*. Variables can ease the management of linked resources by reducing the number of places where hard-coded, absolute file system paths are used. They also make it easier to share projects containing linked resources with other team members by avoiding hard-coded absolute file system paths that may vary between machines. Click **Variables...** while creating the link and select or create a path variable, as shown in Figure 3-6.

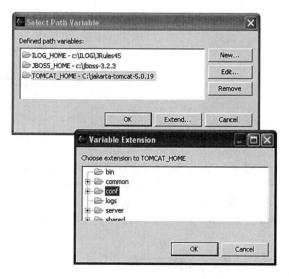

Figure 3-6   Defining and using a path variable for linked folders.

If the chosen variable defines the exact path of the linked resource, click **OK**. Otherwise, click **Extend...** to choose a file or folder below the location described by the path variable, and then click **OK**.

> **Tip:** The **Window > Preferences > Workbench > Linked Resources** preference page allows you to review and define path variables.

Path variables streamline the management of linked resources for users in several ways:

- ❍ They allow a single reference to the absolute path when defining several linked resources under a common root.
- ❍ They allow the location of several resources to be redefined by changing a single variable.
- ❍ They allow users to share projects containing linked resources without updating the paths of each resource (because the absolute path can vary between machines).

The last item in this list requires explanation. When you create a linked resource in a project, a description of the linked resource is added to the project description file (`.project`) in the project's location. Using a path variable, you can share a project by copying the project's content or by using a repository and then redefine the variable to suit each individual workstation. For example, one user might store external resources under `c:\jboss-3.2.3`, while another user running Linux might store the same resources in `/usr/local/jboss`. Defining a path variable on each workspace (`JBOSS_HOME=c:\jboss-3.2.3` and `JBOSS_HOME=/usr/local/jboss`) allows users to work around this difference and share projects with linked resources.

You can load a project that uses path variables even if you do not have all the path variables defined in your workspace. A linked resource that uses a missing path variable is flagged using a special decorator icon. In addition, the **File > Properties > Info** property page for a linked resource, shown in Figure 3-7, displays the variable and indicates whether or not it is defined. A path variable can also specify a location that does not exist on the file system.

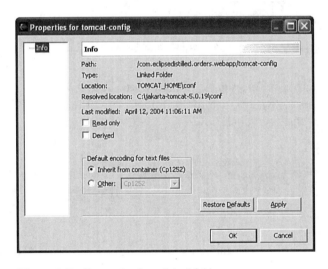

Figure 3-7   Properties for a linked folder.

3.3   Planning Projects and Dependencies

The planned scope of our order management application includes a product catalog, order processing, and a Web-based user interface. Our initial design calls for five modular projects with dependencies as shown in Figure 3-8.

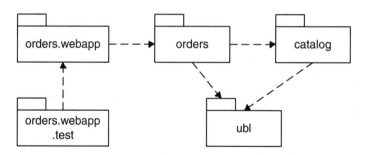

Figure 3-8   Order processing application package dependencies.

The **ubl** project has no other dependencies, whereas the **orders.webapp.test** project ultimately depends on all other projects. The projects are summarized as follows:

catalog. Domain model for product catalogs.

orders. Domain model for order management; depends on product catalog domain model.

ubl. The OASIS Universal Business Language (UBL) reusable components for electronic commerce. These components are used within both the catalog and orders domain models.

orders.webapp. A J2EE Web application interface for order processing; depends on the orders domain model.

orders.webapp.test. A separate project for unit and integration testing of the Web application.

Your first Java project for the product catalog was created in Chapter 2, "Hello Eclipse." Following the same approach, open the Java perspective and use the **New Java Project** wizard to create the remaining four projects. We'll continue with the convention of prefixing the project names with com.eclipse-distilled to assure their names are unique in a shared version control repository. However, it's not necessary to create project names that are equal to the Java packages they contain. You should now have the Eclipse workspace projects as shown in Figure 3-9.

When creating new Java projects using the wizard, be sure to select the project layout option to **Create separate source and output folders**. You should click the button to **Configure Defaults...** and set this choice as the default folder configuration from this point forward. You can get to this same setting by going to the preferences dialog category, **Java > Build Path**.

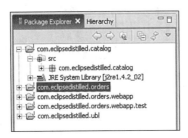

Figure 3-9   Projects in the **Package Explorer** view.

Every Java project has at least one source folder and one output folder. The Eclipse default is to use the project itself as both the source and output folders, so every `.java` file is compiled and its `.class` file is saved within the same folder. For most projects, it is preferable to assign separate folders for source and output. With a separate output folder, you can simply delete its entire contents to clean and rebuild a project from scratch. Also, larger projects will include folders other than source or output, such as documentation, configuration files, and so on.

When a Java project's resources are displayed in the **Package Explorer** view, the source folder (named `src` by default) is shown as a folder icon with a nested package icon. This represents a project folder containing Java packages and source code files. Only the source folder is included in the project build path; other project folders, even if they contain `.java` files, will *not* be compiled. This is explained in detail in Chapter 6, "Java Project Configuration."

The output folder (named `bin` by default) is hidden from view because you do not need to see its contents for most development activities. Similarly, every project contains a `.project` file, and every Java project contains a `.classpath` file, which are also hidden in this view.

If you want to see the output folder and other hidden files, switch to the **Resource** perspective and use the **Navigator** view. This provides a general-purpose view of all workspace resources. This view is shown in Figure 3-10.

Figure 3-10   Projects in the **Navigator** view.

Project dependencies affect the visibility of imported classes in Java projects. It is possible to develop this entire application using a single Eclipse project, but the use of multiple projects provides additional benefits when reusing independent modules. Creating separate projects makes you think clearly about the dependencies between logical subsystems. For example, the UBL e-commerce components and product catalog may be used in other applications that are not part of order processing. For user interface components, placing the model and the view in separate projects helps prevent unnecessary coupling.

Configuration of Java project dependencies is described in detail in Chapter 6.

3.4 Distilled

○ A workspace provides a complete view of all resources required by a set of related projects.

○ Eclipse resources provide a platform-independent, logical view of files and folders, but they must be synchronized with the file system if changes are made outside of the Eclipse workbench.

○ A Java project contains source and output folders (preferably separate locations). The project is automatically configured with an incremental builder that compiles all source files into the output folder. Non-Java projects do not include the incremental builder, but other than that, they could be arranged in the same way.

○ You can map parts of the Eclipse workspace hierarchy onto disjoint locations in the file system by using linked resource locations. This is especially helpful when using Eclipse in combination with other products and development tools that require specific file locations.

○ Configuring an application using multiple projects contributes long-term benefits that improve reuse of independent modules. Project dependencies control visibility of cross-project imported classes.

CHAPTER 4

Customizing Your Workbench

Software developers are passionate about their tools and especially the way in which those tools fit their ideals. The Eclipse workbench is amazingly versatile in its ability to accommodate different development tasks and varying developer preferences. Each release of the Eclipse platform adds more preference settings that enable deeper customization of capabilities and styles, and there is exponential growth in the number of plug-in contributions that extend Eclipse for new and specialized tasks.

But this versatility can be overwhelming to Eclipse newcomers. Powerful customization features may go unnoticed for months, simply because users did not know to look for them. This chapter provides a tour of Eclipse customization through perspectives and preference settings. More radical customization is possible by adding new plug-in contributions to Eclipse; this topic is described in Chapter 9, "Updating the Eclipse IDE."

In this chapter, we'll see how to

- Use multiple perspectives to organize task-specific views
- Create new perspectives for your unique development tasks and work style
- Choose from the many views and editors provided by Eclipse
- Set preferences to fit your individual needs and work habits
- Set preferences shared by your project team

4.1   Perspectives

There is nothing magical about Eclipse perspectives; each perspective simply defines a collection of Eclipse views and action sets organized in a layout that suits its assigned task for a typical user. You may use a perspective as-is, or you may clone and modify it to better suit your needs. As a first step, you should get familiar with the default perspectives and start working with their initial configurations—the defaults represent best practices learned by experienced Eclipse users.

Eight perspectives are defined in the standard Eclipse SDK download:

Resource. This is the default perspective when opening Eclipse and is useful for browsing all workspace resources; that is, projects and their contents.

Java. Primary views and menu/toolbar commands used during Java development.

Java Browsing. Very useful for exploring large projects; contains views for projects, packages, types, and members.

Java Type Hierarchy. Includes a subset of the Java perspective used to explore class inheritance.

Debug. Views used while debugging your Java programs.

CVS Repository Exploring. Used while opening and exploring CVS repositories, especially when discovering shared projects to be imported into your workspace.

Team Synchronizing. Used while synchronizing your file modifications with a CVS (or other) version control repository.

Plug-in Development. Specialized views used while developing new plug-in contributions for Eclipse.

Because Eclipse is an extensible platform, more perspectives may be available in your configuration that were contributed by new plug-ins or by third-party products that are built on the Eclipse platform.

The *perspective bar* is similar to a standard toolbar, but it is specialized to show an icon for each perspective that is open in your workbench. A perspective bar with four open perspectives is shown in Figure 4-1. The current perspective—Java in this case—is highlighted in the list, and a fourth perspective icon is hidden (indicated by the >> icon). Switch perspectives by clicking on the desired icon or on the >> icon to get a pull-down list of those not visible.

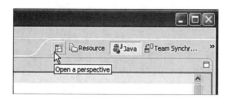

Figure 4-1   Eclipse perspective bar with four open perspectives. The Java perspective is currently
                 displayed.

Tip: After you are familiar with the icons for each perspective, you can recover
space on the toolbar by hiding the perspective labels. In **Window > Preferences
> Workbench > Appearance**, uncheck the option for **Show text on the
perspective bar**.

Each open perspective is represented as a page in the current window,
and only one page can be viewed at a time. Alternatively, you can set your workbench preference to open each perspective in a new window. See **Window >
Preferences > Workbench > Perspectives**.

As you work with Eclipse, you will probably switch perspectives frequently.
During development, the **Java** perspective will consume the majority of your
time, with frequent excursions through the **Debug** perspective. After joining an
established work team, the **CVS Repository** and **Java Browsing** perspectives help
you to quickly become a contributing member. In addition, you may visit the
Team Synchronizing perspective several times a day to update your snapshot of
the repository, to commit changes, or to review differences between your files
and the repository.

The customizable components of any perspective consist of *views*, *editors*,
and *commands*. You can easily add or remove these by selecting from the complete set provided by the plug-ins installed in your workbench.

Each perspective will retain your customizations between Eclipse sessions.
You also can create and save specialized perspectives with names without losing
the built-in perspective. Just open a related perspective (or use the Resource perspective as the most generic starting point) and then add, remove, and rearrange
until you are happy. Select **Window > Save Perspective As...** and enter the name
of your new perspective.

Tip: Don't hesitate to jump in and customize the content or layout of your Eclipse perspectives! After you experiment with adding, removing, or rearranging views, you can restore the default view selection and layout of the current perspective by selecting **Window > Reset Perspective**.

4.1.1 Selecting Capabilities

As you expand the number of plug-in contributions within your Eclipse workbench, the number of perspectives, views, menus, and toolbar options will become quite large. You may find that some of these options are not relevant to your current work, and you might prefer to minimize distraction by hiding them. For example, if you are not writing new plug-ins for Eclipse, you can hide functions that are designed exclusively for helping you in this activity. If you are using Eclipse for work other than Java development (e.g., UML modeling or Web site development), then you can hide the Java development features.

Select the **Window > Preferences** menu option to open the dialog shown in Figure 4-2 and then select **Workbench > Capabilities**. Different capabilities may be available, depending on which plug-ins are installed. Only some of your workbench features are configurable as capabilities, but this is a new capability of Eclipse 3.0, and more capabilities may be added later.

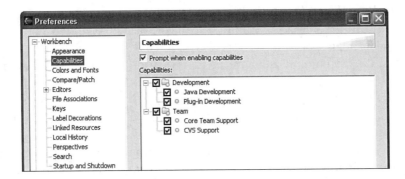

Figure 4-2 Configure which capabilities are activated within the workbench.

A *capability* defines a related set of perspectives, views, and command sets whose functionality is related to a particular development task. When you disable a capability, all of its related features are removed from view, but they remain installed pending future activation.

4.2   **Workbench Views**

A view displays information about the contents of your workbench. For example, the **Navigator** view displays a list of projects and other resources in your workspace. A view might appear by itself or stacked with other views in a tabbed notebook. You can change the layout of a perspective by opening and closing views and by docking them in different positions in the workbench window.

The views available within your workbench are organized into named categories such as **Basic, Java, Debug, Ant,** and **Team.** To see a complete list of views, select **Window > Show View > Other....** The most commonly used views from the **Basic** category are

> **Navigator.** Displays a general-purpose view of projects, folders, and files in your current workspace; useful in any perspective.
>
> **Properties.** Customized by workbench plug-ins to display and edit name/value properties for any resource or object. When this view is showing, you will see its content change to reflect what is selected in other views or editors.
>
> **Outline.** Customized by plug-ins to display a structural view of resource contents. For example, it can display an outline of methods in a Java class file or an outline of tasks in an Ant build file.
>
> **Problems.** Displays a list of problems found in a resource; for example, compilation errors and warnings in a Java file.
>
> **Tasks.** Displays a list of tasks to be performed, along with a reference to the resource and line number for each task. Useful as reminders of work remaining in your programs or documentation.
>
> **Bookmarks.** Displays bookmarks for quick reference and navigation to specific lines in a file.
>
> **Search.** Displays results of searching your workspace.

It is common for a view's display to be coordinated with selections in other views or editors. Selecting an item in the **Outline** view may cause an editor to display the corresponding location and also update the **Properties** view with details of that item.

The **Properties** and **Outline** views may be customized by plug-ins installed in your workbench. Each view provides functionality that is specialized for particular resource types and may contain radically different contents that depend on the current selection in other views or editors. The benefit to you is that your workbench does not need to be cluttered with a dozen related views that show property and structure data for wide-ranging resources such as Java files, XML files, or UML models. They all share the same view and adapt to the current selection.

Each view has an optional toolbar and menu that is separate from those on the main workbench window. A view menu, if present, is accessed by clicking on the triangle icon at the right end of the view toolbar. The view toolbar for the **Package Explorer** is shown in Figure 4-3.

Figure 4-3   View toolbar and menu for the **Package Explorer**.

Views may be maximized to fill the entire workbench window area by clicking the maximize icon on the view or by double-clicking on the view tab. You can also minimize a view, which reduces it to the title bar and allows other views or editors to expand into the view area. If several views are stacked in a tab folder—two views are stacked in Figure 4-3—then they are maximized or minimized as a complete group of tabs.

4.2.1 *Marker Views*

Three of these basic views have related behavior: **Problems, Tasks,** and **Bookmarks** all display a list of *markers*, where each marker is linked to one line in a file. Double-clicking on a marker opens an editor for the associated file and positions the cursor at that line.

Each of these three kinds of markers can be further specialized by contributed plug-ins. For example, the Java plug-in adds a **Java Problem,** which is a specific kind of problem, typically representing a compile error or warning. Other plug-ins may contribute markers that are also subtypes of these three basic categories. An XML editor might contribute an XML validation error as a specialized kind of problem.

When working with large projects in a team environment, you may find your **Problems** view filled with hundreds of warnings caused by deprecated methods, unused import statements, and so on. This is especially true when a few of your co-workers are not using Eclipse to write clean code and instead are leaving this mess for you!

Filter commands are available in many Eclipse views to help you cope with information overload. The **Navigator** view can filter the resources that are displayed, and the **Problems, Tasks,** and **Bookmarks** views filter the markers that are displayed. All of these filters are useful as your projects grow in size and complexity. To set a view's filters, select the **Filters...** toolbar icon or menu. The filter dialog for the **Problems** view is shown in Figure 4-4.

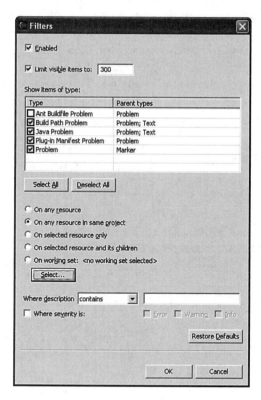

Figure 4-4 Filtering contents of the **Problems** view.

The best solution for filtering your list of problems will depend on the structure of your projects and the kind of problems you encounter. If your workspace is divided into multiple projects (possibly having dependencies for resolving build references), a very helpful technique is to restrict the view of problems to other resources in the same project as the Java class or package selected in **Package Explorer** view. The default view shows problems for your entire workspace. As shown in Figure 4-4, change **On any resource** to **On any resource in same project** to help you reduce information overload. Or choose **On selected resource and its children** for a narrower selection, such as restricting the view to problems in one class or to all classes in a package.

Filters for the **Tasks** and **Bookmarks** views are similar to those for the **Problems** view, except that the **Problems** view may be filtered by severity, whereas **Task** markers may be filtered by priority and status. The list of marker types depends on the workbench plug-ins that are installed. The problem marker types shown in Figure 4-4 are available in the standard Eclipse SDK, which includes specialized types for Java, Ant, and plug-in development.

The **Tasks** view includes a helpful customization for Java developers. When a Java project is built, the parser automatically scans for *Java task tags* in your code comments. You can configure the task tag names and their priorities using the **Java > Task Tags** preferences, as shown in Figure 4-5. Three tags are provided by default (FIXME, TODO, and XXX), and we added a STORY tag to support our agile development process.

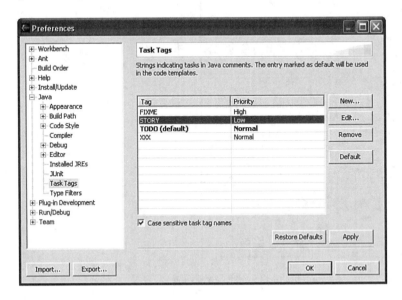

Figure 4-5   Add a new Java task tag for user stories.

This new tag is defined with a Low priority to enable stories to be filtered out while working on coding activities. You can also filter the **Tasks** view to display only tasks containing the word "STORY" when you are reviewing requirements and their implementation. The **Tasks** view is shown in Figure 4-6. This view is not open by default. Open it by selecting the menu **Window > Show View > Other... > Basic > Tasks**. Notice that we added a STORY task tag within the class comment block and that two TODO tasks are included with notes about changes needed in the fields.

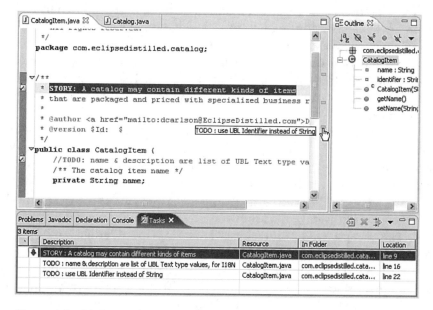

Figure 4-6   **Tasks** view showing STORY and TODO tasks.

The right margin of your Java editor displays small blue rectangles indicating the location of task markers. This is a compressed index area showing all task markers in the file, including those out of view. Click on one of these task markers to navigate to that location in your file. As shown in Figure 4-6, you can hover over a task marker to see its description even if the task tag itself is not within the visible editor area.

4.2.2   View Layout

Adding, removing, and repositioning views in your perspectives is quick and intuitive. To add a view, select the **Window > Show View** menu. The submenu list is defined as part of the current perspective to include those views most like-ly to be used when working in that perspective. To get a list of all views, select **Other...** from the submenu.

A new view will be added to your workbench window. If the same view had been previously opened, the workbench remembers its prior location and opens it there. If the view is already open but is hidden from visibility behind another tab, it is brought to the front.

To move a view, click the left mouse button on the view tab and drag it to the desired location. Release the mouse when finished. While dragging, you'll see an outline border for the destination; move the mouse to different regions *over another view*—top, bottom, left, or right edge—and get an understanding of the possibilities for positioning views. You can split a view area vertically by drop-ping the new view on the left or right side of an existing view, or you can split it horizontally by dropping near the top or bottom. To create a stack of views in a tabbed folder, just drop the view into the center of another view. You have a lot of flexibility.

Eclipse also supports *tear-off views* that appear in individual windows sepa-rate from the main workbench. Simply drag an existing view outside of the workbench window and release the mouse. To reintegrate the view into your workbench, drag it back into the workbench window area.

Any view may be set to display as a *fast view*. All fast views are displayed as icons on the *fast view bar*, as shown on the bottom of your workbench in Figure 4-7. This perspective has three fast views for **JUnit**, **Outline**, and **Tasks**—you'll become familiar with these icons quickly. Clicking on one of these icons causes the fast view to pop out from the fast view bar and overlay the other views. Click anywhere outside of the fast view to hide it. To convert any view into a fast view, right-click on its tab and select **Fast View** from the context menu.

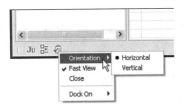

Figure 4-7   Fast view bar with three views. The **Tasks** view has horizontal orientation.

Some views are best shown in a vertical orientation (e.g., an **Outline**), where-as others need to be horizontally oriented (e.g., the **Properties** or **Tasks** views). The fast view bar's context menu allows you to make this choice for each fast view. The fast view bar itself may be docked on the left, right, or bottom of the workbench window.

A fast view remembers its location within the workbench window if you later choose to restore that view location and thus remove it from the fast view bar. To do this, select **Fast View** from the context menu of a view icon in the fast view bar.

4.3   Resource Editors

As a Java developer, most of your time will be spent in the Java file editor. This editor provides menu and toolbar commands, syntax highlighting, and many other features that are customized for Java source code files. But other editors are also available. A generic text editor can be used with any text file, and a Java class file editor can open (but not modify) compiled byte code files to display their attributes and method signatures.

Double-clicking on a file in the **Navigator** view will open the default editor. Or, as shown in Figure 4-8, select the **Open With** context menu and pick one of the other editors that are available.

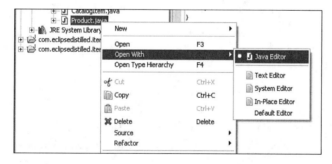

Figure 4-8   Pick an editor from those available for the selected resource.

If there is no associated editor for a resource, then a system editor is selected by referencing the operating system file type assignments. For example, files ending with .xml or .html will be opened in the default Web browser. This *external editor* is launched in a new window, not within an Eclipse workbench view.

On Windows, the workbench will first attempt to launch an external editor in place as an OLE document. This type of editor is referred to as an *embedded editor*. For example, if you have a .doc file in the workbench and Microsoft Word is registered as the editor for .doc files in your operating system, then opening the file will launch Microsoft Word as an OLE document within the workbench editor area. The workbench menu bar and toolbar will be updated with options for Microsoft Word.

You can assign or reassign the default editor for any file type using the **Workbench > File Associations** preference page. If you would like to edit XML or HTML files within Eclipse, you can assign those extensions to the generic Eclipse text editor or use the file context menu to pick the **Text Editor** instead of the default **System Editor**.

Other open source or commercial plug-ins are available that extend your Eclipse workbench with custom editors for XML, HTML, and other file types. The Eclipse Web Tools Platform project will include editors for these types of files and others.

You can split the editor area of your workbench if you would like to view or edit two or more files simultaneously. Left-click on an editor tab and drag it to the top, bottom, left, or right margin. You'll see an outline of the proposed new editor location. To accept it, release the mouse button. To restore a single editor area, close the files in one of the partitions or drag them back into the center of the primary location.

You cannot split the window to show two editors for the same file. This is a frequently requested enhancement for Eclipse, so it may be available in a future version.

4.4   Preferences: Have It *Your* Way

We have already touched on a few preference settings in this and previous chapters. Let's take a step back and review the general capabilities and use of Eclipse preferences. You can review or modify preference settings for all Eclipse plug-ins using a shared dialog; select the menu **Window > Preferences**. The standard set of preferences is shown in Figure 4-9.

The standard Eclipse 3.0 SDK workbench contains over 60 preference pages, which are organized into a hierarchy of categories. Additional preference settings are added with each new release, allowing you to control hundreds of details about the way Eclipse works. When you install a new plug-in, it will typically contribute a new category of preference settings to this window.

As an Eclipse newcomer, you should start with the preference defaults and modify a few settings while exploring the topics in this book. As you get comfortable with the preference categories, it will become natural to explore and adjust preferences while working on specific tasks in the workbench.

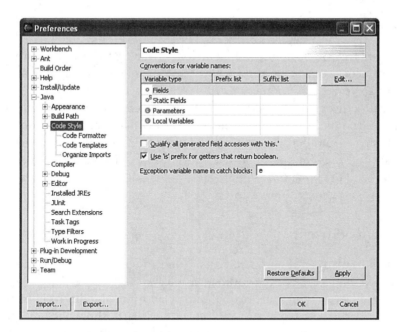

Figure 4-9   Shared dialog for all Eclipse workbench preferences.

4.4.1 Scope of Preference Settings

Most preference settings are limited to the current workspace. If you have several workspaces for your projects, each will have separate preference settings. However, this is not always desirable. You may want to use the same preferences for several workspaces, or you may want unique preferences for individual projects in a workspace.

To accommodate this, Eclipse defines three *preference scopes*:

Configuration. These preference settings are saved in your Eclipse installation directory and are shared by all workspace instances.

Workspace Instance. Each workspace instance defines preferences shared by all of its projects. This is the default preference scope.

Project. Some preference settings may be limited to one project.

The separation of these three levels of preference scope is still a work in progress in the Eclipse platform. More control over the scope of preference settings will be available in future releases. If unspecified, the preference scope is probably limited to your current workspace.

4.4.2 Sharing Your Preferences

Share your hard work with others! Contribute your preferences as best practices for your project team or jump-start new team members with coding styles that are unique to your tools and design.

You can export all of your workspace preference settings by pressing the **Export...** button on the Preferences dialog, as shown in Figure 4-9. You can then import these into another workspace by opening that workspace in a new Eclipse workbench and pressing the **Import...** button in this dialog. To share them with your team, send the preference export file as an email attachment or check it into your team version control repository.

4.4.3 Keyboard Shortcuts

Eclipse defines many keyboard shortcuts. You can customize any of these shortcuts using the preference page **Workbench > Keys**.

For those of you who are already familiar with Emacs editor bindings, these are also predefined. Switch to the Emacs keyboard shortcuts on the same preference page by changing the **Active configuration** setting from "Default" to "Emacs."

4.5   Individual and Team Preferences

It's easy to get lost in the details of so many customization and preference settings. One helpful way to think about these choices is to distinguish between settings related primarily to individual biases, experiences, or quirks and those settings that directly affect the style, structure, or compliance of code that is written. The latter group of preferences should be agreed upon and shared by all members of a project team.

4.5.1 Individual Preferences

The following list is not an exhaustive summary of individual preference categories, but it gives you a starting point when considering your alternatives.

- Keyboard shortcuts
- Workbench and editor appearance, colors, and font
- Perspective layout and view selection
- View filters
- Linked resource locations

4.5.2 Team Preferences

Team preferences are equally beneficial to individual developers, but they also have an impact on coordinated teamwork and shared code.

○ Code style and format
○ Code templates
○ Comment templates
○ Task tags
○ Java JRE version (1.3, 1.4, or 1.5)
○ Compiler options (flagging errors and warning)
○ Team file content types (e.g., binary or text)

4.6 Distilled

○ Don't get tunnel vision within one perspective and try to force all of your work into a single set of views. Take advantage of using several perspectives, where each is organized to maximize productivity for related tasks. Create or customize perspectives to fit your needs.

○ Explore the range of specialized views that are available in Eclipse. Using the right view or set of views can increase your productivity significantly.

○ Use filters in the **Package Explorer** view and the marker views (**Problems**, **Tasks**, and **Bookmarks**) to cope with information overload.

○ Personalize Eclipse to fit your style and work. Match your habits from other editors or IDEs and explore the many options in Eclipse.

○ Share your best practices and team standards with all members by exporting preferences and sharing project settings.

CHAPTER 5

Rapid Development

Eclipse really shines in its ability to improve your development productivity. It offers features that help you navigate and understand large, complex Java projects and automate repetitive or tedious tasks. This chapter does not cover all such features in Eclipse—it's a very long list—but it introduces the fundamental capabilities and explains how they work. Additional related features are described in Part 2 as part of agile development.

In this chapter, we'll see how to

- ❍ Use the Java editor and **Outline** view for synchronized navigation and editing
- ❍ Configure source attachments that display Javadoc comments in hovers and code completion lists
- ❍ Use Content Assist and code templates to speed up your development
- ❍ Use Quick Fix to apply automatic error correction
- ❍ Generate getter and setter methods automatically for fields
- ❍ Explore type hierarchies in the **Hierarchy** view

5.1 Expanding the Product Catalog Design

Our product catalog implementation started with a simple first iteration in Chapter 2, "Hello Eclipse," and then added an empty project structure in Chapter 3, "Managing Your Projects." We discussed the product catalog requirements with our users and sketched the next iteration as a class diagram shown in Figure 5-1.

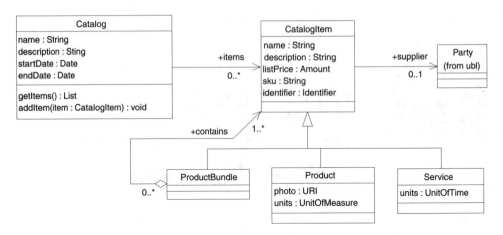

Figure 5-1   Expanded class diagram for product catalog.

This design does not show all getter and setter methods, but we assume they are available for each of the fields and associations between classes. Three subclasses of `CatalogItem` have been added to the design.

We anticipate creating a reusable library of e-commerce components based on the Universal Business Language (UBL) standard and have included three references to those components: `Party`, `Amount`, and `Identifier`. Other reusable components may be discovered and included, but let's get started with the next iteration.

5.2   Dynamic Duo: Editor and Outline

The Java editor is an amazingly powerful and versatile tool. It includes basic text editing features that you would expect and then adds dozens of other capabilities that are unique to Java source code. We'll begin using several especially cool features for navigating within and between Java classes.

In Chapter 4, "Customizing Your Workbench," you learned that the generic **Outline** view adapts its content to whatever resource type is displayed in the current editor. When a Java editor is open, the **Outline** view contains a list of all imports, fields, methods, and inner classes defined in that file. An editor and **Outline** view for our `Catalog` class is shown in Figure 5-2.

When you select any item in the **Outline** view, the corresponding definition is selected and displayed in the Java editor. This is helpful when navigating unfamiliar code or large classes with many methods. The **Outline** view's toolbar contains tools for sorting and filtering the members that are displayed. You can hide field definitions or non-public methods when viewing the public API of a class.

You can also customize the display to show only members matching a name expression.

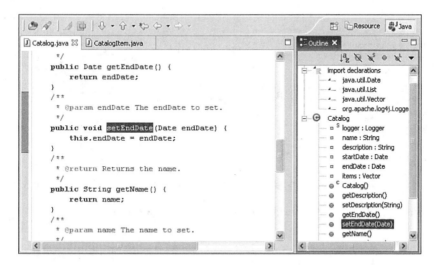

Figure 5-2   Dynamic duo: synchronized locations in Java editor and **Outline** view.

You should also try pressing the fourth icon from the left in the toolbar shown in Figure 5-2. This command toggles a feature to show source for only the selected element, (such as the setEndDate() method in Figure 5-2). Your source file is not modified; the editor simply displays a subset of the file.

An even more powerful feature is the ability to navigate between classes. Position the cursor within a referenced type in the Java editor; the cursor can be located anywhere within the type name. For example, select the class Date in the editor. Then press the **F3** key, which opens a new editor for the selected type. The class file editor for Date is shown in Figure 5-3.

Shortcut: F3: Navigate to a type, method, or field at the current cursor location.

Shortcut: Ctrl+Shift+T: Open an editor for any Java type that is available in your workspace. Also via menu **Navigate > Open Type...** or using a toolbar icon.

Figure 5-3   Use the **F3** shortcut to open an editor for the selected type.

The contents of this editor and the corresponding **Outline** view are produced by analyzing the compiled .class file for java.util.Date. But notice the button within this editor labeled **Attach Source....** If you have the source code for this class in a project folder or JAR or ZIP file, click the button and enter the file location.

Because Date is part of the standard Java library, its source is included when you download the Java software development kit (SDK) from the official Java web site at *java.sun.com*. If you have not downloaded the full Java SDK, then do so now. Depending on how the SDK was installed and how you launched Eclipse, the source may already be attached. If not, enter a source attachment location similar to the following:

```
C:\j2sdk1.4.2_02\src.zip
```

This class file editor will be updated immediately to display the complete source code for java.util.Date or the source of any other class in the standard Java library such as java.lang.String. You can then select a class name within one of these class file editors and navigate to other classes in any imported library, with or without attached source code. This is an excellent way to explore and understand any Java library.

Shortcut: Ctrl+O: Open a lookup dialog containing a list of members in the current Java editor. Start typing characters to limit the list and press Enter to go to the selected member. This is a quick alternative to the **Outline** view.

Shortcut: Ctrl+F3: Open a member lookup dialog for the class name at the current cursor location; e.g., position on `Date` and press **Ctrl+F3** to review and look up one of its methods.

Refer to Figure 5-1 and begin implementing the `addItem()` method for `Catalog`. Another Java editor feature jumps out at you. As your mouse hovers over any Java type, field, or method name, a small pop-up window displays information about that term's definition. Move the mouse away from that term, and the window disappears. For example, hovering over `add(item)` in Figure 5-4 displays a complete signature for this method. These pop-up windows are referred to as *hover help*, or simply *hovers* in Eclipse documentation.

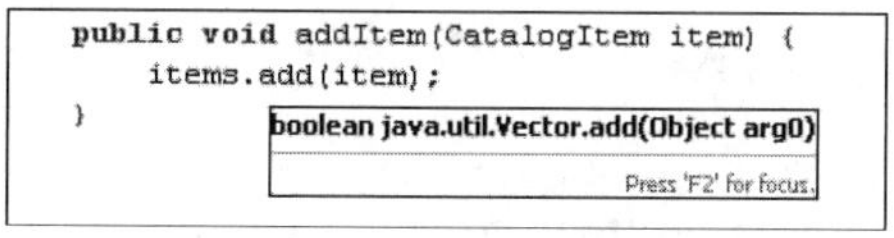

```
public void addItem(CatalogItem item) {
    items.add(item);
}
         boolean java.util.Vector.add(Object arg0)
                                    Press 'F2' for focus
```

Figure 5-4   Hover over a method without attached source.

The hover shown in Figure 5-4 is produced if no source attachment is available. However, if you have attached source, then the Javadoc associated with the selected term is displayed, as shown in Figure 5-5.

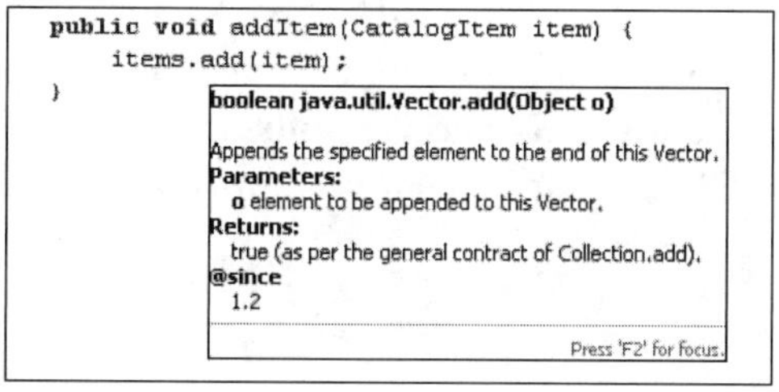

```
public void addItem(CatalogItem item) {
    items.add(item);
}
         boolean java.util.Vector.add(Object o)

         Appends the specified element to the end of this Vector.
         Parameters:
           o element to be appended to this Vector.
         Returns:
           true (as per the general contract of Collection.add).
         @since
           1.2

                                    Press 'F2' for focus
```

Figure 5-5   Hover display with source code attachment.

The gray *ruler* at the left margin of the Java editor area may contain icons that flag errors, warnings, or problems detected during compilation. Icons also appear if you have created bookmarks, added breakpoints for debugging, or recorded notes in the **Tasks** view. You can view details for any icons in the ruler by hovering the mouse over them.

Hovers displayed in the Java editor are very useful when browsing and navigating unfamiliar code. However, preferences for how and when these pop-up windows are opened may differ between developers or stages of development work. Having pop-up windows open automatically as your mouse moves across the editor can be distracting, especially when the pop-up windows are large.

Preference settings exist that allow hovers to be displayed on demand or only when a modifier key is pressed while hovering. These settings, shown in Figure 5-6, are found on the **Hovers** tab of the **Java > Editor** preference page. The **Combined Hover** determines its information content based on the current context of the selected element, chosen in the following order:

- When hovering over a variable while debugging, its current value is displayed.

- When hovering over an element that has a compiler problem, the problem description is displayed.

- Otherwise, display the formatted Javadoc text for the element under the mouse.

The default preference setting for the **Combined Hover** is to display it when no modifier key is pressed. This is the behavior described so far in this chapter. In Figure 5-6, we have changed this preference to require that the **Shift** key be pressed while hovering to trigger display of the **Combined Hover**. Simply hold down the **Shift** key while moving the mouse around the Java editor to obtain the Javadoc hovers.

As you can see in the preferences, a default setting exists to display the source code of the selected element while hovering with the **Ctrl** key pressed. Nothing will be displayed if source code is not attached to the selected element.

You can disable all hovers in the Java editor by unchecking the options for **Combined Hover** and **Source** in Figure 5-6. The **Combined Hover** is still available on demand by pressing the **F2** function key; hover information is displayed for the element at the cursor position.

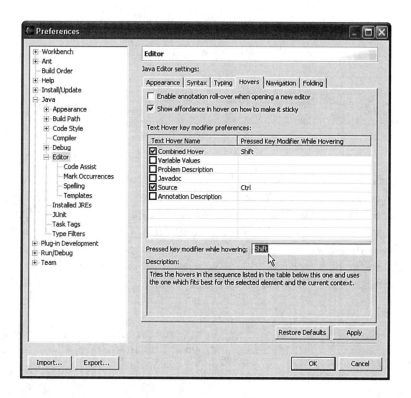

Figure 5-6   Change preferences for hover activation in the Java editor.

5.3   Using Content Assist

Content Assist is a general capability for prompting you with a list of possible ways to complete your current code expression. The list is determined relative to the cursor position by using the previous or enclosing word as a key to find appropriate content. For example, type "get" and then press **Ctrl+Space** or select the menu **Edit > Content Assist**. A list of types, methods, and field names beginning with get is shown, and code templates whose name starts with get are proposed. Select one of these options to insert its code at the cursor position. Otherwise, press the **Esc** key or click away to exit without modifying your code.

Content Assist can do the following for you:

❍ Complete type, variable, or method names anywhere in your code.

❍ Guess new variable or parameter names from their types.

❍ Insert code templates representing common coding pattern.

○ In Javadoc comments, insert HTML tags or standard Javadoc tags.

○ Fill field values in dialogs and wizards.

> **Shortcut: Ctrl+Space:** Opens a Content Assist list using the enclosed or previous word as a key for finding appropriate content suggestions.

A list of suggestions is produced only when the selected element represents a Java type that is included in the **Java Build Path** for the project containing the file being edited. **Java Build Path** configuration is explained in detail in Chapter 6, "Java Project Configuration." For the remainder of this chapter, we assume that the build path includes the necessary types. Our product catalog project, as described so far, does not require any configuration of the build path beyond the default settings from the **New Java Project** wizard.

> **Tip:** You can control several aspects of how Content Assist is invoked or the way its changes are made to your code. See the **Java > Editor > Code Assist** preference page. These preferences include use of a period character "." to trigger Content Assist suggestions for method completion.

5.3.1 Insert Types and Variable Names

When it comes to programming, speed is good. And we all can use a memory prompt from time to time. This first use of Content Assist is simple but very effective.

Let's say you need to write the following statement:

```
CatalogItem catalogItem = null;
```

Start by typing "cat" and press **Ctrl+Space** to activate Content Assist. The search for a match is not case sensitive, so you can save time by using all lower-case. A list similar to that shown in Figure 5-7 is displayed; the exact contents of type names beginning with these letters depends on the libraries that are on your project's **Java Build Path**. Press the down arrow and select `CatalogItem`—notice that the Javadoc we entered for the class comment is displayed to describe the use of this class.

Figure 5-7   Content Assist for completing a class name.

While the list is displayed, you can type additional characters to reduce the number of options. Type an "a" and the list is reduced to two items beginning with cata. Press the Enter key when CatalogItem is selected in the list. The letters "cat" are replaced by the complete class name. If necessary, an import statement for this class is inserted automatically.

Now type one space after the class name and press **Ctrl+Space** again. Content Assist attempts to guess a variable name from the preceding class name. When only one name is guessed, it is inserted automatically, and you are done. Multiple names are proposed for longer class names.

> **Tip:** You can uncheck the option to **Insert single proposals automatically** on the **Java > Editor > Code Assist** preference page if you want to be prompted for insertion of all Content Assist suggestions.

If a type name is composed of multiple parts using the *upper camel case* form (i.e., uppercase letters separate parts of the name), several variable names are proposed that combine one or more parts of the name. This follows common programming conventions. So, for CatalogItem, a list including item and catalogItem is displayed. Select the second option and press **Enter** to complete your statement.

This same kind of assistance is available while typing parameters in a method declaration, where the type name and derived parameter name become an argument for the method.

5.3.2 Method Name Completion

As you type in the Java editor, Content Assist is activated whenever you pause after typing a period character. If you know the full name and continue typing without a pause, then the completion list is not shown. For example, as shown in Figure 5-8, type "`items.`" and then pause for half a second—the period after `items` is significant here because it is the trigger that invokes automatic method completion. You also can activate Content Assist immediately by pressing **Ctrl+Space** without waiting for auto-activation. A list of all possible method names appears that are applicable to this variable. In this example, you must have previously defined a field named `items` whose type is `Vector`.

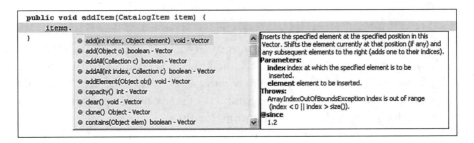

Figure 5-8   Method name completion while typing.

After the completion list appears, start typing characters to narrow the list contents, or press **Backspace** to expand the list. For example, type "`add`" and only the methods beginning with `add` are shown, then press **Backspace** twice and all methods beginning with `a` are shown. You may also use the up and down arrows on the keyboard as well as **Page Up, Page Down, Home,** and **End** to navigate the list. You can also use the mouse to scroll in the pop-up window. Press the **Enter** key after selecting the desired method.

If source code has been attached, the detailed Javadoc comment is shown for each completion method as you navigate the list of possibilities. Similar capabilities exist if you do not have source code to attach, but the Javadoc comment will not appear, and the method parameter names are less informative. For example, the first method in Figure 5-8 would be displayed as `add(int ag0, Object arg1)` instead of `add(int index, Object element)`.

At first glance this code completion appears to be a helpful feature for lazy typists. But it is most beneficial for reminding you of details about the thousands of method names used in your coding, especially when working with unfamiliar libraries. What are the various forms of `add` available for a `Vector`? What are the alternative `substring` methods on `String`?

5.3.3 Source Code Templates

Templates are structured descriptions of coding patterns that occur often in source code. The Java editor supports use of Content Assist to insert templates that fill in commonly used source patterns. Each template has a name that is used to include the template in the list of suggestions.

Many common templates are already defined. Browse the list of templates in **Window > Preferences > Java > Editor > Templates,** where you can also edit the existing definitions and create your own templates.

One common coding pattern is to use a `for` loop that iterates over the elements of a collection or array. In Chapter 2, you implemented a `main()` method for testing our product catalog that contains this code fragment:

```
} else if (data.startsWith("list")) {
    for (Iterator items = catalog.getItems().iterator();
            items.hasNext();) {
        CatalogItem item = (CatalogItem) items.next();
        System.out.println("Product: " + item.getName());
    }
}
```

We'll now use templates to write this same code. The following steps and figures guide you through the process. Follow the steps carefully and do not click away from the template before you are finished. Clicking the mouse outside of the template commits your changes and ends the template guidance.

1. Type the word "`for`" and press **Ctrl+Space** to activate Content Assist. A list similar to Figure 5-9 is displayed. Use the up and down arrow keys to scroll through the list; each selection displays an example of the code that is inserted. Select **for - iterate over collection** and press **Enter.**

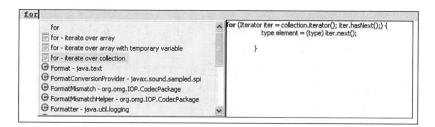

Figure 5-9   Select a for loop template to iterate over a collection.

2. The template shown in Figure 5-10 is now inserted and gives you additional assistance in replacing template parameters. The iterator variable initially named `iter` is highlighted. Type "`items`" which will also modify two other occurrences of this variable.

```
for (Iterator iter = collection.iterator(); iter.hasNext();) {
    type element = (type) iter.next();

}
```

Figure 5-10   Replace the `iter` variable name with `items`; two other occurrences are also replaced.

3. Press the **Tab** key to move to the next template parameter; you can also press **Shift+Tab** to return to the previous parameter. Replace the name `collection` with "`catalog.getItems()`".

4. Pressing **Tab** again takes you to `type`. This is the type to which the objects in the collection must be cast. Type "`CatalogItem`". The second occurrence of `type` is changed automatically. Your template will now look like Figure 5-11.

```
for (Iterator items = catalog.getItems().iterator(); items.hasNext();) {
    CatalogItem element = (CatalogItem) items.next();

}
```

Figure 5-11   Replace the `type` name with `CatalogItem`; one other occurrence is also replaced.

5. Press the **Tab** key, which moves you to the variable named `element`. Replace it with "`item`".

6. Press **Tab** once more to position the cursor in the body of the loop, ready to enter its statements.

7. There is another template we can use to write a message onto the console. First, type the string value that you want printed:

```
"Product: " + item.getName()
```

8. Now select this expression and press **Ctrl+Space** to activate Content Assist. The list shown in Figure 5-12 is displayed. Scroll down to the template named `sysout` and press **Enter**.

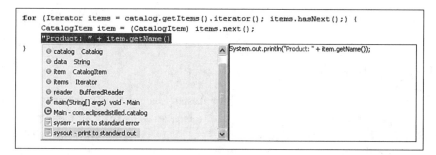

Figure 5-12   Wrap the selected string with a `sysout` template; the resulting code replacement is shown to the right.

9. This template wraps a system output command around the selected expression. The resulting code should look identical to the loop written manually in Chapter 2.

Browse through the list in **Window > Preferences > Java > Editor > Templates** to get familiar with other templates that are available. For example, type "`pub`" and activate Content Assist to select a template that inserts a new public method into your class. With a bit of practice, you'll be coding at record speed.

5.3.4 *Javadoc Content Assist*

A *Javadoc comment* is a Java comment that starts with `/**`. These comments, which occur before declarations for types, fields, and methods, are used to generate HTML documentation from your source code.

The Javadoc specification defines a list of tags beginning with @ that produce formatted output in the HTML. Similar to the way that a period character triggers automatic content assist for method completion, an @ symbol triggers automatic assistance for completion of Javadoc tags. You are presented with a list of the Javadoc tags, such as `@author`, `@version`, `@param`, and so on.

Several of the Javadoc tags, such as `@param`, `@see`, and `@throws`, are followed by type, parameter, or method names from your code. After adding one of these tags and the first few letters of the desired value, activate Content Assist to get a list of terms for completing the tag value. For example, enter `@throws  num` and then activate Content Assist to get a list that contains `NumberFormatException`.

Any formatting that you'd like to see in the generated HTML must be marked using HTML tags within your Javadoc comment, such as `<b>bold</b>` for bold text or `<br>` for a line break. While your cursor is within the body of a

Javadoc comment, activate Content Assist to get a list of standard HTML tags that can be inserted.

5.4   Using Quick Fix

Quick Fix works similarly to Content Assist, except that it is specialized for fixing errors or warnings in your code. It is a smart critic that can analyze your errors and suggest possible corrections. Your code is automatically modified when you select one of the suggestions.

Light bulb icons appear in the Java editor's ruler to indicate when Quick Fix is available for problems on that line. To enable these icons, you must check the option to **Indicate annotations solvable with Quick Fix in vertical ruler** within the preferences page **Window > Preferences > Java > Editor** on the **Appearance** tab. You can then click on one of the light bulb icons to invoke Quick Fix. These icon annotations are shown by default when you install Eclipse.

> **Shortcut: Ctrl+1:** Activates Quick Fix for a warning or error at the current cursor position. Warnings and errors are normally underlined with yellow or red squiggly lines.

The following list includes a sample of the Quick Fix corrections that are available in Eclipse:

- ○ Remove unused, unresolved, or non-visible `import` statements (these are normally shown as warnings in the Java editor).
- ○ Add an `import` statement for a type that cannot be resolved but that exists in the project.
- ○ Create a new method for reference to a method signature that cannot be resolved.
- ○ Add a method `return` statement if missing.
- ○ Handle an uncaught exception by surrounding a method call with a `try/catch` block or adding a `catch` block to an existing `try` block.
- ○ Remove an unneeded `catch` block when the exception is not thrown within its `try` block.

In the next example, we'll use Quick Fix in a way that is similar to Content Assist; that is, to accelerate our development by inserting common code patterns. But this time, code generation is used to eliminate a compilation error.

1. We know that the URL class's constructor throws an exception that must be caught. Type the code shown in Figure 5-13 and notice the immediate display of a syntax error. A Quick Fix light bulb also appears in the ruler of the Java editor. Hover your mouse over either the bulb or the underlined code to display an error message.

2. If you have not yet used URL within this class, the first action is to resolve this import error. Click on the Quick Fix light bulb or press **Ctrl+1** while the cursor is on this line. A list of solutions is proposed, as shown in Figure 5-13. Select the first solution to see a preview of the modified code at the right of the list. Choose this solution by double-clicking or pressing **Enter**.

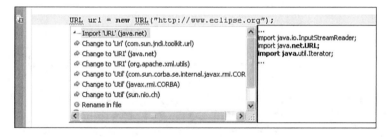

Figure 5-13   Click the Quick Fix light bulb or press **Ctrl+1** to get a list of suggestions. Choose the first option to add the missing import statement.

3. After importing this class, you now see the error shown in Figure 5-14.

Figure 5-14   Hover over the Quick Fix light bulb or over an underlined error in your code to see a description of the problem.

4. Click on the light bulb or press **Ctrl+1** to see the solutions shown in Figure 5-15. Select a solution to see a preview of the code at the right of the list. Choose the second solution by double-clicking or pressing **Enter**.

Figure 5-15   Activate Quick Fix by clicking on the light bulb to get a list of corrections. Choose the second option to surround this statement with try/catch.

5. Your code is modified and reformatted as shown here. Modify the catch body to log, handle, or re-throw the exception.

```
try {
    URL url = new URL("http://www.eclipse.org");
} catch (MalformedURLException e1) {
    // TODO Auto-generated catch block
    e1.printStackTrace();
}
```

Shortcut: Ctrl+Shift+M: Add an import statement for a type that cannot be resolved but that exists in the project. This is a shortcut for using Quick Fix (**Ctrl+1**) and then selecting the option to import the class. Also invoke via the context menu **Source > Add Import**.

Shortcut: Ctrl+Shift+O: Organize imports for the Java type being edited. For all types that are unresolved, import statements are added automatically if the types can be found in the Java Build Path. A choice dialog is opened to prompt you with alternatives when a type name is ambiguous. Also invoke via the context menu **Source > Organize Imports**.

5.5   Generate Getters and Setters

In Chapter 2, you implemented `getName()` and `setName()` methods for the `CatalogItem` class. This is a ubiquitous pattern that encapsulates fields as private members of a class and implements getter and setter methods to access the field values. The setter methods may also implement additional constraint checking and change notification behavior.

Eclipse includes a single command that generates all of these methods. Refer to the class diagram in Figure 5-1 and edit your `CatalogItem` implementation to add field declarations for each attribute. Then, as shown in Figure 5-16, right-click in the editor to choose the menu item for **Generate Getters and Setters....**

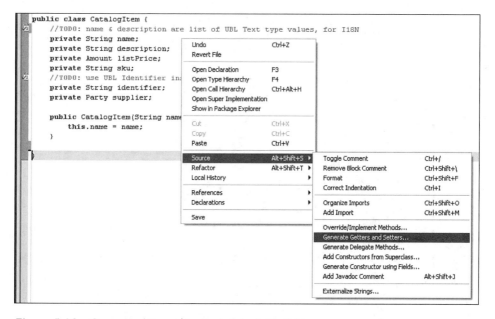

Figure 5-16   Generate getter and setter methods for fields.

In the resulting dialog, shown in Figure 5-17, you can refine the field selection to omit setters for fields that you want to be read-only values. You can also specify whether the generated methods are inserted at the beginning or end of the class implementation, or after a particular method already defined in the class. Select the last option to **Generate method comment,** and standard Javadoc comments are generated for each method, complete with `@param` and `@return` comments derived from the method signature.

In Chapter 2, you modified the code generation templates for new file and type comments. You can also modify the code templates for **Getter body, Setter body, Getter comment,** and **Setter comment.** You may want to customize the comment format to satisfy standards adopted by your team. But more significant for developer productivity, you might expand the **Setter body** to automatically generate code that fires Java bean property change events. You might also include logging commands that produce debug log entries each time a field value is changed.

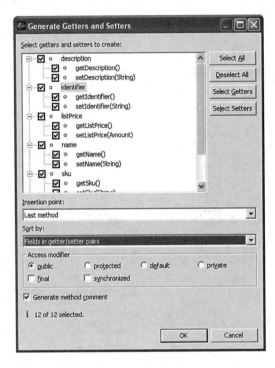

Figure 5-17   Choose options when generating getter and setter methods.

When the templates are modified to suit team standards, you should export a copy of all code templates and share it with your team members. When a new member joins the team, he or she simply imports all code templates into a new workspace and is immediately compliant with team standards.

5.6   Exploring Hierarchies

When exploring object-oriented code, the *type hierarchy* is an important aspect of its design for reuse. The hierarchy in Java code is determined by classes extending classes, interfaces extending interfaces, and classes implementing interfaces. Understanding these hierarchies is one of your first tasks as you learn and extend the design of code libraries created by your team members or acquired from third parties.

The **Hierarchy** view in Eclipse is provided for exactly this purpose. It is open by default in the Java perspective, stacked under the **Package Explorer** view. This view has three modes for displaying the hierarchy of a *focus type*:

- ❍ **Type Hierarchy.** Displays types that extend, are extended by, or implement the focus type. The left side of Figure 5-18 displays this view of the `java.util.Vector` class, where all subclasses and superclasses are shown for types available in the workspace.

- ❍ **Subtype Hierarchy.** Displays a subset of the **Type Hierarchy** containing types that extend or implement the focus type (not shown in the figure).

- ❍ **Supertype Hierarchy.** Displays all types that the focus type extends, plus all implemented interfaces if the focus type is a class. The supertype hierarchy of `Vector` is shown on the right side of Figure 5-18. You can see that `Vector` extends `AbstractList` and implements `Cloneable`, `List`, `RandomAccess`, and `Serializable`.

Double-click any type or method in the **Hierarchy** view to open an editor containing its source.

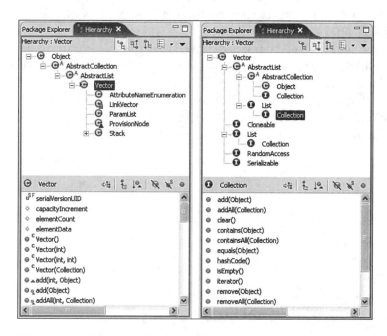

Figure 5-18   View the **Type Hierarchy** and **Supertype Hierarchy** of the `Vector` class. Select a type in the hierarchy to display its fields and methods in the lower pane.

One common question asked by developers is, "What classes implement this interface?" If you need that answer for the List interface shown in Figure 5-18, simply right-click on List and choose **Focus on 'List'** from the context menu. The **Type Hierarchy** in the updated view displays all classes that implement List and all interfaces that extend the List interface.

There are several ways to open the **Hierarchy** view for a Java class or interface:

○ While in the Java editor, position the cursor on a type name and press **F4** or choose **Open Type Hierarchy** from the context menu. For example, position the cursor on Vector while editing the Catalog class to open the Vector hierarchy view.

○ Press **Ctrl+Shift+H** or choose **Navigate > Open Type in Hierarchy...** from the workbench menu. A dialog will open where you can enter any type name available in the workspace.

The **Hierarchy** view is one of the first places to go when you need to learn about a new class or interface. If a co-worker starts talking about the HttpServlet type in a J2EE application and you have the necessary J2EE libraries added to a project in your workspace (see Chapter 6), then simply press **Ctrl+Shift+H**, enter "HttpServlet," and start exploring!

A related **Quick Type Hierarchy** is available as a pop-up in the Java editor by pressing **Ctrl+T**. If the cursor position is on a Java type name, the pop-up hierarchy is the same as that displayed in the **Hierarchy** view. When the cursor is on a method, a hierarchy of types implementing or defining that method is displayed in the pop-up, as shown in Figure 5-19. Click on one of the types in that hierarchy to open an editor positioned to show this method.

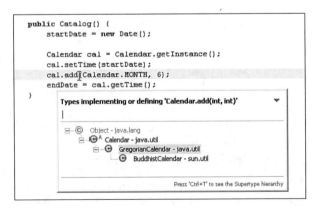

Figure 5-19   A **Quick Type Hierarchy** pop-up window can be opened in the Java editor by pressing **Ctrl+T**.

5.7   Distilled

○ The **Outline** view displays a list of all fields, methods, and inner classes in the current Java editor; selections are synchronized with the editor position.

○ Explore unfamiliar Java class libraries using the **F3** and **Ctrl+F3** shortcuts to open a new editor for referenced types and methods.

○ Use Content Assist to accelerate development by inserting type and variable names or completing methods while you type.

○ Configure source code files to obtain detailed Javadoc information in hovers and Content Assist lists.

○ Use source code templates to insert and guide you through common coding patterns such as `for` loops, `switch` statements, or `try`/`catch` blocks. Customize or create new templates to suit your needs and style.

○ Quick Fix provides suggestions and automatic correction of common compilation errors, such as failure to catch a thrown exception.

○ Generate getter and setter methods for selected fields in your class. Customize method templates, e.g., to add logging or change notification in all setter methods.

○ The **Hierarchy** view allows you to rapidly explore and navigate the type hierarchies in Java code, as determined by classes extending classes, interfaces extending interfaces, and classes implementing interfaces.

CHAPTER 6

Java Project Configuration

Eclipse includes features such as Content Assist and code templates that enhance rapid development and others that accelerate your navigation and learning of unfamiliar code. Automatic compilation and building of complex projects provides additional acceleration by giving immediate feedback on code changes and project status. All of these features depend on correct configuration of the projects in your workspace.

We continue development of the product catalog and order processing application by configuring the project dependencies required to build and run that code. Part of the configuration consists of including a JAR file for the Apache log4j logging utility and a shared library of components from the Apache Axis Web Services toolkit.

This chapter does not describe configuration and use of a source code version control repository. Eclipse has excellent support for team repositories such as CVS, which is described in Chapter 13, "Team Ownership with CVS." If you are joining an existing development team, you can skip directly to that chapter after reading this one.

In this chapter, we'll see how to

❍ Configure your project's source and output folders

❍ Configure dependencies between Java projects

❍ Add libraries to your build path

❍ Create named user libraries composed of related JAR files

❍ Override workspace compiler preferences with project-specific settings

6.1   Java Build Path

Up to this point, our product catalog project had no dependencies other than the Java runtime libraries. It is now time to expand our development to include the other projects set up in Chapter 3, "Managing Your Projects." External dependencies are also added into the mix, such as Apache log4j and Axis Web Services toolkit. Correct configuration is essential for error-free compilation, execution, and full use of Eclipse features such as Content Assist.

Edit the configuration properties for a Java project by selecting the project and choosing **Project > Properties** from the main workbench menu bar. The dialog shown in Figure 6-1 is opened.

The same property editor dialog may be opened using another approach. Most Eclipse resources have property pages that describe or allow you to set that resource's properties. This is true for any resource, not only for projects. The last menu item in a resource's context menu is always named **Properties,** and it displays a shared dialog with one or more pages that are assigned based on the resource type. Projects with a Java nature have property pages as shown in Figure 6-1. Open this dialog by right-clicking on the `com.eclipsedistilled.` `orders` project in your workbench **Package Explorer** view and selecting **Properties.**

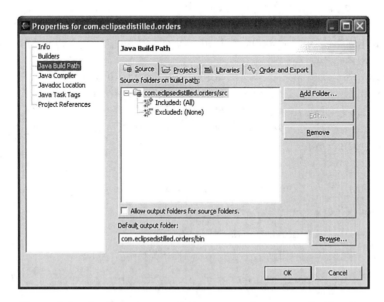

Figure 6-1   Configuring source folders in your Java project build path.

Each Java project has its own build path that specifies all dependencies required to compile the project. Those dependencies may come from other Java projects in the workspace, from Java archive `.jar` files, or from folders containing `.class` files.

The **Java Build Path** properties page contains four tabs:

○ **Source.** The source and output folders. If you initially create a project without separate source and output folders, you can change it here. Multiple source folders can be used in one project; e.g., to separate application source code from unit tests.

○ **Projects.** Check-off other projects in the workspace whose output folders should be added to this build path.

○ **Libraries.** Location of other archive files required by this project.

○ **Order and Export.** Order in which projects and libraries appear in the build path and the default runtime classpath; e.g., use classes from a workspace project before using the same classes from an archive library.

6.1.1 Source and Output Folders

Each Java project is configured with a *builder* that automatically compiles every `.java` file from the source folders and saves the `.class` files into an output folder. Your source folder must contain subfolders for the complete package hierarchy as used by your Java source files. As described in Chapter 2, "Hello Eclipse," you can create these folder hierarchies easily using the **New Java Package** wizard.

All non-Java files from the source folder are copied unchanged to the corresponding folder hierarchy in the output folder. These non-Java files are usually properties files and resource files. This sometimes creates confusion when Eclipse users store other configuration or documentation files within their source folder tree and then are surprised to see them copied into the output folder. These other non-source files should be saved in regular project folders that are not configured as source folders in the configuration. You can create regular folders outside the source tree by right-clicking on a project and selecting **New > Folder** instead of **New > Package**.

Figure 6-1 shows the source folder tab in the Java project properties. This project was created with separate source and output folders named `src` and `bin`, respectively. This setup will suffice for most new projects created within Eclipse, but you can change that configuration here.

If you want to keep your unit test code within the same project as the application code, then it's a good idea to create a separate source folder, named `test` for example. Click the **Add Folder...** button on the source configuration tab and then click **Create New Folder...** on the resulting dialog. If you create a test folder without adding it as a configured source folder, then Java source files within it will not be compiled.

Although it's fairly common for developers to keep unit test code in the same project as the code being tested, it is preferable to create a separate project for JUnit test cases because they often need a different **Java Build Path**. This is especially true if you are building applications using Java runtime libraries other than the J2SE libraries. For example, if you're building a J2ME application that depends on the Mobile Information Device Profile (MIDP), you'll have to put your JUnit test cases in a separate project because JUnit requires J2ME's Foundation as a minimum class library. It's also common to use additional JUnit framework libraries when testing Web and database applications.

The most common reason for using multiple source folders is to accommodate preexisting source code that was created outside of Eclipse. Developers can be very creative when organizing their projects! A test folder is sometime embedded within the application source folder, or several logically separate source trees may be included in the same folder.

Eclipse provides other ways to split these sources into logically separate projects or source folders without changing the original structure, which might be required by other tools or Ant build files. You can add inclusion and exclusion filters on a source folder to explicitly select the files that are or are not used to build this project. For example, if documentation files are stored within the source, you could exclude `**/*.html` files so that they are not copied into the output folder.

There are many other possibilities for configuring preexisting code within an Eclipse project. Search for "project configuration tutorial" in the Eclipse help documentation where other detailed scenarios and suggestions are provided.

6.1.2 Project Dependencies

When we created the projects for our order management application in Chapter 3, the project dependencies were not yet specified in the configuration. These dependencies are shown as a UML package diagram in Figure 6-2. These package names are shortened versions of the fully qualified project names used in our workspace. They represent the import dependencies between top-level packages in our application, but not necessarily the dependencies of all sub-packages and external utility libraries.

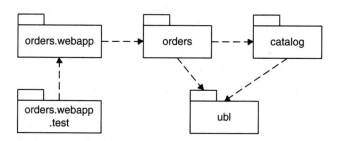

Figure 6-2   Order processing application package dependencies.

Click on the **Projects** tab in the build path configuration, as shown in Figure 6-3. All of the projects in your current workspace are listed except for the project we are now configuring, which is `com.eclipsedistilled.orders`.

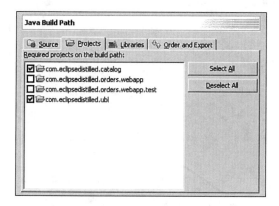

Figure 6-3   Configuring project dependencies for `com.eclipsedistilled.orders`.

Referring to the package diagram, we see that `orders` depends on `catalog` and `ubl`. Configure the dependencies in your Eclipse project by selecting the checkboxes for those two projects.

The end result is that the output folders from these other two projects are included in the build path of the current project, and their classes are available while compiling classes for `com.eclipsedistilled.orders`. Configuring these project references also causes their classes to be included in Quick Assist completion lists, so typing "`cat`" and then **Ctrl+Space** will now include the `Catalog` and `CatalogItem` classes in the pick list while writing the `Order` class.

6.1.3 Project Libraries

The **Libraries** tab of the **Java Build Path** dialog allows you to add other libraries into a project's classpath. A library is a JAR or ZIP archive containing Java class files or a project folder containing class files. An archive file may be in a project within your current workspace or elsewhere on your file system.

The library configuration for `com.eclipsedistilled.orders` is shown in Figure 6-4. The JRE System Library is included automatically in every Java project; it contains the standard Java APIs. We'll review two approaches for adding individual JAR libraries to this project and then create a named *user library* that bundles a collection of related JARs.

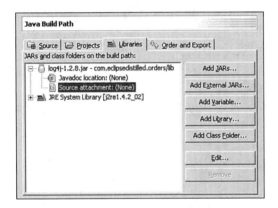

Figure 6-4   Configuring libraries for `com.eclipsedistilled.orders`.

The **Libraries** tab contains five buttons for specifying the location of required library files:

- ❍ **Add JARs.** Select archive files located within any project from the current workspace; projects are not required to be Java projects.

- ❍ **Add External JARs.** Select archive files anywhere on your file system external to the current workspace.

- ❍ **Add Variable.** Use a Java classpath variable as the base path for external archives.

- ❍ **Add Library.** Select from a list of user libraries that define collections of related archive files.

- ❍ **Add Class Folder.** Select any folder from a project in the current workspace that contains Java `.class` files.

An important consideration when planning your project configuration is portability between different developer workstations in a team environment, which might include portability across operating systems such as Windows, Linux, and Macintosh. The first library option, **Add JARs,** is usually the most portable but not always possible or desirable when using libraries from other vendor products. Using external libraries with absolute file paths is the least portable. We'll use the first approach to add the Apache log4j library to our project (see References).

It is common practice to create a subfolder named `lib` within a Java project that contains other JAR files required to build the project. Right-click on your project and select **New > Folder** to create this folder. Download the `log4j.jar` binary file and copy it into your project `lib` folder (the file name may include a version number).

If you copy the file into your project using the operating system command line or file explorer, then your Eclipse **Navigator** view or **Package Explorer** view is updated automatically if you have automatic refresh enabled; otherwise, you must manually refresh the `lib` folder (see Chapter 3).

> **Tip:** If you are using Eclipse on Windows, you can copy/paste or drag-and-drop files between the Windows file explorer and your Eclipse workbench folders in the same way you would between folders in the Windows Explorer. You can also cut/copy/drag between two Eclipse folders within the workbench on any operating system.

Now click the **Add JARs...** button, where you'll see a list of all projects in your workspace. Expand the project and `lib` folder containing `log4j.jar` and add it to this project's build path. It should appear as in Figure 6-4.

If you expand the `log4j.jar` entry in the configuration dialog, there are two optional entries about this library.

○ **Source attachment.** The folder or JAR file containing Java source code for classes in this library.

○ **Javadoc location.** The URL or external location containing a folder or ZIP file of Javadoc HTML for classes in this library.

This source attachment location is the same kind of entry we configured in Chapter 5, "Rapid Development," to enable Javadoc hover and Content Assist for the Java runtime library. If you have source code for other libraries, such as log4j, then edit this library entry to get the same benefits when working with its classes.

You can open a Web browser with the full Javadoc HTML documentation for a library's entries by pressing **Shift+F2** while the cursor is positioned on a class or method name in the editor. However, for this to work, you must configure the URL or directory where the HTML files are located.

> **Shortcut: Shift+F2**: Open the full Javadoc HTML for a Java class, method, or field at the current cursor position. This command is also accessible via the menu **Navigate > Open External Javadoc**.

You can also configure the Javadoc location for the Java runtime libraries by expanding the JRE System Library in this same configuration dialog. Expand the `rt.jar` archive and edit the Javadoc location. This location is preset with the value `http://java.sun.com/j2se/1.4.2/docs/api` when you install Eclipse (with version number appropriate to the JVM you used during installation). However, this will work only while you are connected to the Internet. You can change this URL to a local file path if you want to enable this feature while working offline.

This approach to project configuration is the easiest way to ensure that library locations are portable between different developer workstations and operating systems. All libraries are stored within the project folders, and locations (except for Javadoc files) are relative to the workspace home. If you zip your workspace and send it to another developer, he or she can simply unzip and open it in his or her Eclipse workbench. All project building and Content Assist will work without change.

Another way to configure library locations that also has benefits of machine and platform portability is to use *classpath variables*. Click the **Add Variable...** button in the **Java Build Path** dialog, which presents a new dialog, as shown in Figure 6-5.

In this example we'll add the standard J2EE Servlet API library to our `orders.webapp` project; a similar technique could be used for adding the log4j library. In Chapter 3, we reviewed the benefits of linked resource locations for gaining developer and platform portability of project files located outside of the workspace. Classpath variables are very similar to linked resource locations but require separate definitions.

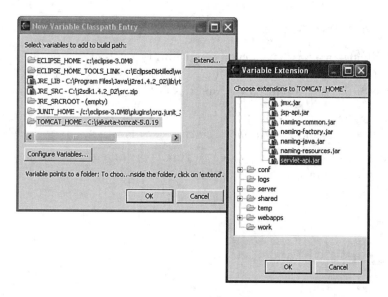

Figure 6-5   Extending a Java classpath variable in project build path.

Follow these steps to add a TOMCAT_HOME library location:

1. Click the **Configure Variables...** button in this dialog, where you can create a new variable or change a variable location value.

2. Add a new variable named TOMCAT_HOME with a location pointing to the root of your Tomcat application server installation, e.g., `C:/jakarta-tomcat-5.0.19`, and then click OK.

3. Back in the dialog shown in Figure 6-5, select this variable and click the **Extend...** button, which opens the second dialog also shown in the figure.

4. Expand the `common` and `lib` folders and then select `servlet-api.jar`. Click **OK**.

The Servlet library is now part of your project configuration. You can easily share this workspace or project with other developers who use a different path or different version of the Tomcat server. They only need to create a TOM-CAT_HOME classpath variable with their location. All other aspects of this project configuration remain unchanged.

You can review and update any of your classpath variables in the Eclipse preferences category **Java > Build Path > Classpath Variables**.

6.1.4 Order and Export

After specifying project dependencies and library references, you may need to configure two other aspects of the build path. These are shown on the **Order and Export** tab of the **Java Build Path** properties in Figure 6-6.

○ Change the order of class path entries in situations where the same class name exists in more than one project or JAR location.

○ Choose which project or JAR entries are contributed to other projects that have this project as one of their dependencies.

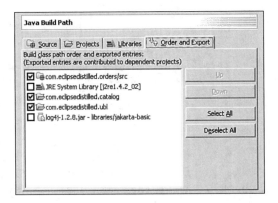

Figure 6-6   Configuring order and export of libraries for `com.eclipsedistilled.orders`.

The same class name may exist in more than one class path entry when you have a project in your workspace that includes an updated version of some classes in one of the referenced libraries. If you want to compile and run an application using the updated version, then you must place the project above the older library version in the build path order. We assume that the library JAR file contains other classes that you need; otherwise, just remove the old library from this project's build path.

A project's build path can also include the library entries defined within one or more of its required projects. For this to work, you must explicitly export a project's libraries that are shared with its clients. However, you need to be careful when exporting a project's libraries because doing so means that those libraries can be logically thought of as part of this project. Another approach is for the client project to import the library itself, in addition to importing the required project.

Refer to the package diagram in Figure 6-2 that shows dependencies between the projects in our order processing application. The `orders.webapp` project depends on only the `orders` project, but it will likely include references to classes from `catalog` and `ubl`. When configuring the build path for `orders.webapp`, we can include dependencies to these other two projects, or we can export these two projects from the `orders` project. We take the latter approach and select the export checkboxes for `catalog` and `ubl` when configuring the `orders` project in Figure 6-6.

The **Java Build Path** order also determines the order that source folders and libraries are displayed within a project in the **Package Explorer** view. In most situations, the order of libraries does not affect the way a project builds or runs, so you can reorder the source folders and libraries to appear in the **Package Explorer** view in a way that makes it easy to find references, such as ordering libraries alphabetically.

6.2   Create Shared User Libraries

When working with third-party commercial or open source libraries, or with standard APIs such as J2EE, it's common to require several JAR archives in combination. If these are used in only one project, then you can configure the build path as described in the previous section. However, you may need to include the libraries several times in a modular multi-project structure. It would be easier to define the combined library as a single entry.

This kind of configuration is called a *user library* in Eclipse. The JAR files contained within a user library are identified by an absolute file path external to the Eclipse workspace. It's helpful to have a consistent location for these libraries on your local or network file system. A library's files also might be located within a vendor product installation directory. We'll use the following file structure:

```
/eclipse-contrib/
    libraries/
        axis-1.2beta/
        j2ee/
        jarkata-basic/
        jakarta-j2ee/
```

Download the Apache Axis distribution (see References) and unzip its JAR files into the `axis-1.2beta` folder (or a similar folder name based on a newer version). Standard vendor-independent interface libraries are available for J2EE specifications such as Servlets, EJB, JNDI, JavaMail, and others; place these JARs into the `j2ee` folder. Many other useful utilities are available from the Apache

Jakarta project, including the log4j library. Place these JAR files in the `jakarta-basic` and `jakarta-j2ee` folders.

We could use a classpath variable to include J2EE library files from Tomcat or JBoss installations, just as we did with the Servlet library earlier in this chapter. However, because we may deploy to several different application servers, and because our project code is written to the standard J2EE APIs, we gain more flexibility by creating a vendor-independent J2EE user library. A user library allows us to add a single **Java Build Path** entry that includes all JAR files required for our J2EE development.

Open the Eclipse preferences page for user library configuration located in the category **Java > Build Path > User Libraries**. The configuration for the Apache Axis library is shown in Figure 6-7. Press the **Add JARs...** button, browse to the Axis library folder, and select the archive files.

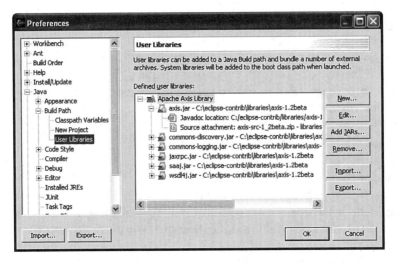

Figure 6-7   Create a new user library for the Apache Axis Web Services toolkit.

Download source and Javadoc ZIP files for each user library, if they are available. Doing so enables maximum benefit from Content Assist and Javadoc display when using these libraries in Eclipse. For convenience, place these files in the same directory as the binary JAR files. While adding each JAR file to the user library, also edit the associated Javadoc location and source attachment parameters. These values are shown for the `axis.jar` file in Figure 6-7.

The user library preferences page includes buttons for importing and exporting library definitions to a separate file that can be shared with your team members—note that this import/export is separate from the more general import/export of all workbench preferences. Export your new libraries to a file named `EclipseDistilled.userlibraries` and then notify other team members that they should import this file into their user library settings. This file does not contain the library's files—it only contains the file path locations to JARs, source attachments, and Javadoc HTML.

If others who import this file use a different file structure for organizing their external library files, they must edit the library definitions to remove and add the JAR files with correct path locations. Unfortunately class path variables are not available to parameterize the library file locations.

6.2.1 Linked Library Project

A useful hybrid strategy is to configure a user library that is also available as a linked folder in your Eclipse workspace. Follow these steps:

1. Create a *simple project* in your workspace. Unlike Java projects, a simple project has no Java build path configuration in its properties. Use the command **File > New > Project > Simple Project**.

2. Uncheck the option to use a default project location within the workspace folder and enter the path for your `\eclipse-contrib\libraries` folder (see Figure 6-8).

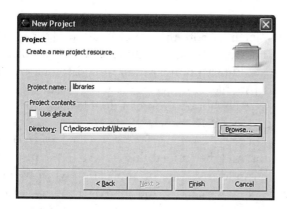

Figure 6-8   Create a new simple project with linked folder location.

3. Your new `libraries` project should look similar to the one in Figure 6-9.

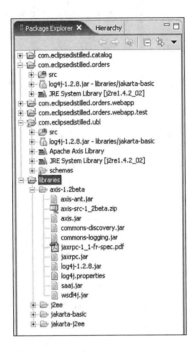

Figure 6-9   Java projects with sharing common libraries.

The Apache Axis distribution includes both the source code and Javadoc HTML files in one ZIP file, which is named `axis-src-1_2beta.zip` in this illustration. This file is used within the user library configuration to add source attachment and Javadoc to classes in this JAR file. Also notice the inclusion of a PDF specification file related to the JAX RPC library. You can double-click this file from within Eclipse to launch an external PDF reader.

In previous configuration of the `orders` project, we created a `lib` subfolder, copied the log4j JAR file into it, and then added this archive to the project build path. However, this approach can lead to a lot of duplication when we need the same JAR in several projects. Now we can use the shared `libraries` project to add log4j, or other `jakarta-basic` archives, into any of our projects.

In Figure 6-9, the shared log4j JAR has been added to both the `orders` and `ubl` projects. In addition, the Apache Axis Library is also included in the `ubl` project configuration as a user library; it includes a combination of six interdependent JAR files.

Eclipse has very flexible capabilities for configuring user libraries and leaves opportunity for creative arrangements. The hybrid approach described here has several benefits:

❍ Gather all of your open source libraries in a common folder named `/eclipse-contrib/libraries`.

❍ Download binary, source, Javadoc, and other related specifications into the same folder. Leave source and Javadoc files compressed in ZIP files.

❍ Create a simple project in each Eclipse workspace using a linked folder location for the project's contents. If you use multiple workspaces to separate your work as described in Chapter 3, then they can share the same reference libraries.

❍ Create user libraries when you often use several JAR files in combination. Export the user library definitions to share them between workspaces.

❍ Use the libraries project to add other individual JAR files to the build path of Java projects; use the **Add JARs...** button for portable location references.

6.3   Java Compiler Settings

The Java compiler settings enable you to control the problem messages produced by Eclipse while building your project. The problem severity level can be set to Error, Warning, or Ignore for more than 30 different conditions. These messages appear as markers within the generic **Problems** view, which also includes additional capabilities to sort and filter the messages (see Chapter 4, "Customizing Your Workbench").

Default compiler settings for all projects in the current workspace are assigned in the preference page category **Java > Compiler**. You have the option of overriding workspace preferences for the Java compiler with project-specific settings. The project properties dialog includes the **Java Compiler** page shown in Figure 6-10. Initially, the option to *Use workspace settings* is selected. Change this to *Use project settings* when you want to modify the problem messages for an individual project.

A common reason to modify these settings is when you are working on Java code from outside your team or from an open source repository. For example, the **Unused Code** tab is shown in Figure 6-10, where the **Unused imports** option is set to a default value of Warning. This option displays a warning message for each import statement in a Java source file that is not used within that class.

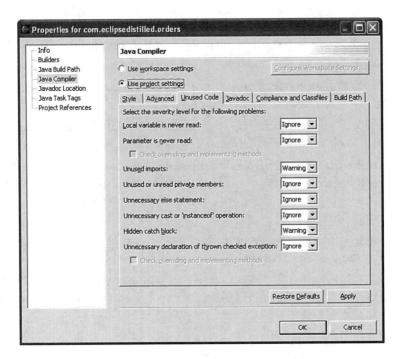

Figure 6-10   Use project-specific settings for compiler detection of unused code.

Other developers not working with Eclipse will often leave many unused imports in their code, sometimes leading to hundreds of warning messages when you create an Eclipse project containing that source code. It's best to leave this warning activated for your other projects, but you can eliminate the warnings in this single project by changing the option to ignore unused imports.

Your development team might also choose to establish very rigorous coding standards that rank unused imports as errors and issue a warning for unused local variables and unnecessary `else` statements. Set these coding standards as default Java compiler preferences and then export the preferences to a file that is imported by all team members.

6.4   Create Code Templates for Logging

Although not part of Java project configuration, the creation of code templates is naturally a part of our setup to improve development productivity. We will create several new templates that insert common statements used by the log4j logging facility.

Open the preferences page for **Java > Editor > Templates** and press the **New...** button. Fill in the template as shown in Figure 6-11. Press the **Insert Variable...** button while filling the template pattern to get a list of variables that automatically substitute values when the template is applied in your code.

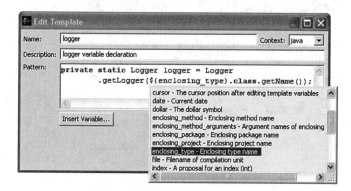

Figure 6-11   Create a new code template to insert log4j variable declaration.

Save the template and apply it within your `CatalogItem` class. Position the cursor below the class declaration, type "`logger`", and press **Ctrl+Space** to activate Content Assist. Select the `logger` template from the suggestion list and press **Enter**. Notice that the enclosing class name is automatically substituted when the following code is generated:

```
public class CatalogItem {
    private static Logger logger = Logger
            .getLogger(CatalogItem.class.getName());
```

However, you still receive an error that the `Logger` class cannot be resolved. Position the cursor over the `Logger` class name and press the shortcut **Ctrl+Shift+M**. Two different classes with this name are available:

```
java.util.logging.Logger
org.apache.log4j.Logger
```

A logging facility was added to Java version 1.4 that is similar in name and function to the Apache log4j library. But many developers still choose to use log4j instead of the `java.util.logging` package. You can prevent accidental choice of the wrong class and simplify use of Content Assist by filtering available types within Eclipse to exclude the `java.util.logging` package. Open the preferences page for **Java > Type Filters** as shown in Figure 6-12 and add a new type filter.

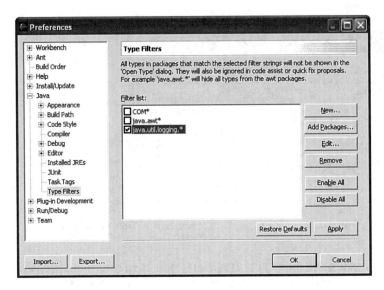

Figure 6-12   Filter the available types to exclude built-in Java logging, leaving the Apache log4j logging types as default.

Now when you press **Ctrl+Shift+M** to add an import statement for `Logger`, it is inserted immediately without prompting you because only one class by this name is available.

Now we'll create one more template for logging error messages. In Chapter 5, we used Quick Fix to automatically wrap a `try`/`catch` block around a `URL` class constructor to catch the `MalformedURLException`. We can now replace the default generated `catch` block with an error log message.

Create a new template named `logerr` and assign this pattern:

```
logger.error(${message}, ${e});
```

When you want to apply this pattern to log errors, simply type "logerr," press **Ctrl+Space** to activate Content Assist, select the template name, and press **Enter**. A single line is inserted, which is shown as bold here:

```
try {
    URL url = new URL("http://www.eclipse.org");
```

```
    } catch (MalformedURLException e) {
        logger.error("message", e);
    }
```

As with the other templates described in Chapter 5, you are prompted to replace the template variables. The two variables named `message` and `e` are highlighted in this pattern so that you can replace them with appropriate values, although the default name `e` is correct in this case.

6.5 Distilled

Eclipse includes a wide assortment of configuration options that control project compilation or enhance productivity. Don't get overwhelmed by the number of choices, but get started and gradually expand the customizations to suit your personal style and team development standards.

- ○ Each Java project includes a *builder* that compiles its resources from source into output folders. A simple project has no builders, and other project types can add relevant builders that apply appropriate compilers or transformation utilities to the files.

- ○ A project is built automatically; that is, the builder is applied automatically whenever a file is saved. For Java projects, the builder uses the *Java compiler settings* configured in the workspace preferences or overridden in a project.

- ○ A Java project's *Java build path* defines which projects from the workspace and which JAR archive files are included in the class path when building or running the project.

- ○ *User libraries* provide a convenient mechanism to define named collections of related JAR files that are used in combination. For example, J2EE standard APIs or the Apache Axis Web Services toolkit are good candidates for user libraries.

- ○ A hybrid configuration is possible where third-party JAR files are collected in an external directory. Some of these archives are packaged in one or more named user libraries, and all are easily accessible from within Eclipse using a simple project and linked file location.

6.6   References

Apache Log4j is an open source logging facility available at *jakarta.apache.org/ log4j/*.

Apache Axis is an open source Web Services development toolkit available at *ws.apache.org/axis/*.

CHAPTER 7

Debugging Your Code

Understanding the operation of complex software often requires introspection that goes beyond the display of log information using `println()` statements and `log4j` output. You need the ability to step through a program statement-by-statement and view or modify the state of fields, method parameters, and local variables. Debugging tools that enable such control are common among most IDE and command-line development environments. However, Eclipse raises the bar with its excellent customizable debugging capabilities and additional workbench views.

Our debugging activities are focused on the product catalog project that was introduced in Chapter 2, "Hello Eclipse." We initially ran the application within Eclipse using the **Console** view for command-line input and output. Now we will run the same project within the debugger, which enables detailed analysis of its control flow and state. If you are new to Java, and especially if you are new to object-oriented programming, stepping through your code in the debugger is an excellent way to understand how it runs.

In this chapter, we'll see how to

- ○ Start and customize a debug launch configuration
- ○ Use debug stack frames that provide execution context for variables and display expressions
- ○ Set breakpoints and step through program execution
- ○ Inspect and change values of fields, method parameters, and local variables
- ○ Use the **Expressions** view to watch variables during debugging
- ○ Assign **Detail Formatters** that customize object display when existing `toString()` methods are inadequate

❍ Use hot code replacement to modify code without restarting the Java VM

❍ Use a remote debugger connection to suspend and step through a Servlet running in a Tomcat server on another machine

7.1 Start a Debug Session

You can use the debugging features in any perspective; however, the **Debug Perspective** is designed specifically to support these activities. It's easiest to start a new debug session from the **Java Perspective** and then switch to the **Debug Perspective**. Of course, you can move freely between perspectives at any time.

Start a debug session by right-clicking on the `Main.java` entry from the `com.eclipsedistilled.catalog` package in the **Package Explorer** view and selecting **Debug > Java Application** from the context menu. Alternatively, select **Debug > Debug...** from the context menu to open a dialog, as shown in Figure 7-1. Press the **New** button to create a new launch configuration for running the `Main.java` class. Press the **Debug** button to start a debug session.

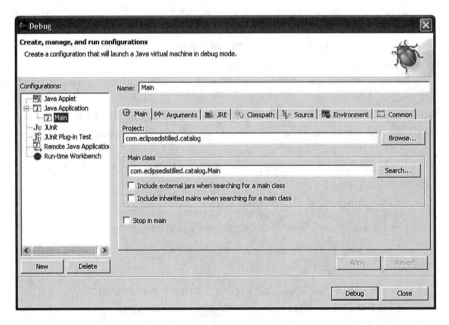

Figure 7-1   Create a launch configuration for your application.

Our `Main.java` application does not require configuration because the project build path is used by default when running this program. However, you can launch and debug much more complex applications within the Eclipse workbench. Anything that can be run as a Java application (i.e., anything that has a main() method) can be run in the debugger, such as a Swing-based GUI application or a complete application server such as Tomcat or JBoss. The launch configuration dialog includes tabs for specifying command-line arguments, classpath locations, and environment variables needed to start the application. Other debug configurations are shown on the left side of this dialog for running Java Applets, JUnit tests, or a runtime instance of the Eclipse workbench itself used when debugging plug-ins.

After you have run an application, it appears in the list of recently run configurations under the **Run** and **Debug** toolbar menus. The **Debug** menu is shown in Figure 7-2 with one entry for **Main** (you can rename this entry in the configuration dialog, for example to **Catalog App**). Select **Main** to start the debug session, or select **Debug...** to open the configuration dialog and modify the launch parameters before starting. You can also press **F11** to debug the previously launched configuration.

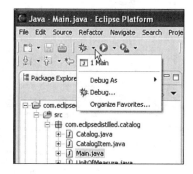

Figure 7-2   Rerun or configure a previous debug session using the toolbar menu.

If we run this application before setting any breakpoints, it will look much like the way we ran it in Chapter 2. The **Console** view displays our messages and accepts user input from the command line. While waiting for user input, the application is blocked on the readLine() statement, but so far the Eclipse debugger has had no noticeable effect on the execution.

Now switch to the **Debug Perspective** by selecting **Window > Open Perspective > Debug** from the workbench window menu. You can use the perspective bar to switch between open perspectives; refer to Chapter 4, "Customizing Your Workbench," for more information on customizing the workbench layout.

Start your debugging work by using the **Console** to add two products to the catalog. Now, press the **Suspend** button on the **Debug** view toolbar or pick **Run > Suspend** from the workbench menu. The debug views will appear, as shown in Figure 7-3. The application execution thread is suspended, and you can select any *stack frame* from the call stack in the **Debug** view. The **Variables** view shows fields, local variables, and method parameters for the selected frame. This figure shows an expanded view of the `catalog` field from a `Main` class instance.

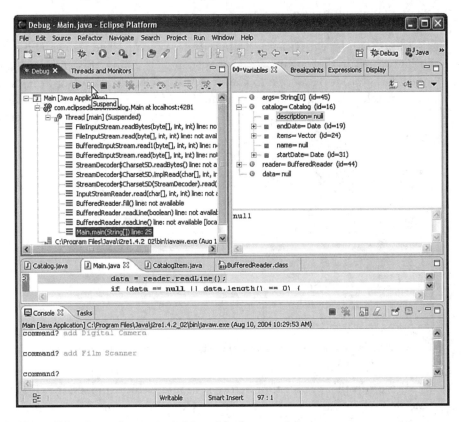

Figure 7-3   Suspend execution while waiting for console input.

You can add or remove breakpoints in the source code at any time. Add a breakpoint within the Java editor by double-clicking in the left ruler beside a line where you want a breakpoint. A blue ball appears to mark the breakpoint. If the class containing this breakpoint is loaded in the Java VM during an active debug session, then a checkmark is overlaid on the blue ball, as shown in Figure 7-4. If you create this same breakpoint before starting the debugger, then the marker will appear without a checkmark.

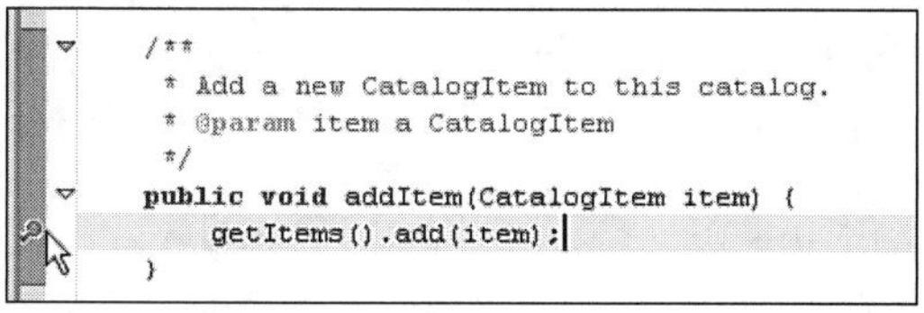

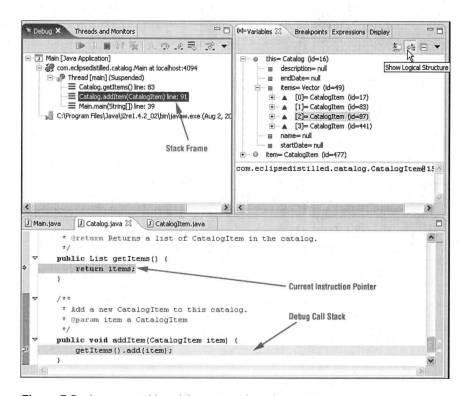

Figure 7-4   Create a new breakpoint by double-clicking in the left ruler.

Now press the **Resume** button on the **Debug** view toolbar. Add a new catalog item in the console view and press the **Enter** key. The execution will suspend when it hits the breakpoint, displaying the views shown in Figure 7-5.

Figure 7-5   Inspect variables while stepping through your program.

When a program thread is suspended, the **Debug** view shows one or more *stack frames* for that thread. A stack frame shows the execution context containing local variables and arguments for the method in that position of the call stack. This call stack is similar to the stack trace you receive when a program throws an exception, except that here the thread is suspended during execution.

As you step through a program's execution, the source code lines are highlighted to track your progress. Two kinds of progress steps are highlighted in Figure 7-5. The **Current Instruction Pointer** contains the statement that will be executed next when the thread resumes. The **Debug Call Stack** marks the line where the selected stack frame was suspended. In this example, we have selected a previous stack frame that shows the program state before stepping into the current statement, getItems(). Program step commands are described in the next section.

In the default Eclipse configuration, the current instruction pointer line is shown with a darker color than the call stack line. These colors are configurable on the preferences page **Workbench > Editors > Annotations**.

In Figure 7-5, the tooltip hover is displayed for the **Show Logical Structure** toolbar button. This command changes the way collections, such as the Vector class, are displayed in the **Variables** view. Instead of showing the fields of the Vector instance, its content is shown as a simple value list for easier viewing.

7.1.1 Stepping Through Execution

After execution has suspended on a breakpoint, there are several options for resuming or stepping through the program statement-by-statement. You can terminate a program at any time while it's running or suspended. Figure 7-6 shows the menu items available in the workbench **Run** menu when a program thread is suspended. The **Suspend** command is disabled for that thread because it is already suspended.

The first three commands provide the most general control:

❍ **Resume.** Resume execution of a thread until it either ends or encounters a breakpoint.

❍ **Suspend.** Suspend an executing thread.

❍ **Terminate.** Terminate the Java VM.

⊪▶ Resume	F8
⊪▮ Suspend	
▮ Terminate	
⊐ₐ Step Into	F5
⊕ Step Over	F6
₊⊕ Step Return	F7
⇒⊺ Run to Line	Ctrl+R
⊐⊕ Use Step Filters	Shift+F5

Figure 7-6   Commands used to step through the execution of a program.

Behavior of the step commands is relative to the stack frame for the selected thread in the **Debug** view. For all commands, the current line of execution in the selected stack frame is highlighted in the editor.

○ **Step Into.** Step into the next executed method. Stepping into a method causes the stack frame to grow by one.

○ **Step Over.** Finish execution of the current line and suspend on the next executable line.

○ **Step Return.** Step out of the current method. Execution resumes until a return statement is executed in the current method.

○ **Run to Line.** Resume execution up to the selected line. This is a convenient way to suspend execution at a line without setting a breakpoint.

○ **Use Step Filters.** When this command is toggled on, each of the step commands will apply the set of step filters that are defined in the user preferences page **Java > Debug > Step Filtering**. When a step action is invoked, stepping will continue until an unfiltered location is reached or a breakpoint is encountered.

If a breakpoint is encountered while performing a step operation, the execution will suspend at the breakpoint, and the step operation is ended.

The **Run to Line** command is not on the **Debug** view toolbar. Place your cursor on the line at which you want the program to be suspended. Select **Run to Line** from the workbench **Run** menu or the Java editor context menu, or press **Ctrl+R**. By default, **Run to Line** stops if a breakpoint is encountered before reaching the selected line (as with other step operations). However, there is a setting on the **Run/Debug** preferences page to skip breakpoints during **Run to Line** if you'd like to avoid this behavior.

7.2   Inspecting and Displaying State

The **Variables** view shows fields, local variables, and method parameters for the selected stack frame. The stack frame provides the *execution context* for these variables. Select one of these variables to display its value in the **Details** pane of this view—note that the **Details** *pane* at the bottom of this view is distinct from the **Display** *view*, although they have a similar purpose. If the variable contains an object, as opposed to a primitive, you can also expand that object to display its member variables. Refer to Figures 7-3 and 7-5, which display values of the `Catalog` member variables. The **Display** *view* is not open by default; open it while in the **Debug** perspective using the menu **Window > Show View > Display**. Please be aware of the difference between the **Details** *pane* and **Display** *view* in the following discussion.

The **Details** pane can also be used to evaluate code snippets. This evaluation occurs within the context of the selected variable, or if no variable is selected, then the selected stack frame context is used. You must be aware of this context because it determines the value of the identifier `this` and also determines which other variable names are available within the code snippet. In Figure 7-7 we entered a snippet to create a new `Party` instance, add a name (a `Party` can have multiple names), and assign this `Party` as the supplier for a `CatalogItem`. The `setSupplier(p)` method is evaluated in the context of the selected `CatalogItem` instance in the `items` Vector.

To execute this code snippet, do the following:

1. Select the desired `CatalogItem` instance within the `Catalog items` variable.

2. Select the entire expression in the **Details** pane; alternatively, you can select and execute only a subset of the text within this pane.

3. Right-click on the selected text and pick **Execute** from the context menu, or press **Ctrl+U**.

4. The value of the `supplier` field is updated immediately.

When a variable is a primitive or a `String`, you can simply enter the new value in the **Details** pane, select it, and pick **Assign Value** from the context menu. That menu item is disabled in Figure 7-7 because the current variable has a complex object type.

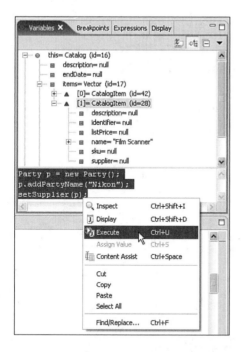

Figure 7-7   Execute a code snippet during debugging.

While typing in the **Details** pane, you can invoke Content Assist in the same way as in the Java editor. For example, type "P" and press **Ctrl+Space** to get a list of all classes beginning with P. You also can press **Ctrl+Space** on a blank line to get a list of all member variables and methods of the CatalogItem class. This works because the current context is determined by the CatalogItem variable selection. We used this technique to add setSupplier(p) to the code snippet.

The **Display** *view*, shown in Figure 7-8, serves as a scratch pad for code snippets and output results. The contents of this view are saved between Eclipse workbench sessions so you can use it to record and save several snippets used during debugging activities. To evaluate one of the expressions, select it and press one of the three view toolbar buttons to **Inspect, Display,** or **Execute** that expression. Alternatively, right-click on the selected text and pick one of these commands from the context menu, or use the shortcut keys.

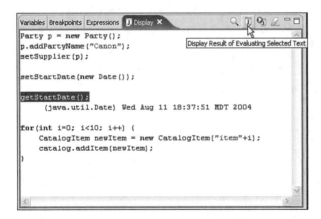

Figure 7-8   **Display** view containing several code snippets, one of which is evaluated to display its output.

> **Tip:** There are three ways to evaluate code snippets in debug views:
>
> **Execute.** Run the code.
>
> **Display.** Run the code and display the result.
>
> **Inspect.** Run the code and show a "live" version of the result, which can be browsed like a variable.
>
> The shortcuts for these commands vary across operating system platforms. The **Display** command is **Ctrl+Shift+D** on Windows and **Ctrl+Shift+V** on Linux.

Selecting the **Display** command will insert the result into this view on the line following the expression, as shown for the `getStartDate()` expression in Figure 7-8. When evaluating an expression in this view, it will run within the execution context of the stack frame selected in the **Debug** view. The stack frame must be bound to a `Catalog` instance for the `getStartDate()` expression to be executed. Other snippets in this view have different requirements for execution context. The first snippet executes in the context of a `CatalogItem` instance.

The **Display** view also provides an output area for results of expressions evaluated in other views. Select an expression in a Java editor, right-click on the selected text, and pick **Display** from the context menu, or press **Ctrl+Shift+D** (**Ctrl+Shift+V** on Linux). The current value of this expression in a suspended debug thread is displayed in a pop-up window, as shown in Figure 7-9. Press **Ctrl+Shift+D** again to copy this output into the **Display** view.

```
/**
 * @param startDate The startDate to set.
 */
public void setStartDate(Date startDate) {
    this.startDate = startDate;
}
```

                        (java.util.Date) Wed Aug
                        11 19:24:53 MDT 2004
                        Press Ctrl+Shift+D to Move to Display View

Figure 7-9   Open a pop-up **Display** window for an expression selected in a Java editor while debugging.

You can also **Inspect** the value of an expression to study a result that returns a complex object structure. Select an expression in a Java editor, in the **Display** view, or in the **Variables** view and pick **Inspect** from the context menu, or press **Ctrl+Shift+I**. When selected in the Java editor, a pop-up window similar to Figure 7-10 is opened. Press **Ctrl+Shift+I** again to move this result into the **Expressions** view, as shown in Figure 7-11.

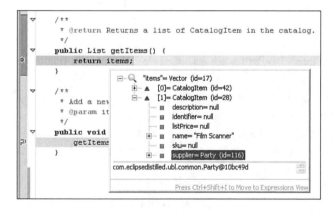

Figure 7-10   Open a pop-up **Inspector** window for an expression selected in the Java editor while debugging.

The **Expressions** view accumulates references to several expressions that you want to inspect or watch while debugging your code.

○ An *inspected expression* might be a field in one of the objects from the execution context or an expression selected in the Java Editor. An inspected value might be "live" if it holds an object whose fields are updated as you step through your code.

○ A *watch expression* displays the result of an expression that is reevaluated each time a thread is suspended. Right-click in the **Expressions** view and choose **Add Watch Expression** to create a new entry.

The **Expressions** view in Figure 7-11 contains one watch expression, catalog. getItems().size(), and one inspected expression, items. These types of expressions are displayed with different icons in the view. This particular view content was displayed while the thread was suspended, so the watch expression shows a value of "3"; while running, this value is not shown.

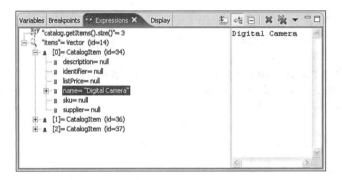

Figure 7-11   **Expressions** view showing a watched expression and an inspected value.

The **Expressions** view includes a **Details** pane for viewing values of selected fields or for evaluating expressions as we did in the **Variables** view. In both the **Variables** and **Expressions** views, you can use commands in the view menu to position the **Details** pane at the bottom or right side, or to hide the **Details** pane altogether.

When a value is shown in a **Details** pane or the **Display** view, it is produced by the toString() method of the displayed object. However, sometimes you need different output displayed, especially when you don't have source code for a third-party class. In these cases, you can add a **Detail Formatter** that produces an alternate toString() value.

Figure 7-12 shows the preferences page for **Java > Debug > Detail Formatters**. You can add a custom formatter for any class used while debugging. In this figure, we are editing a formatter to modify its code snippet to include more detail while displaying an instance of CatalogItem. You can define several formatters in your preferences and enable or disable their use with the check box beside each formatter. **Detail Formatters** may be added, enabled, or disabled at any time during a debug session.

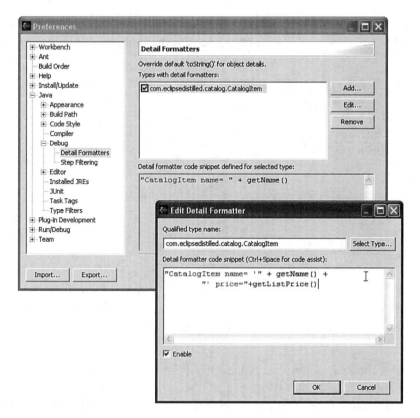

Figure 7-12   Edit a **Detail Formatter** for the `CatalogItem` class.

7.3   Managing Debug Sessions

While debugging a large application, you may create many breakpoints that are spread across several projects. The **Breakpoints** view provides a list of all breakpoints set in your workspace. This view, shown in Figure 7-13, allows you to enable or disable each breakpoint, remove one or all from your code, or set the number of times a breakpoint must be hit before it causes your application to be suspended.

Another helpful feature of the debugger is **Add Java Exception Breakpoint**, accessible by clicking the **J!** icon in the **Breakpoints** view toolbar. Use this type of breakpoint when you don't know what code is causing an exception to be thrown. For example, if you set a breakpoint for `NullPointerException` (NPE), the debugger breaks exactly at the point before the NPE occurs. This is particularly helpful when debugging other developers' code. When you get an NPE, don't bother searching for the cause, just enable the NPE breakpoint!

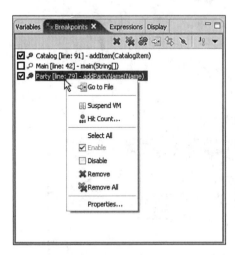

Figure 7-13 Manage all breakpoints in your application.

Select the **Properties...** command from the context menu in the **Breakpoints** view to modify the characteristics of the selected breakpoint. This dialog is shown in Figure 7-14. You can check the option to **Enable Condition** and enter a Java expression that will be evaluated at runtime, using fields or variables available at this breakpoint's position in the code. In this example, we have specified that the breakpoint will be activated only when more than one name has been assigned to a `Party` object.

Another option is to choose **Suspend when value of condition changes**. Using an expression of `partyNames.size()` would then suspend execution any time this list is modified. More complex expressions are also possible in the conditional breakpoint. You can use the following expression, and the breakpoint will be activated any time a `Party` includes a name containing "IBM".

```
Iterator i = partyNames.iterator();
while (i.hasNext()) {
    Name name = (Name)i.next();
    if (name.getValue().indexOf("IBM") != -1)
        return true;
}
return false;
```

Figure 7-14 Enable a conditional breakpoint.

One of the most powerful aspects of the Eclipse debugger is the ability to change code in the midst of a debug session, without stopping and restarting the Java VM. This is called *hot code replacement* because no restart is required. It is enabled by default when you install Eclipse, but it can be customized using the **Java > Debug** preferences page, as shown in Figure 7-15.

Hot code replacement was added as a standard technique in Java VM specifications to facilitate experimental development and to foster trial-and-error coding. The Eclipse debugger supports **Hot Code Replace** when running with a 1.4.1 or later Java VM, or the IBM J9 VM. This lets you make changes to code that you are currently debugging. However, there are restrictions on what changes can be hot swapped, depending in part on the support provided by a particular VM.

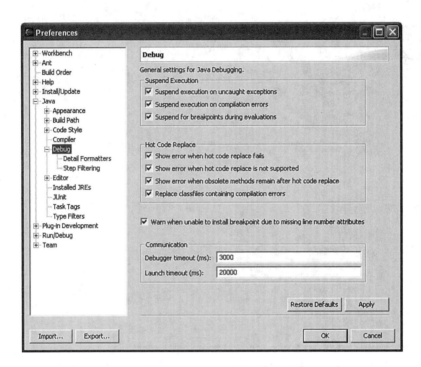

Figure 7-15   Java Debug preferences.

Generally, replacement only works when the signature of existing classes does not change:

○ You can add new classes.

○ You can change the body of a method.

○ You cannot add or remove fields to existing classes or change their types after those classes are loaded in the VM.

○ You cannot add or remove methods to existing classes or change their signatures (name, parameters, return type, or visibility) after those classes are loaded in the VM.

○ You cannot add or remove inner classes.

However, this list depends on the VM being used. When future VMs are available that expand hot code replacement, the Eclipse debugger will automatically use those new features. In spite of these limitations to hot code replacement, this feature of the Eclipse debugger provides a large productivity boost when debugging applications. You can fine-tune the logic of method calculations, modify the layout and content of GUI windows, or modify many other aspects of application logic without violating the constraint of changing class signatures.

Your debug process is set up in the launch configuration shown in Figure 7-1. You can choose which JRE is used to run the application and specify the arguments, classpath, and environment variables used when starting it. You can inspect the command line used to launch a process by selecting it in the **Debug** view and choosing **Properties** from the context menu. The dialog shown in Figure 7-16 is opened to display the process information.

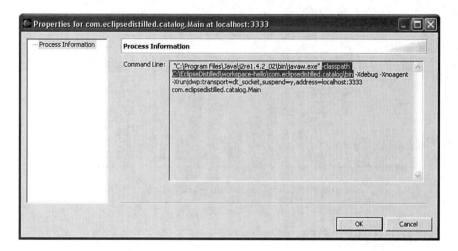

Figure 7-16 Command-line parameters used to launch a debug process.

The -classpath argument is highlighted to show that it includes only the bin directory of our com.eclipsedistilled.catalog project. If this project had other dependencies or required libraries, they would also be included in this argument value, along with any other customizations in the launch configuration.

Other settings affecting the launch configuration may be changed in the **Run/Debug > Launching** preference page, shown in Figure 7-17. The **Remove terminated launches when a new launch is created** option is enabled by default; it's sometimes useful to disable this option if you want to keep a trace of the old runs.

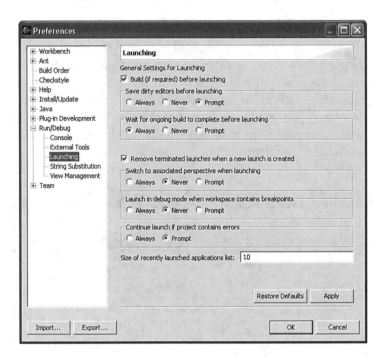

Figure 7-17   General preferences for launching applications.

7.4   Remote Java Applications

The client/server design of the Java debugger allows you to launch a Java program from a computer on your network and debug it from Eclipse running on your workstation. This is particularly useful when you are developing a program for a device that cannot host the Eclipse IDE or one that is shared by several developers. It is also useful when debugging programs on dedicated machines such as J2EE application servers.

To debug a program remotely, you must be able to launch the program in debug mode on the remote machine so that it will wait for a connection from your debugger. The technique for launching the program and connecting the debugger are specific to the JVM you are running. The basic steps are as follows:

1. Ensure that you are building your Java program with available debug information. You can control these attributes from the **Compliance and Classfiles** tab of **Window > Preferences > Java > Compiler**.

2. After you build your Java program, install it to the target computer. This involves copying the `.class` files or JAR files to the appropriate location on the remote computer.

3. Invoke the Java program on the remote computer using the appropriate JVM arguments to specify debug mode and a communication port for the debugger.

4. Start the debugger in your Eclipse workbench using a remote launch configuration that specifies the address and port of the remote computer.

7.4.1 Debug Remote Tomcat Servlet

We'll use the remote debugger to step through a Servlet running on a remote Tomcat application server. This example uses version 5.0.19 of Tomcat (*jakarta.apache.org/tomcat*). Installing the server is simply a matter of unzipping the distribution file, such as to `C:\jakarta-tomcat-5.0.19` on Windows. We'll use the `servlets-examples` Web application included with Tomcat to review use of the remote debugger.

The Eclipse **New Java Project** wizard makes it very easy to create a project using the Tomcat example. Start the wizard and select the option to **Create project at external location**, as shown in Figure 7-18. Enter a project name "`tomcat-examples`". Set the project location by browsing to `servlets-examples` within the server's `webapps` folder.

Figure 7-18   Create a new Java project using an external location for the Tomcat `servlets-examples` Web application.

This Tomcat example includes all Java source code within the `WEB-INF/classes` folder in the same location as the compiled class files. The **New Project Wizard** will analyze the project subdirectories and configure directories containing Java source files as source folders in your new project. For this project's structure, the wizard defaults work perfectly.

You also need to configure this project with a library containing the standard Java Servlet APIs that are used when writing any Servlet. You can click the **Next** button in the wizard and use the **Libraries** tab to select the JAR location while creating the project, or set the project's properties after creating it. See Chapter 6, "Java Project Configuration," for a detailed explanation of configuring Java project libraries. The required library is found in the Tomcat server installation location `common/lib/servlet-api.jar`. You can select this JAR location, or preferably as described in Chapter 6, create a subfolder containing standard J2EE libraries in our shared `libraries` project.

The resulting project is shown in Figure 7-19. Notice how the wizard correctly assigned `WEB-INF/classes` as both the source and output folder location. Now open the `RequestParamExample.java` file and set a breakpoint within the `doGet()` method that is executed when the Servlet is invoked.

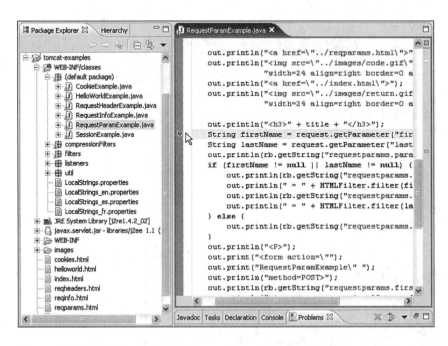

Figure 7-19   Set a breakpoint in the source file for one of the Servlets.

You would not keep your Java source code in the application server WEB-INF directory in normal development configurations, but this structure is used by the Tomcat examples for simplicity. It works well for our exploration of remote Java debugging.

A **Remote Java Application** launch configuration must be used when debugging an application that is running on a remote JVM. Because the application is started on the remote system, the launch configuration does not specify the usual information about the JRE, program arguments, or classpath. Instead, information about connecting to the application is supplied, as shown in Figure 7-20.

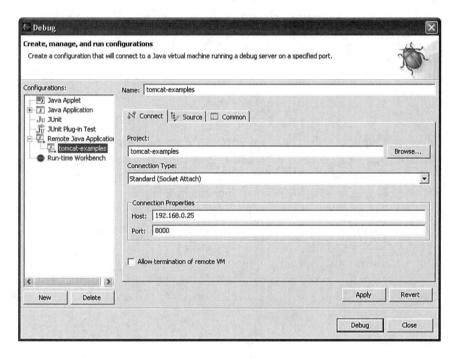

Figure 7-20 Create a new **Remote Java Application** launcher.

In the **Project** field of the **Connect** tab, type or browse to our new tomcat-examples project. The project used to launch a remote debugger determines the source file location; you can also configure additional source folders in the **Source** tab of the debug configuration.

In the **Connection Properties** fields, enter the host and port used to connect to the Tomcat server. This is not the port used when connecting from a Web browser (e.g., 8080); this is the port used by the JVM for remote debug connections. This port must be configured in the Tomcat startup script. You need to edit two lines of the `bin/catalina.bat` script if Tomcat is running on Windows. If running on Linux, the defaults are already set this way in `bin/catalina.sh`.

The first line of these two excerpts, prefixed with `rem`, is the original setting. Change the two lines as follows in `bin/catalina.bat`:

```
rem set JPDA_TRANSPORT=dt_shmem
set JPDA_TRANSPORT=dt_socket

rem set JPDA_ADDRESS=jdbconn
set JPDA_ADDRESS=8000
```

Now start the Tomcat server using this command on Windows:

```
bin/catalina.bat jpda start
```

Or this command on Linux:

```
bin/catalina.sh jpda start
```

The `jpda` option tells Tomcat to listen for debugger connections on port 8000, or whatever port you configured on the startup script. This port must be the same as the one used in the Eclipse launcher shown in Figure 7-20.

If you are running Tomcat on the same machine as your Eclipse workbench, then you can use `localhost` as the host name in Figure 7-20. This is still a "remote" debugging session when using `localhost`. Figure 7-20 shows a remote host IP address, where Tomcat is running on `192.168.0.25`. You can also enter a remote host name here if the machine has a known name on your network.

Everything is ready to begin our remote debugging session. If you are running Tomcat on your local machine, substitute the IP address with `localhost` in these steps:

1. Start Tomcat on the remote machine.

2. Start the `tomcat-examples` launch configuration from the **Debug** toolbar menu in your workbench.

3. Open a Web browser to the Tomcat home page using `http://192.168.0.25:8080` (substitute your Tomcat server host address or name).

4. Click on the Web page link for **Servlet Examples** and then execute the **Request Parameters** example.

5. Enter parameter values into the Web form shown in Figure 7-21 and press **Submit Query**.

6. The breakpoint will be activated in your Eclipse workbench, and the Tomcat server thread will be suspended, as shown in Figure 7-22.

7. Use debugger commands to step through the Servlet execution and review state changes in the **Variables** view.

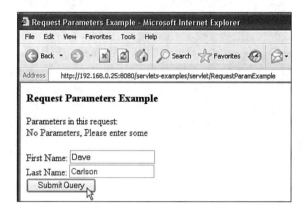

Figure 7-21   Tomcat Servlet Request Parameters Example.

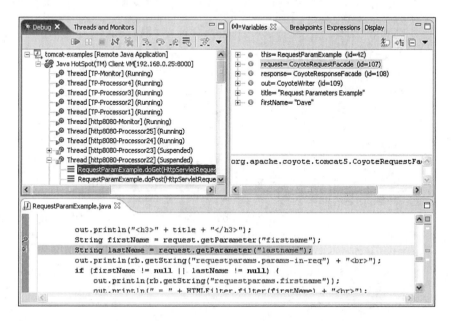

Figure 7-22   After hitting the breakpoint, use the debugger to step through execution of the Servlet running on the remote Tomcat server.

This example also provides a good illustration of debugging multithreaded applications. When Eclipse connects to the Tomcat server, the **Debug** view shows a list of **Running** threads in the server thread pool. When you submit a Web page to the Servlet, one of the threads is changed to **Suspended**. While stepping through that thread in the debugger, go back to the Web page and submit the form again. A second thread will be **Suspended**, and you can switch between debugging these two threads in the **Debug** view. In Figure 7-22, you see a second **Suspended** thread immediately above the thread we are debugging.

The Eclipse Web Tools Platform (WTP) will provide new plug-ins for starting, stopping, and publishing Web applications to a server from within the workbench. The plan for these tools is presented in Chapter 1, "A Java IDE and So Much More!" WTP is used when developing Web applications, although the remote debugging capabilities will be needed when you debug applications running within a dedicated test server.

7.5   Distilled

- ○ The **Debug Perspective** includes several views specialized for debugging activities: a **Debug** view of running threads and, when suspended, their stack frames; **Variables**, **Expressions**, and **Display** views for exploring object state; and a **Breakpoints** view for managing a list of all breakpoints in your code.

- ○ After execution has stopped on a breakpoint, there are several options for resuming or terminating execution, or stepping through the program statement-by-statement.

- ○ The **Variables** view shows fields, local variables, and method parameters for the stack frame selected in the **Debug** view. The stack frame provides the *execution context* for these variables.

- ○ You can evaluate code snippets that display, inspect, or update program state. Pop-up windows may be used to display or inspect selected expressions within a Java editor during a debug session.

- ○ You can assign a **Detail Formatter** that defines a customized output string used to display values of any class during debugging. This formatter overrides a class's `toString()` method.

- ○ **Hot Code Replace** facilitates experimental development by allowing you to make changes to code in the midst of a debug session without restarting the Java VM.

- ○ The client/server design of the Java debugger allows you to launch a Java program from a computer on your network and debug it from Eclipse running on your workstation.

PART 2

Getting Agile

Eclipse itself is developed using an agile development process and includes features that add agility to any development effort. The rest of us benefit from the fact that creators of Eclipse have added tools to make their own lives easier and more productive.

Chapter 8 introduces the principles of agile development and its use of iterative development cycles. Each remaining chapter in this section focuses on one aspect of agile development and how to accomplish it within the Eclipse IDE. You could read these chapters in any order or jump straight into one of these chapters before finishing Part 1. For example, if you are joining an established project team, you may not create your own Java project from scratch. Instead, you'll check out projects from a repository such as CVS. In that case, you should read through Chapter 13 earlier in your study.

CHAPTER 8

Characteristics of Agile Development

Agile software development is a general name for a family of related method-ologies, including Extreme Programming (XP), Scrum, Crystal Methodologies, Adaptive Software Development, and others. Its core principles emphasize empowering the programmer through small self-organizing teams, close collabo-ration with customers, use of iterative development cycles, and continuous unit testing and integration by the developers.

Older methodologies from the so-called "traditional" approaches emphasize rigorous planning and a document-driven, waterfall lifecycle. Some of the tradi-tional methodologies are attempting to reinvent themselves by incorporating agile principles, but they usually retain a centralized predictive planning process. The Rational Unified Process (RUP) is often classified as a traditional waterfall methodology but is actually a process framework that can be specialized for iter-ative agile development.

In many ways agile development is more about attitude than about develop-ment tools. However, having the right tools can go a long way toward giving you a good attitude—and Eclipse fits the bill perfectly. Both XP and Eclipse grew out of the Smalltalk development community. The first XP project was a Smalltalk project, and many of the original Eclipse platform developers were previously Smalltalk tool developers. Many of the tools and techniques included in Eclipse have been done before in Smalltalk, such as the Smalltalk Refactoring Browser, Envy/Developer's repository tools, "3-pane" browsers, the Outline view, incre-mental compilation, and more.

8.1 The Agile Manifesto

The *Agile Manifesto* was born in February 2001 when a group of methodologists gathered to share and promote their common vision for software development.

At this meeting they agreed to use the term "agile" to describe their common ideas. The manifesto is a statement of values and principles for agile software development (see *http://www.agilemanifesto.org* and the related site *http://www.agilealliance.org*).

The manifesto includes twelve principles that fall roughly into two categories: programmer empowerment and iterative development. We'll review five of those principles that are especially relevant to programming activities. An agile development project is composed of small teams (5 to 10 programmers per team) where the programmers are actively involved in elaborating the initial requirements and adapting to changes.

- ○ Business people and developers must work together daily throughout the project.
- ○ The best architectures, requirements, and designs emerge from self-organizing teams.

Project deliverables are planned as a series of releases where each release is the result of one or more short development iterations. Only the current or next iteration is planned in detail. Future iterations have features, user stories, or use cases assigned to them but are not planned with detailed task assignments.

- ○ Deliver working software frequently, from a couple of weeks to a couple of months, with a preference to the shorter timescale.
- ○ Working software is the primary measure of progress.
- ○ Continuous attention to technical excellence and good design enhances agility.

A typical release cycle is shown in Figure 8-1 (Leffingwell & Muirhead, 2004). The product owners contribute the initial feature requests or use cases, but these requirements are not documented in complete detail at this stage. For larger projects, the features are assigned to a release within the roadmap, or the roadmap is adjusted to accommodate requirements changes during interim releases. Just as your car's dashboard and steering wheel provide feedback and control while driving, the Track & Adjust component of an agile process requires feedback about the project's status and opportunities to adjust the next steps of its progress. This feedback may come from users, test metrics, an issue list, iteration progress, or work backlog.

Agile development is often based on two kinds of plans (Kruchten, 2004):

- ○ A coarse-grained plan: the phase or release plan.
- ○ A series of fine-grained plans: the iteration plans.

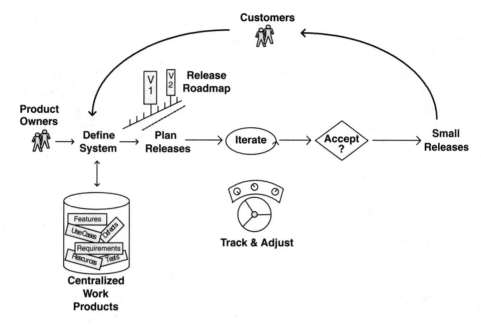

Figure 8-1   Generalized agile process model (courtesy of Rally Software Development).

The investment in long-range (longer than one or two iterations) speculative plans is reduced, and the lack of precision and accuracy in such plans is acknowledged. Release plans are therefore intentionally coarse-grained, less comprehensive, and less precise. Iteration plans are focused on the short-run and are less speculative and thus are worthy of greater estimating investment and precision.

The development team can and should be expected to embrace change. But in order for the team to fulfill its responsibility of delivering a deployable product at each iteration, the team must be able to commit and deliver on the iteration plan. Changing the iteration plan midstream invites chaos and severely threatens the ability of the development team to deliver at the end of an iteration.

It is important that the development team deliver working software at every iteration for several reasons:

1. It is the only way to objectively demonstrate progress.

2. It is the only way users can provide concrete feedback based on actual usage of the software.

3. Like a missed manufacturing deadline, it hurts the company's rhythm and morale when the team cannot deliver on an iteration.

Moreover, the shorter the iteration, the more practical it becomes to freeze an iteration while maintaining the team's ability to embrace change.

The agile development process includes an underlying activity for tracking and adjusting the plan based on input from developers and customers. It is essential that the agile process itself is adaptable and responsive to changes in the project environment. At the end of each iteration, the team must reflect on what worked and what did not and then must make decisions about what to do differently next time.

8.2   Iterative Development

Each release cycle consists of a series of time-boxed development iterations. XP recommends iterations of one to three weeks in duration, and Scrum recommends fixed-length 30-day iterations. Whatever timeframe you use, it should be short and focused. The most important benefit is that fixed time iterations introduce near-term milestones that force both the team and implemented code to converge on working software deliveries at regular intervals. As stated in the Agile Manifesto: *Working software is the primary measure of progress.*

> **Tip:** Time-boxed iterations of 2-8 weeks establish a rhythm for the development team and become the drum beat that synchronizes the activities of all participants.

The iterative development process is shown in Figure 8-2. Several iterations may be completed within each release cycle. The scope and focus of an iteration must be negotiated and agreed to by product owners and developers before the iteration begins. Because the development teams are self-managed, developers participate in estimating task duration and take responsibility for tasks as the iteration cycle unfolds. A daily team meeting tracks issues and progress toward completion of the time-boxed iteration.

The nested development cycle represents the work of individual developers (or pairs of programmers in XP) on the team. One iteration cycle includes several passes through the nested development cycle. The number of development cycles depends on the number and breadth of requirements that must be elaborated.

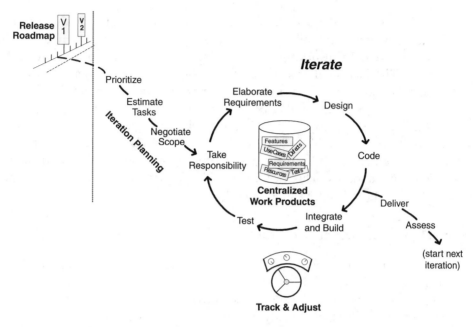

Figure 8-2 Iterative development process cycle (courtesy of Rally Software Development).

Agile development teams are empowered to work with users directly and to elaborate initial requirements as they proceed. This represents a sharp departure from the traditional waterfall process model, where we assume that developers are interchangeable resources who are given a reasonably complete set of requirements to implement. This assumes that someone spent the time inventing, defining, and vetting requirements documents with the key stakeholders. We also assumed that this time was invested before the development process began. It may or may not have worked, but at least it was easy to describe!

Requirements are more abstract in agile practices. They are never frozen (except within the bounds of short iterations), and the team has much more accountability in making certain they are building the right thing. This means the agile team has a higher degree of involvement in defining the system under construction. In turn, this means the development team members and product owners work hand-in-hand in a nearly continuous process.

8.3 Agile Development and Eclipse

Eclipse provides a development platform that supports and accelerates the agile development cycle. We'll examine the details of those platform features in the remainder of this chapter and the six that follow it.

Eclipse is a flexible platform that can accommodate varying preferences for developer style, compiler settings, and project configuration. However, the entire agile development process is itself subject to reflection, adjustment, and adaptation. The Eclipse platform accepts plug-in contributions that can radically alter and extend its capabilities to support new unforeseen development needs.

Extreme Programming (XP), as a member of the agile development family, outlines a set of twelve practices for achieving successful results (Beck, 1999). We'll explore five of those practices that are especially relevant to programming activities: testing, refactoring, continuous integration, collective ownership, and coding standards. This section provides a roadmap for the next chapters that describe how Eclipse supports each practice.

8.3.1 The Self-Adaptive Process

Most of the time we think about using agile processes for adapting the software being developed to satisfy the changing requirements of its customers. However, the process itself is also adaptive. A project that begins using an adaptive process probably won't have exactly the same process a year later, especially if your team is new to agile development. And different processes may be needed when designing embedded systems, developing software products for resale, or building operational support systems.

Our immediate interest is to understand how the Eclipse platform can be adapted to support these different processes and their needs. For example, agile development recommends writing unit tests before implementing the corresponding functionality. Eclipse includes excellent support for JUnit testing (*http://www.junit.org*), but your team may need flexibility in deciding how to test previously implemented code that is integrated into your project. A common approach is to write unit tests for existing code only when resolving bug reports or when refactoring that code. Your team has the responsibility and authority to make decisions about the best test strategy.

These and other adaptations are described in the following chapters. Each chapter concludes with a section on new plug-in contributions that can be added to extend the platform capabilities described in that chapter.

8.3.2 Continuous Testing

Programmers continually write unit tests that must run flawlessly for development to continue. Customers write tests demonstrating that features are finished. Creation of tests is an on-going development activity that becomes part of the program itself. Regardless of who refactors, enhances, or corrects a bug in a program, an automated test suite is available to verify correct behavior.

When a bug is fixed, either a relevant test was missing or the test was incorrect or incomplete. This will often be the case when existing code is brought into the project without a test suite or when a team is just getting started with agile development processes. No problem—just write a unit test so that the same errant behavior will be easily caught in the future.

The benefits of continuous testing are considerable, but a commitment and investment of time is required of every member of your team. Many developers and their managers see writing unit tests as a waste of time, when in reality they are verifying that the software works—and continues to work—as per the use cases. Agile development methods accept the reality that requirements will continue to evolve over the course of a project. That evolution will require refactoring to keep the flexibility that allows evolution. When code is refactored, it must be reverified, which is accomplished by running unit tests. The greatest gains are realized when unit testing is continuous and automated.

We focus on JUnit functionality that is built into Eclipse. JUnit is the most widely used unit testing framework for Java, and its simple but powerful framework has been ported to many other programming languages. Writing unit tests is still a time-consuming activity, but the wizards and views provided by Eclipse help you get started so that you can reap the rewards.

8.3.3 Refactoring

Programmers restructure the system without changing its behavior to remove duplication, improve communication, simplify, or add flexibility. Developers welcome change at any time when using agile development practices, but doing so requires that the code itself is adapted easily. In addition, because the code is the primary deliverable, it must communicate its intent to anyone who reads it. Refactoring makes this possible.

You don't refactor on speculation or for elegance. You refactor by asking if there is a way to change the code to make adding a new feature easier or to remove duplicate code. Having a complete unit test suite for the code being refactored gives you confidence that the revised code still passes these tests and thus provides the same behavior.

Some examples of refactoring include renaming a variable, method, class, or package; changing a method signature; extracting an interface from a concrete class; and pulling up methods from a subclass into an abstract superclass (Fowler, 1999). A refactoring is not one big change as much as it is a series of small steps.

Refactoring your code can be a very time-consuming activity when changing a method or type name that is widely used in your project. Eclipse makes this process stunningly easy. You can review the proposed changes from a refactoring and then accept only a subset of the changes or reject the entire set of changes to take a different approach. After using the refactoring support in Eclipse, you'll never be able to do without it.

8.3.4 Continuous Integration

Integrate and build the entire system many times a day, every time a task is completed. Integrating one set of changes at a time makes it easy to identify problems and prevents a surprise at the end of an iteration. All developers and customers working on a team keep a current view of the iteration's progress.

If integration took several hours, it would not be possible to work in this style. It is important to have tools that support a fast integration build and test cycle. You also need a reasonably complete test suite that verifies successful integration of a new component.

Eclipse includes flexible support for automatically building your project as each file is saved, using either the built-in compiler and project configurations or a customized Ant build script (*http://ant.apache.org*). The Ant editor, Outline view, and runtime configurations help you to create and execute large, complex build scripts, all from within the Eclipse IDE.

8.3.5 Collective Ownership

Anyone can change any code anywhere in the system at any time. This ensures that every developer takes responsibility for the entire system and is not held up when another component needs refactoring or causes a test to fail. Not everyone knows every part equally well, although everyone knows something about every part.

Collective ownership requires good tools that enable efficient code sharing and a team culture that encourages such behavior. Eclipse provides world-class tool support in this area. Generic team features are provided that can be bound to many different version control repositories. CVS support is provided in the standard download, and additional plug-ins are available for other repositories.

8.3.6 Coding Standards

In agile development processes, the code is of central importance in documenting system design and behavior, and this is possible only when consistent coding
standards are used. In addition, collective ownership and refactoring mean that
all developers are likely to touch much of the source code.

Eclipse provides extensive customization of automated code formatting
rules, code generation and Content Assist templates, Javadoc templates, and
built-in spell checkers for comments. Additional plug-in contributions are available for checking the code style against standards.

8.4   Distilled

- ○ Agile software development is a general name for a family of related
  methodologies that emphasize empowering the programmer through small
  self-organizing teams, close collaboration with customers, use of iterative
  development cycles, and continuous unit testing and integration by the
  developers.

- ○ Projects are guided by two-level planning: a coarse-grained release plan
  and a fine-grained iteration plan.

- ○ Eclipse provides a development platform that supports and accelerates the
  agile development cycle and that may be radically customized through
  plug-in contributions.

- ○ Five agile development practices are especially relevant to programming in
  Eclipse: testing, refactoring, continuous integration, collective ownership,
  and coding standards.

8.5   References

Beck, Kent, *Extreme Programming Explained: Embracing Change*. Boston, MA:
Addison-Wesley, 1999.

Fowler, Martin, *Refactoring: Improving the Design of Existing Code*. Reading,
MA: Addison-Wesley, 1999.

Highsmith, James. A., *Adaptive Software Development: A Collaborative
Approach to Managing Complex Systems*. Dorset House, 2000.

Kruchten, Phillippe, *The Rational Unified Process: An Introduction*, Third
Edition. Boston, MA: Addison-Wesley, 2004.

Leffingwell, Dean and Muirhead, Dave, *Tactical Management of Agile Development: Achieving Competitive Advantage*, Rally Software Development, Boulder, CO, 2004. This white paper is available from *www.rallydev.com*.

Schwaber, Ken and Beedle, Mike, *Agile Software Development with Scrum*. Prentice Hall, 2001.

CHAPTER 9

Updating the Eclipse IDE

Agile development requires adaptable processes and tools that can be customized to fit the needs of your organization and projects. The chapters in Part 1, "Getting Started," described many ways in which the Eclipse IDE can be customized to fit your personal and project preferences. However, the greatest strength of Eclipse lies in its plug-in architecture that allows you to extend and update its capabilities with new features. This chapter explains how to add new and update existing features in your Eclipse IDE.

Most of the chapters in Part 2, "Getting Agile," include a final section named *Contributions* that lists plug-ins related to the topics of that chapter. The Eclipse community is growing rapidly, and hundreds of open-source and commercial plug-ins are now available. See the Contributions at the end of this chapter for references to index sites that provide searchable plug-in registries.

In this chapter, we'll see how to

- Review and modify your workbench plug-in configuration
- Add bookmarks for remote and local update sites
- Search for and install new features
- Install plug-ins that are not packaged as features
- Configure locations where features and plug-ins are installed on your computer
- Set preferences for update site proxies and notifications

9.1   Finding and Installing Features

As you gain familiarity with Eclipse, your workbench becomes a dynamic environment where features are added, removed, enabled, or disabled. Members of your team may add features that are specific to their roles, such as modeling, database design, coding, or testing. You can disable features that are only used occasionally, which removes their menu items from the workbench when not needed, and then you can re-enable a feature when its functionality is required.

Eclipse Features

The term *feature* has a special meaning and significance in Eclipse. A feature is a way of grouping and describing related functionality that makes up a product. Grouping plug-ins into features allows the product to be installed and updated using the Eclipse update server and related support. The platform itself is partitioned into three major features:

Platform

JDT (Java Development Tooling)

PDE (Plug-in Developer Environment)

Feature definitions do not contain code themselves; instead they specify the packaging for one or more related plug-ins or nested features. *Features* are organized for the purposes of distributing and updating products, whereas *plug-ins* are organized to facilitate the development of the product function by the product team. The development team determines when to divide program functionality into a separate plug-in.

By default, a feature is treated as universally portable. But a feature definition can include constraints for which operating/windowing systems, languages, and/or system architectures are supported. This information is used to ensure that a feature is not installed or shown in a context that does not match these constraints. Features also provide description, license, and copyright information.

The Eclipse platform includes an update facility that helps you manage your workbench configuration, find and install new features, and update installed features. The **Product Configuration** window shown in Figure 9-1 is opened by selecting the workbench menu command **Help > Software Updates > Manage Configuration....**

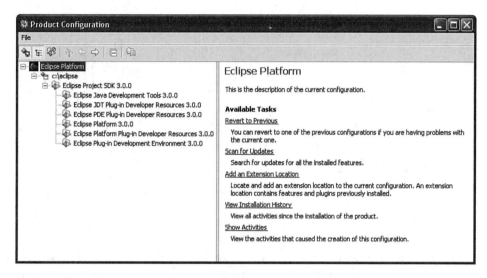

Figure 9-1 Initial product configuration before installing new features.

The workbench configuration is organized into a three-level hierarchy:

Install Location. A configuration's features may be installed at several disk locations. This workbench configuration has one location at `c:\eclipse`.

Feature. This configuration contains one top-level feature named Eclipse Project SDK, which is version 3.0.0. A top-level feature may be disabled and re-enabled from this configuration window.

Nested Feature. A feature may include nested features that add functionality. Nested features cannot be disabled individually—they can only be disabled as part of their top-level feature. The choice of configuring a feature as top-level or nested is made by the development team, not by the user.

Although you can add individual plug-ins to your Eclipse configuration, the install/update facility is organized around the higher-level feature packaging. We'll see how to install individual plug-ins without a feature definition in the next section of this chapter.

To search for new or updated features and install them, select the workbench menu command **Help > Software Updates > Find and Install...**. The dialog shown in Figure 9-2 is displayed. The first option in this dialog searches for updates to installed features, which are listed in the configuration shown in Figure 9-1. Choose the second option to search for new features to install and then press the **Next** button.

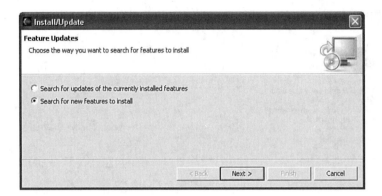

Figure 9-2 Search for updates and new features.

Eclipse will search for new features on one or more *update sites*. An update site may be located at either a remote URL or a local computer file path. Each update site includes an index file with category names and a list of features within each category, plus JAR files containing the features and plug-ins. One update site is listed when running the default Eclipse SDK configuration, as shown in Figure 9-3. This remote site, located at *update.eclipse.org/updates/3.0*, contains three categories of features that can be added to your workbench. (Note that the list of categories changes from time to time, so what you see may differ from this figure.)

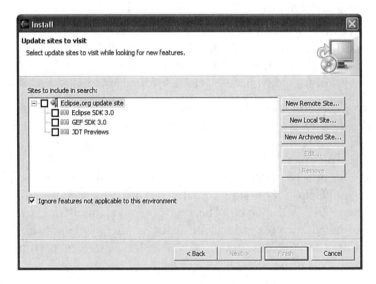

Figure 9-3 Eclipse.org update site with new features.

You can add new *bookmarks* for other update sites not located on the Eclipse.org Web site. We'll add one remote site and one local site before starting a search for new features across all three update sites.

The JBoss project (*www.jboss.org*) created an Eclipse feature called the JBoss-IDE that adds preferences, views, and launch configurations for starting, stopping, and deploying applications to a JBoss J2EE server. To add this update site, do the following:

1. Press the **New Remote Site...** button shown in Figure 9-3.

2. Enter the site name "JBoss IDE".

3. Enter the site URL `jboss.sourceforge.net/jbosside/updates/`.

The PMD project (*pmd.sourceforge.net*) created an Eclipse feature that includes tools for finding problems in Java code. PMD analyzes your source code to enforce coding practices such as prohibiting empty `try`/`catch` blocks and unused local variables. PMD is described in more detail in the Contributions section of Chapter 12, "Continuous Integration with Ant." The PMD project does not host a remote Eclipse update site, but their download archive contains the contents of an update site that you can unzip and access as a local site. Do the following to add this update site:

1. Open your Web browser to *pmd.sourceforge.net*.

2. Download the update site archive for Eclipse 3.0, e.g., `pmd-eclipse3-site-2.0.5.zip`.

3. Create a directory location on your computer to hold this local update site, e.g., `c:\eclipse-sites\pmd`.

4. Unpack the site archive into this directory.

5. In Eclipse, press the **New Local Site...** button shown in Figure 9-3.

6. Browse to the `c:\eclipse-sites\pmd` folder and press **OK**.

Your **Install** dialog should now look similar to that shown in Figure 9-4. The feature categories listed within each update site may be different, but similar choices will be available. Select the categories for your search; for this example, we have selected one category from each of the update sites.

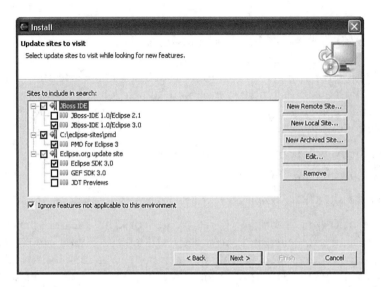

Figure 9-4   Search for new features from three sites.

The search results are displayed, as shown in Figure 9-5. Select the features that you wish to install and press the **Next** button.

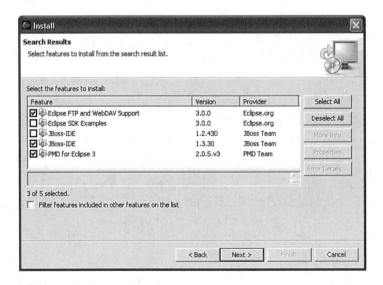

Figure 9-5   Select features to install.

Select each feature in the list and review its license agreement, as shown in Figure 9-6. If you accept the terms of all agreements, then select the option to acknowledge your acceptance and press **Next**; otherwise press the **Cancel** button.

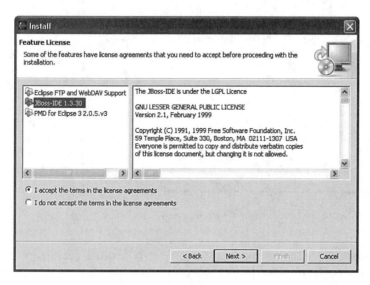

Figure 9-6   Accept or reject feature license agreements before installation.

Your final choice is to select the install location for each feature. The primary install location for Eclipse is referred to as the *product location*. By default this is c:\eclipse on Windows systems, but you may have chosen a different location when you unpacked the distribution. The product directory contains subdirectories named features and plugins. You can install the new features into the product directory, which will add new entries within features and plugins.

You can also create one or more additional install locations that are referred to as *extension locations*. As shown in Figure 9-7, press the **Add Site...** button and browse to a folder where the new features will be installed. In this figure, we created a new location c:\eclipse-contrib\tools. When the site is added, the update facility automatically creates a subdirectory named eclipse and adds a file named .eclipseextension within that directory.

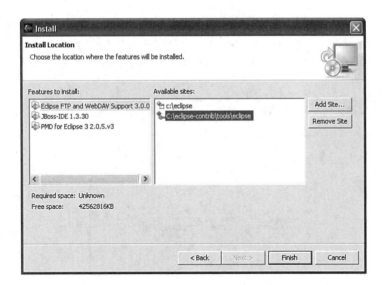

Figure 9-7   Choose the location where each feature will be installed.

You must choose the install location separately for each feature on the installation list, or else features without a site selection will be installed in the primary Eclipse product directory. When installing several features at one time, it's not necessary to select the same location for all features. You can create any number of separate extension locations; for example, you might want to create different locations for programming tools and modeling tools.

> **Tip:** Choose an installation site for new features that is different from your primary Eclipse product directory. This allows you to reinstall the standard Eclipse platform without losing third-party product extensions.

After completing the installation, you will be prompted to restart the Eclipse workbench to activate the new features. Press **Yes**. Review the new configuration by selecting the workbench menu command **Help > Software Updates > Manage Configuration...**. As shown in Figure 9-8, we now have two install locations with the three new features in the extension location.

This configuration view also can be used to disable or uninstall a feature, or to scan the original update site for updates to a feature. If you are not using a feature for an extended period of time, it may be helpful to disable it and remove that feature's menus, views, and all other IDE appearance and resource consumption. Select a feature and click on the **Disable** task. You will be prompted to restart the workbench; press **Yes** unless you want to disable other features before restarting.

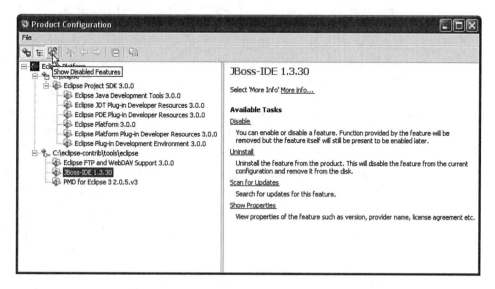

Figure 9-8 Updated product configuration.

Disabled features are not listed in the configuration view by default. To see a complete list, press the view toolbar button **Show Disabled Features,** as shown in Figure 9-8.

If you remove and reinstall your Eclipse SDK distribution, then you can quickly reinstall the product extensions that were saved to other location directories. As shown previously in Figure 9-1, select the **Eclipse Platform** entry and click on **Add an Extension Location.** You can browse to any extension directory and add all of its features at one time, but this must be a valid extension directory with an `eclipse` subdirectory that contains an `.eclipseextension` file.

> **Tip:** When you update to a new release of Eclipse, e.g., from 3.0.0 to 3.0.1, do not unzip the new release over the old installation. Create a clean installation and reinstall extra plug-ins by opening the **Product Configuration** dialog and selecting **Add an Extension Location** where your plug-ins are located.

9.2   Installing Plug-ins Without Features

Several hundred Eclipse plug-ins have been created, and the pace of development continues to accelerate. However, these plug-ins are packaged and distributed in many different ways and with a few different folder structures. Some developers have created update sites as described in the previous section, but more often plug-ins are distributed as ZIP files that do not include feature definitions. A feature usually groups several related plug-ins, so it's not necessary to define a new feature for one plug-in.

We'll step through a simple approach for leveraging the Eclipse update facility to organize and install these plug-in distributions. To make this approach concrete, install an open-source plug-in that converts Java source code to formatted HTML with color syntax highlighting similar to that in the Eclipse Java editor.

❍ Download the JavaToHtml converter from *http://www.java2html.de/ eclipse.html.*

❍ The ZIP file `java2html_eclipse_141.zip` (or a more recent version) contains a directory and file list as follows:

```
de.java2html_1.4.1/plugin.xml
de.java2html_1.4.1/eclipselib.jar
de.java2html_1.4.1/java2html.jar
de.java2html_1.4.1/java2html_eclipse.jar
de.java2html_1.4.1/icons/java2html.gif
de.java2html_1.4.1/icons/source_browser.gif
```

The installation instructions tell you to unpack the ZIP file into `c:\eclipse\ plugins` directory and restart Eclipse. This approach works fine and is similar to the instructions in many other plug-in projects, but with a minor change in the installation procedure, we can gain a more flexible organization that leverages the update facility.

Instead of installing the plug-in into the Eclipse product directory, you will create a new extension directory and add it to the configuration. You could unpack the plug-in into the extension directory created in the previous section, `c:\eclipse-contrib\tools\eclipse\plugins`, but you would not be able to disable the new plug-in without disabling the entire extension directory.

There is no way to create a new empty extension directory from within Eclipse except when installing from an update site, so we need to construct it manually. Create the following directory structure:

```
/eclipse-contrib
    /tools-plugins
```

```
/eclipse
    .eclipseextension
    /plugins
```

Copy the `.eclipseextension` file from `c:\eclipse-contrib\tools\`
`eclipse` to `c:\eclipse-contrib\tools-plugins\eclipse`. This marker file
must be present to notify the Eclipse update facility that this is an extension
directory. If you do not have another extension directory, copy the `.eclipse-`
`product` file from `c:\eclipse` and rename it to `.eclipseextension`.

Now that you have the extension directory set up, install the plug-in:

1. Unpack the JavaToHtml ZIP file into `c:\eclipse-contrib\tools-`
   `plugins\eclipse\plugins`.

2. In Eclipse, open the **Product Configuration** view, select **Eclipse Platform**,
   and click on **Add an Extension Location**. Browse to your new extension
   directory and press **OK**.

Your configuration will now appear as in Figure 9-9. When prompted to restart
Eclipse, press **Yes**.

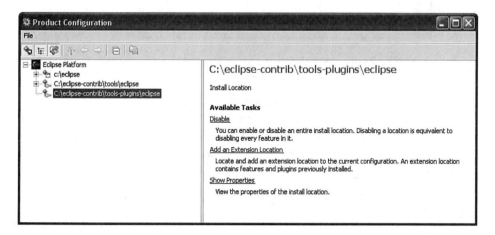

Figure 9-9 Extension location containing plug-ins without feature definitions.

Because the plug-in is not part of a feature, the configuration does not list
anything within the extension location. You can disable and enable the entire
extension directory, including all plug-ins within it, but you cannot disable individual plug-ins. If you install several different plug-ins in the same extension

directory, then all will be disabled or enabled as a group. You could create a separate extension directory for each third-party plug-in if you prefer complete control over disabling and enabling each plug-in.

The **About Eclipse Platform** dialog, shown in Figure 9-10, includes a button **Plug-in Details** that lists all plug-ins installed and enabled within your workbench. Open this dialog using the workbench menu **Help > About Eclipse Platform**. This is the quickest way to verify successful installation of plug-ins that are not packaged as features.

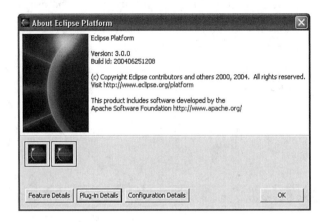

Figure 9-10   Review details of all plug-ins installed in the workbench.

When downloading plug-ins as ZIP archives (the most common approach used for packaging and distribution), you need to look at the ZIP folder structure for each plug-in that you intend to add. Sometimes the ZIP entry file paths for a plug-in include a `plugins` folder at the top level, in which case that plug-in would be unpacked into `c:\eclipse-contrib\tools-plugins\eclipse`.

9.3   Setting Update Preferences

The workbench preferences include two pages that control the update facility. The **Install/Update** page, shown in Figure 9-11, includes preference settings that may be necessary when accessing update sites.

The **Proxy settings** are needed when running Eclipse behind a firewall that uses a proxy server for HTTP connections. If this is true in your workplace, check the option to **Enable HTTP proxy connection** and fill in the proxy host address and port number. Check your Web browser for its proxy configuration or ask your network administrator for the address and port. Without this setting, you will not be able to connect to remote update sites.

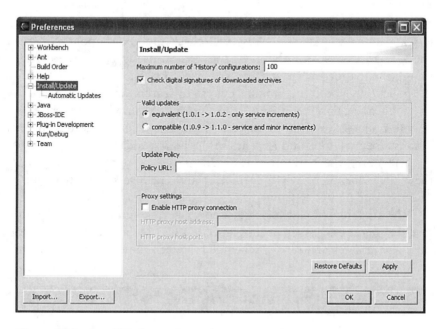

Figure 9-11   Install/Update preferences.

Eclipse allows you to search for updates to installed features. Each installed feature includes a URL that is used to connect to a server and search for new versions. If you have copied an update site from a remote site location to a local site location, as we did with the PMD feature, then the update URL in the feature definition will not refer to the correct local path. Your workbench should update its installed PMD feature from the local site when a newer version is downloaded.

This problem is resolved by creating an **Update Policy** file that redirects feature updates to the local site or to an alternative remote site behind your firewall. The update policy file is formatted as an XML document. To redirect updates to the PMD feature, create the following file and save it to `C:\eclipse-sites\UpdatePolicy.xml`:

```
<update-policy>
   <url-map pattern="net.sourceforge.pmd"
            url="file:/C:/eclipse-sites/pmd/" />
</update-policy>
```

In the **Policy URL** field of Figure 9-11, enter this file URL:

```
file:/C:/eclipse-sites/UpdatePolicy.xml
```

This update policy file is used to override a URL in a feature manifest. When looking for new updates, Eclipse will check the update policy (if present) and check if a `url-map` for the matching feature prefix is specified. If a match is found, the mapped URL will be used *instead* of the one in the manifest. Using the policy file, you can configure Eclipse to search for updates on your computer or on a local server behind the firewall. Meanwhile, other features from remote update sites will continue to be updated using the default mechanism because they will not find matches in the policy document.

For more information on using update policy settings, including details on the policy document XML format, search Eclipse online help for the topic "Eclipse Update Policy Control."

The preferences can also be used to search automatically for updates to installed features. As shown in Figure 9-12, check the option to automatically find new updates and set the schedule for when these searches will occur.

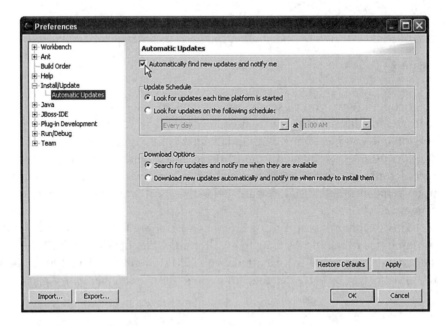

Figure 9-12   Enable and configure automatic update notification.

9.4   **Distilled**

❍ The **Product Configuration** dialog lists all install locations and all features within each location. When plug-ins are installed that are not packaged with feature definitions, they will not appear in the configuration list.

❍ The **About Eclipse Platform** dialog includes a button that lists all plug-ins enabled in your workbench, whether or not they are packaged as part of a feature.

❍ You can add bookmarks for remote or local update sites that are searched for new or updated features.

❍ You should install new features into an extension location instead of the primary Eclipse product location. If you remove and reinstall Eclipse at a later date, you will not lose the third-party extensions.

❍ Many plug-ins are packaged and distributed without feature definitions or update sites. Instead of unpacking their ZIP files into the primary Eclipse `plugins` directory, as is often recommended, use an extension directory that allows you to enable or disable these plug-ins.

❍ Preference settings may be required when a proxy server is used with your firewall, and update policy files allow you to redirect a feature URL to a locally cached site.

Eclipse allows considerable flexibility in how you organize product extensions and libraries used by your projects. In Chapter 6, "Java Project Configuration," we configured external libraries for Apache Axis and log4j, and in this chapter we updated Eclipse with new features and plug-ins. The resulting file directory structure follows:

```
/eclipse
   .eclipseproduct
   /features
   /plugins

/eclipse-contrib
   /libraries
      /axis-1.2beta
      /jakarta-basic
   /tools
      /eclipse
         .eclipseextension
         /features
         /plugins
   /tools-plugins
      /eclipse
```

```
          .eclipseextension
          /plugins

/eclipse-sites
    /pmd
```

9.5   Contributions

Many chapters in Part 2 include a Contributions section that lists third-party plug-ins related to the topics of each chapter. Index sites are also available that list several hundred contributions organized by category:

- ❍ The community page at Eclipse.org lists many available resources (see *www.eclipse.org/community/*).

- ❍ Eclipse Plug-in Central is an information portal and marketplace for the Eclipse ecosystem. It offers a plug-in directory, reviews, ratings, news, forums, listings for products and services, and support for the Eclipse Foundation (see *www.eclipseplugincentral.com/*).

- ❍ A categorized registry of plug-ins is available at *www.eclipse-plugins.info/*.

CHAPTER 10

Continuous Testing with JUnit

Continuous testing is an essential component of agile development practices. But writing and running software tests is often akin to taking medicine—an unpleasant but necessary task. However, if writing unit and functional tests becomes an integral part of your daily work, then it can accelerate your development and give you confidence in the outcome.

Writing unit test cases increases the quality of your deliverables by verifying successful completion of use cases and/or user stories. Don't wait until your development iteration is nearly complete before verifying whether you've met the requirements. Instead, you should write and run tests each day. This makes debugging easier because each unit test specifies the expected results, and a failed test tells you where the problem occurred and how your result is different from the required one. Refactoring can impact a lot of code written by many of your teammates. Without a unit test suite, you won't know if the refactoring changed the code's behavior.

But you can't achieve these benefits without committing to this strategy and investing the time to make it work, which can be difficult because you often don't reap the rewards until later in the project when requirements change and refactoring is in full-swing. The greatest reward may not come until a year later when your maintenance team takes over or when you begin working on the next release. But the return on this investment is significant.

The objective of the JUnit support built into Eclipse is to make it easier to write tests than not to write them. JUnit is a simple, flexible framework for writing and running unit tests in Java. Eclipse adds wizards for creating test cases and test suites, and it provides a view for running and viewing the details of test results.

We shall explore JUnit by writing tests for the UBL library of electronic business components. These tests include verifying and demonstrating the functionality of Java code generated from XML Schemas and testing the implementation of new code that computes the total of order line item prices spanning multiple currencies.

In this chapter, we'll see how to

❍ Choose one or more strategies for adding JUnit testing to your development process

❍ Configure Eclipse projects to organize your tests

❍ Write test cases using the JUnit wizard

❍ Run tests and analyze their results using the integrated JUnit view

10.1 Choosing a Test Strategy

Unit testing can support several general strategies for validating the behavior of your software. When developing new code, write tests that

❍ Specify the intended outcome of code yet to be written. Then you should write code until the tests pass. This is the ideal test-first strategy advocated by agile development principles.

❍ Specify the correct operation for bug reports. Then you should modify the code until these bug-fix tests pass.

> **Tip:** When you get a bug report, start by writing a unit test that exposes the bug. Keep the test case around after the bug has been fixed because it will let you know if the bug returns in the future.

The JUnit framework is also applicable to exercising any software APIs. You gain substantial benefit from writing tests that

❍ Help you define the API for as-yet unwritten types. Although this might feel strange to start with, you'll soon find it liberating to be able to use the API before they are even written.

❍ Help you understand or confirm your understanding of a new complex API, such as an XML parser, a business rules engine, or a JAX-RPC-compliant implementation for Web Services.

❍ Verify correct operation of a library acquired from another team or vendor.

    ○ Verify expected results from classes produced by a code generator. Code generation is becoming more prevalent for large frameworks like J2EE and for database or XML data binding.

We apply these strategies to our order processing application while building a library based on the Universal Business Language (UBL) specification. See the sidebar "UBL Order Pricing Calculation" for a description of our tasks.

UBL Order Pricing Calculation

The Universal Business Language (UBL) specification was created by OASIS to enable global interoperability of e-commerce transactions. The specification does not include Java APIs, but it provides XML Schemas and associated documentation that defines the syntax and semantics for procurement data.

The global nature of UBL requires a flexible structure for handling international pricing and calculation of order and invoice amounts. The complexity of these data requires careful verification and testing of software that implements the specification.

Figure 10-1 shows a class diagram with the relevant types and attributes for computing total amounts on an order and each of its line items. This diagram was derived from the UBL XML Schemas. Our task is to design and implement a corresponding Java library.

Simplified pseudo code for the calculations is as follows:

```
LineItem amount =

    quantity ÷ baseQuantity * priceAmount

Order totalAmount = sum( LineItem amount )
```

The unit test implementation in this chapter is based on this UBL order pricing example. Complete schemas and UML class diagrams for the UBL specification are available at the OASIS Web site:

www.oasis-open.org/committees/tc_home.php?wg_abbrev=ubl

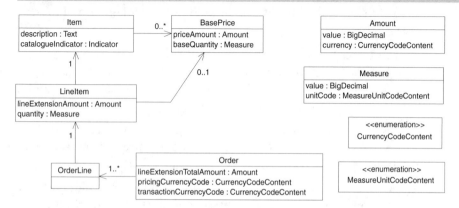

Figure 10-1 Domain model for UBL order pricing (small subset of the complete UBL model).

Our implementation of the order pricing calculation consists of two steps:

1. Use the Apache Axis toolset to generate Java classes from the XML Schemas for UBL data types `Amount` and `Measure`, and for code lists `CurrencyCodeContent` and `MeasureUnitCodeContent`.

2. Write Java classes that implement the order and line item types using the generated data types.

Our testing and verification follows two of the strategies described previously:

❍ Write JUnit tests that verify correct operation of the data types and code lists generated from the XML Schemas.

❍ Follow a test-first strategy and write unit tests for the order and line item amount calculations before implementing those methods.

> **Tip:** Focus on writing the tests that will catch most bugs; don't worry about the fact that you can't catch *every* bug.

10.1.1 JUnit Tactics: Test Hierarchy

Before proceeding with implementation of the tests, we'll quickly review the JUnit framework so that it is clear how the Eclipse wizards and commands work with this structure. JUnit tests are contained within a composite structure of arbitrary depth. You can run an entire test suite or any of its parts; the smallest part is one test method within a test case. A test suite may contain any class that implements the `Test` interface, including other suites. This structure is displayed in Figure 10-2.

The following definitions provide additional explanation of these framework classes:

Test Case. A test case, such as `AmountTest`, collects a set of one or more related test methods and is usually a subclass of the framework class `TestCase`. Each test method name must start with "`test`" and has no arguments, e.g., `testSetCurrency()`.

Test Suite. A test suite is a collection of tests that are run at the same time. A test suite is often constructed dynamically from selected test cases or may contain only a single test method.

Test Runner. A test runner is a utility used to run a suite of tests. The runner may provide a graphical presentation, such as an Eclipse view, or a command-line execution that is incorporated into automated build files.

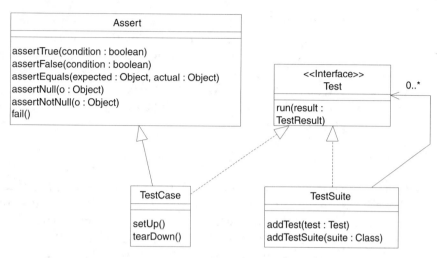

Figure 10-2   Composite structure of JUnit framework showing a subset of framework methods.

10.2 Project Configuration

A last bit of housekeeping is to review the ways in which you organize JUnit tests within an Eclipse project. The test cases are ordinary Java classes, so there are no fixed constraints on where you create them. You could co-mingle test case classes with the application code being tested, but this is not recommended. Instead, you should collect the test classes in a separate source folder or in a new project dedicated to unit tests. Clear separation enables you to easily omit tests from your production code distribution. Using a consistent configuration also allows other team members to quickly find and run the test suites.

The first configuration requirement is that the Eclipse project containing JUnit tests must include the `junit.jar` library in its Java build path. This configuration requirement is good justification for creating a separate project to contain your JUnit tests. When you use the Eclipse wizard to create new JUnit test cases, it automatically checks the build path and asks whether the library should be added for you. This is the easiest route; otherwise, you can manually add the library as described in Chapter 6, "Java Project Configuration." If you add the library yourself, then you should extend the predefined classpath variable named `JUNIT_HOME` to avoid absolute file paths in your project configuration.

As you are getting to know JUnit, it's helpful to take advantage of Eclipse source code navigation and text hover tips to learn about the framework implementation. The source code for JUnit is included in the Eclipse distribution, so you can attach this source archive to the library. This procedure is also described in Chapter 6. When the Eclipse wizard automatically adds the `junit.jar` library, it also attaches the source for you. All Eclipse JDT plug-in sources can be found here, including those for JUnit:

```
/eclipse/plugins/org.eclipse.jdt.source_3.0.0/src
```

So where do you put your tests? Figure 10-3 illustrates two approaches that work well. The first option is to create a second source folder in your project that contains unit tests for the code within that project's primary source folder. To create the second source folder, select the `com.eclipsedistilled.ubl` project in the **Package Explorer** and then select **File > New > Source Folder** from the main menu bar. Enter `test` as the folder name.

Figure 10-3   Two alternatives for organizing unit tests within your workspace.

A single project can have any number of separate source folders with names of your choosing. Just remember that a source folder is not the same as a regular project folder. This is described in more detail in Chapter 6, where Figure 6-1 shows the project source configuration tab.

The second option is to create a new project that is dedicated to testing. A common convention is to append `.tests` on the end of the project name whose code is tested. The second project named `com.eclipsedistilled.ubl.tests` contains the standard `src` folder for its Java source files.

Figure 10-3 includes both alternatives. Obviously, you would not do this in your own development—you should choose one or the other. It is quite reasonable, however, to combine these approaches for different projects. In our example order processing application, we created a separate project for testing the Web application, but we will use a second source folder for unit tests within the other projects.

A final recommendation when configuring your tests is to use the same Java package hierarchy for the unit tests and the code being tested. This package name is `com.eclipsedistilled.ubl.datatypes` in Figure 10-3. The reason is simple: this allows your unit test cases to access protected and package-protected methods in the classes being tested.

Because the package names are the same, your test case classes must have names that are different from the classes being tested. A common convention is to append `Test` onto the class name, so `AmountTest` is a test case for the methods in `Amount`.

10.3 Writing Test Cases

We now have all of the concepts in place to proceed with writing and running our tests. Figure 10-4 shows a class diagram of the JUnit tests that we intend to implement. This is only a small fraction of the complete test suite; these examples were selected to illustrate a range of test strategies and techniques.

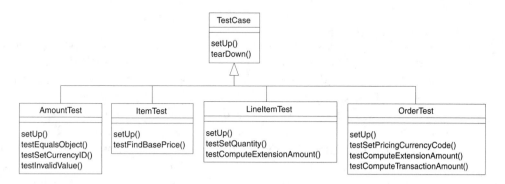

Figure 10-4   Our first iteration of UBL unit test cases.

The UBL specification defines a set of XML Schemas for electronic business documents. One of those schemas includes data types for `Amount`, `Measure`, internationalized `Text`, and others. Because we anticipate building a Web Services interface for order processing, we will use the Apache Axis toolset to generate Java classes for some of these UBL schema types.

The details of Web Services and Axis are beyond the scope of this book, but see *Building Web Services with Java* (Graham, 2004) for a detailed explanation of Axis. In Chapter 12, "Continuous Integration with Ant," we edit and run Ant build files within Eclipse to include the Axis code generation as part of continuous integration during development. For now, assume that another team member has already done this, and your task is to write unit tests for the generated code.

A relevant subset of the `Amount` class implementation is as follows:

```java
public class Amount {
    private BigDecimal value;
    private CurrencyCodeContent currency;

    public Amount(String val, CurrencyCodeContent curr) {
        value = new BigDecimal(val);
        currency = curr;
    }

    public void setCurrencyID(String currencyID) {
        currency = CurrencyCodeContent
                        .fromString(currencyID);
    }

    public void setValue(BigDecimal value) {
        this.value = value;
    }
}
```

A test case is often associated with one application class that is being tested. Thus, `AmountTest` is associated with `Amount`, for example. This is not a requirement of JUnit, but it is a common practice. The Eclipse test case wizard supports this convention and also helps you generate a test case template from the methods in a class.

Three different new type wizards are available from the workbench toolbar in the Java perspective. We've used the new class wizard in previous chapters. Click the down-arrow beside this toolbar icon to get a menu of related wizards, as shown in Figure 10-5. Select **JUnit Test Case** to create a new test case. Of course, you can also create this class in the same way as any other Java class, but the JUnit wizard accelerates this process.

Figure 10-5   Select the **JUnit Test Case** wizard from the toolbar.

The **JUnit Test Case** wizard shown in Figure 10-6 is very similar to the standard new class wizard, but it includes options that are unique to JUnit and omits others that are not relevant. The unique options are as follows:

- **Superclass default** is set to `junit.framework.TestCase`. This will be the right choice in many circumstances, although you might subclass a specialized framework that in turn subclasses `TestCase`. See the final section of this chapter for a list of other specialized test frameworks used with databases or Servlets.

- **Method stubs unique to JUnit.** You will frequently select `setUp()` and `tearDown()` methods. The static `main` method is usually not needed when running tests within Eclipse.

- **Class under test.** This is not required, but if specified, it enables the **Next** button on this wizard where you can select which methods are tested.

When creating our `AmountTest` test case, these choices are made in the wizard:

- Select the application class under test *before* opening this wizard. Do this by either making that class the current open editor or selecting the class in the Java **Package Explorer** view. This pre-fills the **Class Under Test** field when the wizard is opened and also fills the test class name by appending `Test` onto the application class name.

- Change the source folder from `src` to `test`. The `src` folder is chosen by default because the application class is in the `src` folder. If your tests are located in a different project, press the **Browse** button and pick the appropriate project source folder for this test case.

- Check the option for creating a `setUp()` method stub.

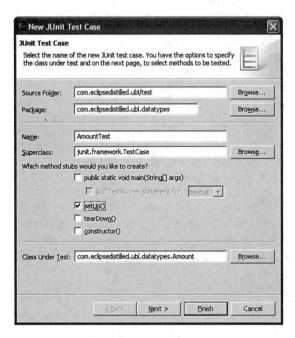

Figure 10-6   JUnit Test Case wizard.

Now press the **Next** button at the bottom of this wizard page and select the methods from **Class Under Test** that are included in the new JUnit test case. The next wizard page offers a list of all public and protected methods in the application class. For our `Amount` class, check the methods `equals(Object)` and `setCurrencyID(String)`. The wizard generates a skeleton test case, as shown here:

```
package com.eclipsedistilled.ubl.datatypes;

import junit.framework.TestCase;

public class AmountTest extends TestCase {

    /*
     * @see TestCase#setUp()
     */
    protected void setUp() throws Exception {
        super.setUp();
    }

    /*
     * Class under test for boolean equals(Object)
     */
```

```
public void testEqualsObject() {
    //TODO Implement equals().
}

public void testSetCurrencyID() {
    //TODO Implement setCurrencyID().
}
}
```

Now fill in the test methods so that we can run the test case to verify correct operation of the Amount data type class. Our immediate purpose is to understand how Eclipse supports JUnit testing, so details of the Amount class implementation are omitted. Complete implementation of all example code is available for downloading from this book's companion Web site (*www.EclipseDistilled.com*). The test case implementation is shown on the following page.

A typical test case consists of three parts:

1. Code that creates the objects used by the tests. This testing context is referred to as a test's *fixture*. The setUp() and tearDown() methods are part of the fixture. The setUp() method is run before every test method, and the tearDown() method is run after each test method. This assures a clean, repeatable test scenario.

2. Code that exercises the application objects in the fixture.

3. Code that verifies the result.

Tip: Make sure that all tests are fully automatic and that they check their own results.

Tip: JUnit test cases, and the classes they are testing, should resist writing to the system console. This is important to encourage self-validating tests and to keep the console clear of noise when running JUnit's command-line TestRunner.

Tip: Don't forget to test whether exceptions are raised when things are expected to go wrong.

```java
public class AmountTest extends TestCase {
    private Amount usd10;
    private Amount usd15;
    private Amount eur10;
    private Amount eur25;

    protected void setUp() throws Exception {
        usd10 = new Amount(10d, CurrencyCodeContent.USD);
        usd15 = new Amount(15d, CurrencyCodeContent.USD);
        eur10 = new Amount(10d, CurrencyCodeContent.EUR);
        eur25 = new Amount(25d, CurrencyCodeContent.EUR);
    }

    public void testEqualsObject() {
        assertEquals(usd15, usd15);
        assertEquals(usd15,
                new Amount(15d, CurrencyCodeContent.USD));
        assertEquals(usd10.toString(), eur10.toString());
        assertFalse("Amount is not equal to null",
                    usd10.equals(null));
        assertFalse("Amount values are not equal",
                    usd10.equals(usd15));
        assertFalse("Amount currency codes are not equal",
                    usd10.equals(eur10));
    }

    public void testSetCurrencyID() {
        usd10.setCurrencyID("AUS");
        usd10.setCurrencyID(null);

        try {
            usd10.setCurrencyID("XYZ");
            fail("Expected illegal currency for: XYZ");
        } catch (IllegalArgumentException e) {
            // expected
        }
    }

    public void testInvalidValue() {
        usd15.setValue(new BigDecimal(155.50d));
        usd15.setValue(new BigDecimal("155.50"));

        try {
            Amount amount = new Amount("10,500.50",
                    CurrencyCodeContent.USD);
            fail("Expected exception for: " + amount);
        } catch (NumberFormatException e) {
            // expected
        }
    }
}
```

These test conditions contain two intentional errors related to currency comparison. Can you spot them? If not, then this should reinforce the value of JUnit testing to ensure error-free code. Subtle errors are difficult to detect by scanning code or test data visually. When expected results are different from actual results, the offending tests are highlighted clearly in the JUnit view. Then you must determine whether the application code is wrong or whether you had incorrect expectations. Either way, it is an important discovery.

> **Tip:** When using `assertTrue`, `assertFalse`, `assertNull`, and `assertNotNull`, be sure to use the method signature that takes a `String` message argument describing what went wrong. This not only makes problems easier to solve—it also self-documents the test cases.

When applying a test-first strategy—writing the tests before implementing the code—it is still helpful to create an empty implementation of the intended methods. The JUnit wizard can then use this interface to generate test case stubs for the planned methods.

A subset of the `LineItem` class is shown below. Specify this as the **Class Under Test** in the JUnit wizard to generate a test case skeleton named `LineItemTest` that is similar to `AmountTest`. Write complete tests for the results that you expect when these methods are invoked and then work on the `LineItem` implementation until the tests pass.

```
public class LineItem {
    /**
     * @param quantity The quantity to set.
     */
    public void setQuantity(Measure quantity) {
    }

    /**
     * Compute the lineExtensionAmount for this LineItem.
     *
     * @return the computed amount
     */
    protected Amount computeExtensionAmount()
        throws PriceException {
    }
}
```

Notice that we have specified `computeExtensionAmount()` as a protected method. JUnit can test this only if the test case is contained in the same package as the application class.

> **Tip:** Think of the boundary conditions under which things might go wrong and concentrate your tests there.

10.4 Running Your Tests

A key to successful unit testing is to run your test frequently—several times per day for projects under active development and at least once per day for the complete application. The Eclipse workbench includes commands and views that make it easy to achieve this goal.

We already reviewed the composite structure of the JUnit test hierarchy, where a test case contains test methods and a test suite contains either test cases or other test suites. You can run tests at any level of this hierarchy. This makes it easy to select specific tests and run them after every code change. The primary commands used to run tests are as follows:

- ❍ **Run a test case.** Right-click on a test case Java class within the **Package Explorer** view and select **Run > JUnit Test**.

- ❍ **Run a single test method.** While editing a test case class, right-click on a test method in the **Outline** view and select **Run > JUnit Test**. This is very helpful while debugging the tests themselves.

- ❍ **Run all tests inside a package, source folder, or project.** Right-click on package, folder, or project within the **Package Explorer** view and select **Run > JUnit Test**.

Each time you run a different test, it is added to the most recently used list of launch configurations. The **Run** icon on the main workbench toolbar includes a menu of recent tests (and other non-test programs). You can also simply click the toolbar button to re-run the last test. This is the fastest way to iterate during a test-first programming cycle. The run menu is shown in Figure 10-7.

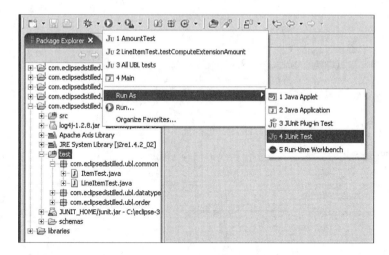

Figure 10-7   Run menu showing the most recent tests. Click the down-arrow beside the **Run** toolbar icon to get this menu. The **Run As** submenu can be used to run the current package explorer selection.

10.4.1   JUnit View

When you run JUnit tests, the results are displayed in a **JUnit** view. This view is shown automatically in the current perspective whenever you start a test run. Selecting the menu as shown in Figure 10-7 will run all tests within the test source folder and display the results shown in Figure 10-8.

A convenient arrangement for the **JUnit** view is to dock it as a fast view (see Chapter 4, "Customizing Your Workbench," for a description of fast views). When you run tests, the view will pop up automatically if there are failures or errors; in any case, the fast view icon shows the test result at a glance. Three alternative icons are shown in Figure 10-9. When all tests are successful, the icon displays a green checkmark. Any failures or errors display a red X. As a reminder to rerun your tests, the view icon is decorated with an asterisk (*) whenever you change the workspace contents after a test run.

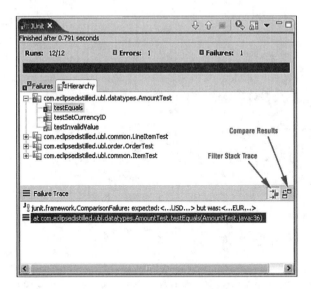

Figure 10-8   JUnit view showing results of running all test cases in the test source folder.

Figure 10-9   JUnit view icons: (a) successful, (b) failures, and (c) workspace contents changed
since last test run.

Unsuccessful tests fall into two categories:

Failures. Anticipated problems checked with JUnit assertions. For example, `assertEquals(a, b)` fails when the expected and actual results are not equal.

Errors. Unanticipated problems like a `NullPointerException` or `ArrayIndexOutOfBoundsException`.

Our `AmountTest` test case produces one failure and one error. Double-clicking on a failure trace line causes Eclipse to open the offending Java class file and position the cursor on the test case line where the failure or error occurred. The *failure* is caused by this assertion:

```
assertEquals(usd10.toString(), eur10.toString());
```

When an assertion compares two string values, an additional comparison viewer is available to help diagnose the problem. Press the **Compare Results** icon to open the window shown in Figure 10-10. More complex comparisons are also possible where more text is displayed and several distinct differences are high-lighted. The `assertEquals()` method also can be invoked with non-string values, but the result comparison view is not available for those failures.

The *error* in our test case produces this stack trace:

```
java.lang.IllegalArgumentException
    at com.eclipsedistilled.ubl.codelist.CurrencyCodeContent
        .fromString(CurrencyCodeContent.java:367)
    at com.eclipsedistilled.ubl.datatypes.Amount
        .setCurrencyID(Amount.java:112)
    at com.eclipsedistilled.ubl.datatypes.AmountTest
        .testSetCurrencyID(AmountTest.java:43)
```

It is caused by this line in our test:

```
usd10.setCurrencyID("AUS");
```

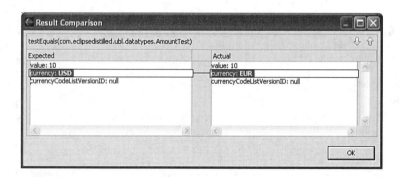

Figure 10-10   Compare actual with expected test result.

A quick investigation shows that AUS is not a valid currency code and that this method throws `IllegalArgumentException`. Replacing the code with AUD (for Australian Dollar) and rerunning the test eliminates this error.

You can toggle on/off the **Filter Stack Trace** option in the lower pane of the **JUnit** view. Many calls listed in the full stack trace are caused by JUnit frame-work methods or Java reflection methods. Because some methods are not help-ful when diagnosing failures, the JUnit view allows you to configure a set of stack trace filter patterns. These patterns are defined on the **Java > JUnit** preference page. It's helpful to add two additional patterns if you are running Eclipse with the Sun JDK. Press the **Add Filter** button to add the following two patterns:

```
sun.reflect.*
junit.framework.TestResult$*
```

10.4.2 *Customize a Test Configuration*

The tests we have run so far were configured by default using the project build path. However, it is sometimes necessary to customize the classpath, command-line parameters, or environment variables used by a test suite. You can even select a different Java runtime environment (JRE) version than the one used by Eclipse. These kinds of customizations may be needed when you import a Java project containing tests that were previously run outside of Eclipse, or when your test environment requires network or database connections.

To specify a custom configuration, select the **Run...** command under the toolbar submenu shown in Figure 10-7. This configuration dialog, as shown in Figure 10-11, is the same runtime configuration used for launching other applications. JUnit configuration includes an additional tab labeled **Test**. Here you can change the configuration name that appears on the **Run** menu, change the **Test class** that is run, or select a folder containing a set of test classes.

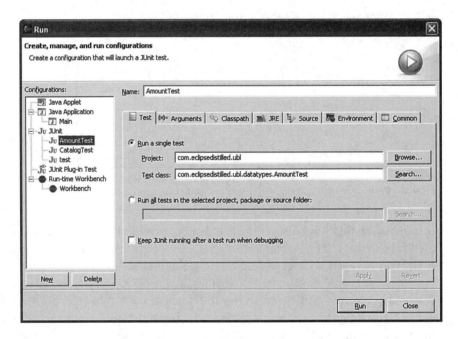

Figure 10-11   Optional configuration of JUnit runtime parameters.

10.4.3 Create a Test Suite

A test suite is a group of related JUnit tests. You can create an explicit Java class that defines which tests are in a suite, but it's often easier to use an Eclipse feature that automatically extracts all tests from a package, source folder, or project. This way, when you add a new test or test case, it is included in the test suite without any additional configuration, and there is no risk of accidentally omitting a new test from your suite. The test results shown in Figure 10-8 were produced by running all tests within the `test` source folder.

You can create one or more named suites that include specific test case classes. For example, your project may include several packages, where each contains many test cases. While developing part of this project, you might like to run all tests from one package but omit other package tests. This allows very frequent unit testing without taking too much time.

Eclipse includes a test suite wizard that makes suite maintenance very easy. Select the menu **File > New > Other > Java > JUnit > JUnit Test Suite** to open the wizard. When you pick the test cases from a package in our UBL project, the following test suite is generated. If you open the wizard again while this class is selected, then the lines between the two JUnit comments are replaced with a new selection.

```
public class AllTests {
    public static Test suite() {
        TestSuite suite = new TestSuite(
            "Test for com.eclipsedistilled.ubl.common");
        //$JUnit-BEGIN$
        suite.addTestSuite(ItemTest.class);
        suite.addTestSuite(LineItemTest.class);
        //$JUnit-END$
        return suite;
    }
}
```

To run this suite, select this class and choose the **Run > JUnit Test** just as you did with other test case classes.

10.5 Distilled

- ○ JUnit supports many different unit testing strategies, ranging from test-first processes advocated by agile development to writing unit tests that verify your understanding of third-party APIs.

○ JUnit tests are contained within a composite structure. You can run an entire suite or any of its parts; the smallest part is one test method.

○ Two alternatives are recommended for organizing your tests: create a second source folder in your project or create a new project dedicated to testing. For either configuration, write your test cases in the same Java package as the classes being tested so that tests have access to protected and package-protected methods.

○ The **JUnit Test Case** wizard accelerates your development by generating class templates with method stubs for the tests to be written.

○ The **JUnit** view is displayed automatically whenever any tests fail. It helps you to quickly identify points of failure and to compare expected with actual results.

10.6 Contributions

These contributions are not written as Eclipse plug-ins, but they are very useful libraries for JUnit testing. Each contribution extends the JUnit framework and includes a specialized subclass of `junit.framework.TestCase` used for writing tests. Because the Eclipse **JUnit** view and commands work with any subclass of `TestCase`, these contributions work inside Eclipse without any modification.

> **HttpUnit.** When testing Web applications, you need to bypass the browser and access your site from a program. HttpUnit makes this easy by emulating the relevant portions of browser behavior, including form submission, JavaScript, basic HTTP authentication, cookies, and automatic page redirection. It also allows test code to examine returned pages. See *www.httpunit.org.*

> **Cactus.** A test framework for server-side Java code (Servlets, EJBs, Tag Libs, Filters). See *jakarta.apache.org/cactus/.*

> **DbUnit.** A framework for writing tests using data from relational databases. This framework uses XML datasets (collections of data tables) and performs database operations before and after each test to assure that database content is in a known state. See *www.dbunit.org.*

10.7 References

JUnit home page, *www.junit.org*.

Fowler, Martin. *Refactoring*, Chapter 4, Building Tests. Reading, MA: Addison Wesley, 1999.

Graham, Steve, et al. *Building Web Services with Java*, Second Edition. Pearson Education, 2004.

Massol, Vincent. *JUnit in Action*. Greenwich, CT: Manning, 2004.

CHAPTER 11

Refactoring Your Code

The goal of refactoring is to make system-wide code changes without affecting the behavior of a program. The principal motivation is to make the software easier to understand and cheaper to modify. The term *refactoring* had been used for years by the Smalltalk community, but it only became widespread following publication of Martin Fowler's definitive book, *Refactoring: Improving the Design of Existing Code*. The concepts are powerful, but they also can be time-consuming to apply.

Eclipse provides an extensive list of commands that automate your Java code refactoring. Many commands that appear to be simple, such as **Move** and **Rename**, are actually refactoring operations—for example, moving and renaming Java elements requires changes in dependent files. Other refactoring operations, such as **Extract Interface**, help you generalize a design in preparation for the next iteration of development. After using automated refactoring to rename a Java package containing many classes with dependencies, you'll never want to do this again the old manual way.

In this chapter, we'll see how to

- ❍ Look for cues indicating the need to refactor your code
- ❍ Apply several refactoring operations that generalize the design of our UBL library
- ❍ Choose from a complete catalog of refactoring operations that are categorized as in Martin Fowler's book

11.1 When to Refactor

Refactoring is not an activity you schedule or set aside time to do. Refactoring is done in small bursts when you encounter "bad smells" in your code—to use a term popularized by Kent Beck and Martin Fowler. These odors may be caused by duplicated code, large classes, long methods, tightly coupled components (a.k.a. Feature Envy), and so on. Whenever you have difficulty understanding or modifying some code, try to find the cause of this difficulty and refactor it away.

Fowler describes a *Rule of Three* for deciding when to refactor:

> *"The first time you do something, you just do it. The second time you do something similar, you wince at the duplication, but you do the duplicate thing anyway. The third time you do something similar, you refactor."*

The most common reason to refactor is when you need to add a new feature to your software. As the code grows, it may be easier to understand and extend if a package is divided into two logical units. When previously defined methods are exposed as part of the public API, it may be necessary to extract new interfaces from concrete class implementations. When you find yourself saying, "If only I had designed the code this way, adding the feature would be easier," then you should fix it by refactoring.

The refactoring work done in this chapter is motivated by the need to add a new feature to our order processing application.

New Application Requirements

We met with our users and discussed a new set of business and technical requirements in preparation for the next development iteration. We agreed on a need for more flexibility in our design to support different kinds of electronic business transactions. These changes enable integration with a wider variety of order processing systems and allow us to publish a set of public interfaces.

We need to implement the following design changes:

- **A Web Services interface.** We must send and receive electronic order transactions using the SOAP protocol. This is in addition to our first release features, where order management is available via a direct Web browser interface.

- **Alternative forms of data persistence.** At a minimum, we must support direct database interaction via J2EE standards and XML serialization to documents compliant with the UBL standards.

Our first iteration used concrete class implementations for UBL components such as `Amount`, `Measure`, and `LineItem`. To implement these new features, we must extract a set of Java interfaces from these components.

We need to refactor the UBL component library...

11.2 Refactoring in Action

The best way to understand refactoring in Eclipse is to do it. When working on complex tasks, you'll often need to apply several different refactoring operations in succession to achieve your goal. Our goal is stated as follows:

> **Extract Interfaces.** Extract interfaces from the UBL class implementations for `Amount`, `Measure`, `Item`, `LineItem`, and `Order`. Create a new Java package that separates these interfaces from their implementations. Introduce a factory class for creating instances of these types.

All of these changes must be completed without breaking or modifying the behavior of our current implementation. The unit tests implemented in Chapter 10, "Continuous Testing with JUnit," give us confidence that we can verify a successful outcome.

The following sequence of refactoring operations is required to accomplish our design goal:

1. If possible, commit all code to the repository before refactoring.

2. Run all of your JUnit test cases and confirm that they all pass.

3. Rename UBL packages to add `.impl` suffix.

4. Rename classes with `Impl` suffix.

5. Extract an interface from each class.

6. Move interfaces out of `impl` packages, e.g., move data type interfaces from `ubl.datatypes.impl` to `ubl.datatypes` package.

7. Introduce a factory class for creating all UBL types.

8. Search for remaining class references and change to interfaces.

9. Rerun all JUnit test cases and confirm that they all continue to pass.

10. Commit the refactored code back to the repository.

11.2.1 Prepare for Refactoring

Refactoring operations often create changes to large amounts of code. This always carries some risk that the changes will have undesirable side effects on the code structure or its behavior. In addition, refactoring is sometimes an exploratory exercise where you try a design idea but may not keep the results. Therefore it's important to allow yourself an opportunity to abandon the changes and revert to a known version of working code.

If you have access to a source code repository, commit all code to it before refactoring. This will enable you to roll back to the last known state if the refactoring operations prove to be problematic. If you do not have a repository, create a ZIP archive of your workspace. Chapter 13, "Team Ownership with CVS," describes the CVS repository client support built-in to Eclipse, including a server that can be easily installed on your Windows computer for private use.

Refactoring should not change the behavior of your program. Without running unit tests that verify correct operation both before and after refactoring, it will be impossible to know whether the refactoring operations were successful. So before starting, run all your JUnit test cases and verify successful results. It's risky to start major refactoring operations on code with uncertain behavior.

11.2.2 Rename Packages and Classes

Prior to extracting interfaces from the UBL class implementations, we rename the packages with an `.impl` suffix and rename the classes with an `Impl` suffix. These changes are not mandatory, but they represent common conventions when organizing Java code. Another common convention is to leave the class names as they are and name the interfaces with an "I" prefix, so `Amount` implements the interface `IAmount`. In this example, we'll follow the first convention of using an `Impl` suffix on class implementations because this is the approach used in the Java Architecture for XML Binding (JAXB) specification (*java.sun.com/xml/jaxb*). The refactoring operations in Eclipse can accommodate either convention.

When this step is finished, the UBL project will contain two packages for data types:

```
com.eclipsedistilled.ubl.datatypes
com.eclipsedistilled.ubl.datatypes.impl
```

Refactoring commands are available from the context menus of several Java views (e.g., **Package Explorer, Outline**) and editors. The context menu only contains refactoring operations that are applicable to the current selection. There is also a **Refactor** command on the workbench menu bar; this contains all refactoring commands and enables those that are applicable to the selection in a view or editor. Most of the commands used in this chapter can be invoked from the **Package Explorer** view's context menu by selecting a package or class.

Shortcut: Alt+Shift+T: Shows the refactoring menu for the selection.

Shortcut: Alt+Shift+R: Starts a Rename refactoring operation on the selection.

Our first task is to rename the `com.eclipsedistilled.datatypes` package. Right-click on this package and select **Refactor > Rename...**. The dialog window shown in Figure 11-1 is displayed. Be sure to check the *Update references* option because this is a primary benefit of using the Eclipse refactoring commands! This command renames the underlying operating system folder in addition to changing package and import declarations in each Java file.

We also selected the second option to update matches found in comments and strings. If this package name is found in a Javadoc comment (e.g., references in `@see`, `@link`, `@param`, and `@throws` tags), then it is updated with the new name. This option forces you to preview changes to verify that no undesirable substitutions are made.

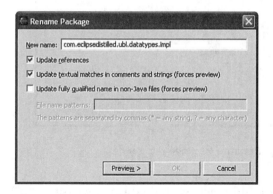

Figure 11-1   Choose options when renaming a package.

When performing a refactoring operation, you can optionally preview all of the changes resulting from this action before choosing to carry them out. The preview displays a list of potential problems and a summary of all changes that the refactoring action will perform. If you do not preview a refactoring operation, the change is made in its entirety, and any resultant problems are shown. If a problem is detected that does not allow the refactoring to continue, the operation is halted, and a list of problems is displayed.

A preview of the package renaming operation is shown in Figure 11-2. You can compare each proposed change by viewing *before and after* source code. If one or more change is not wanted, then simply uncheck that change. If the entire refactoring operation is unwanted, then press the **Cancel** button. You can explore the impact of significant refactoring operations even when you have no intention of completing them; just cancel the preview.

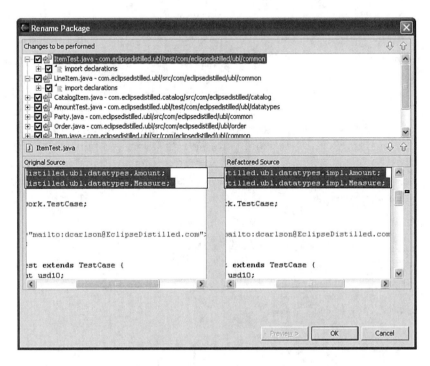

Figure 11-2   Preview changes for **Rename Package** refactoring.

Next, rename each class in this package and add an `Impl` suffix. Select each class in the **Package Explorer** view and press the shortcut keys **Alt+Shift+R**, or select **Rename** from the **Refactor** menu. The preview of changing `Amount` to `AmountImpl` is shown in Figure 11-3. Notice how all references to this class are also renamed, for example as shown in the `LineItem` class. Imagine the burden of searching for and changing each occurrence manually!

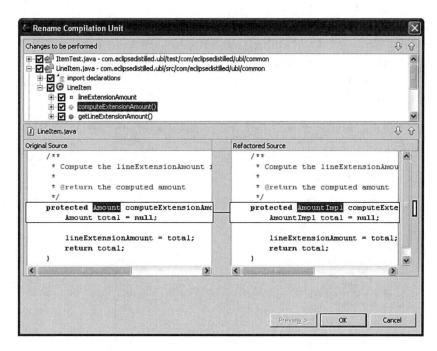

Figure 11-3   Preview changes for **Rename Class** refactoring.

11.2.3 Extract Interfaces

Now we extract an interface from each of these implementation classes. Select each class in the **Package Explorer** view and press the shortcut keys **Alt+Shift+T** to display the refactoring menu, or right-click on the class to open the context menu and navigate to the **Refactor** submenu. Choose the **Extract Interface** command, which displays the dialog shown in Figure 11-4.

Check the option: **Change references to the class 'AmountImpl' into references to the interface (where possible)**. When the class implementation has already been used in the methods of other classes, this option replaces class references with interfaces. The replacement is made only when the refactoring algorithm can determine with 100% certainty that the change is valid. For example, the class name is not changed to an interface when passed as an argument to another class constructor and assigned to an instance variable; the class may be needed here instead of the interface. We will search for remaining class references and change them to interfaces in the last step of this refactoring task.

Select the methods from each class that should be extracted to its interface. In Figure 11-4 we omitted `equals(Object)` and `toString()` from the refactoring operation because these methods are always inherited from the class `Object` and it is generally bad form to include methods defined by the class `Object` in an interface.

Figure 11-4   Select methods to be extracted into a new interface.

Now press **Preview** to review the changes, which are shown for the `AmountImpl` class and `Amount` interface in Figure 11-5. Notice how the return type of the `computeExtensionAmount()` method is changed in the `LineItem` class. It may appear that we are undoing the rename operation shown in Figure 11-3 where the same method's return type was changed from `Amount` to `AmountImpl`. However, there is a significant difference: the first refactoring renamed the *class* returned by this method, and the second refactoring changed the return type to a new *interface* named `Amount`.

Finally, move the generated interfaces out of the `.impl` package. It would be helpful if the refactoring operation allowed you to specify a target package at the time these interfaces are generated, but this is not possible in Eclipse version 3.0.0. Interfaces are always generated into the same package as their implementations. This also explains why we renamed the classes prior to extracting the interfaces—so that we can create a new interface having the original class name without encountering a name collision.

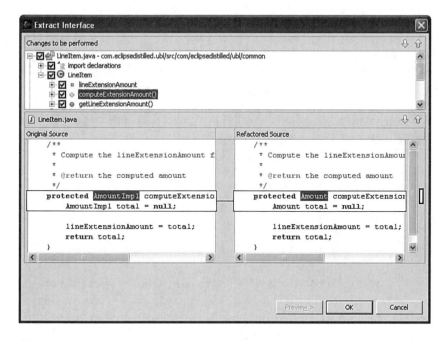

Figure 11-5   Preview changes for **Extract Interface** refactoring.

Moving files—and logically moving their package name references—is very quick using the **Move** refactoring operation. The **Move** command can be invoked on a group of files instead of running the command on files one at a time. Select all of the interfaces within the com.eclipsedistilled.ubl.datatypes.impl package and press the shortcut keys **Alt+Shift+V,** or right-click on one of the selected interfaces and select **Move** from the **Refactor** submenu. In the resulting dialog, select the com.eclipsedistilled.ubl.datatypes package and then press **OK,** or press **Preview** if you wish to review the changes.

Shortcut: Alt+Shift+V: Start a Move refactoring operation on the current selection.

Alternatively, you can drag and drop Java elements in either the **Package Explorer** or **Outline** view. It may not be obvious, but this action invokes an immediate **Move** refactoring operation without an option to preview the changes. References to the moved elements are updated automatically. You can use this drag-and-drop approach to move packages, classes, or interfaces. You can also move fields and methods between classes.

11.2.4 Introduce Factory

The final refactoring operation is to introduce a factory pattern for creating new instances of the UBL data types. Our design objective is to remove dependence on a particular set of data type implementations and enable alternative bindings to a database or Web Services. Thus application code should never directly create instances of `AmountImpl`. The factory will create these instances and return objects implementing the `Amount` interface.

Before refactoring, `Amount` instances are created like this:

```
new AmountImpl(10d, CurrencyCodeContent.USD);
```

After refactoring, the constructors are replaced with calls to the factory:

```
DatatypesFactory.createAmount(10d, CurrencyCodeContent.USD);
```

The first step is to create a new class named `DatatypesFactory` within the `com.eclipsedistilled.ubl.datatypes` package. The class is initially empty; the refactoring operation will add static methods to the factory that create our data type instances.

The **Introduce Factory** refactoring operation is invoked on individual class constructors. As shown in Figure 11-6, position the cursor on one of the `AmountImpl` constructors and press the shortcut keys **Alt+Shift+T** to display its refactoring menu. Select the **Introduce Factory** command, which displays the dialog shown in Figure 11-7.

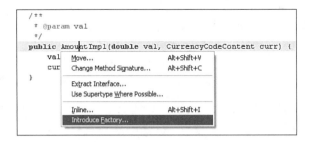

Figure 11-6   Introduce a factory pattern for creating instances with this constructor.

Enter the name for this new factory method and specify the factory class to which this method will be added. Because we will use the same `DatatypesFactory` class to create all UBL data type instances, we name the factory methods with qualified names such as `createAmount` and `createMeasure`. Uncheck the option to make the class constructor private. This option always defaults to true (i.e., it is checked), so you must uncheck it for each refactoring operation in this task. Our factory class is in a different package than the data type implementations, so the constructors must remain public.

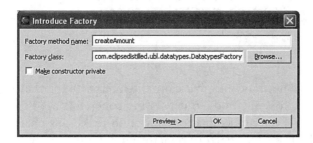

Figure 11-7   Enter the factory method name and the factory class in which it will be created. Uncheck the option to make this class constructor private.

Press the **Preview** button to review the changes proposed by this refactoring operation. As seen in Figure 11-8, the `AmountImpl` constructor is used in the `setUp()` method of the `ItemTest` unit test that we implemented in Chapter 10. The **Introduce Factory** refactoring replaces these statements with calls to `DatatypeFactory.createAmount()`.

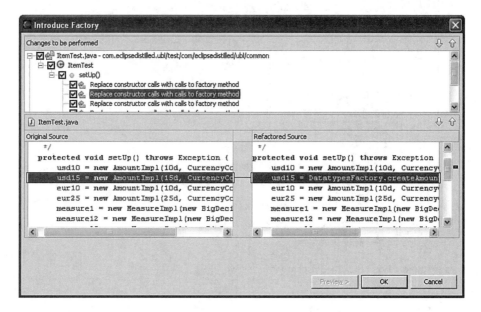

Figure 11-8   Preview changes for Introduce Factory refactoring.

The refactoring operation inserts this method into the factory class:

```
public class DatatypesFactory {

    public static AmountImpl createAmount(double val,
                        CurrencyCodeContent curr) {
        return new AmountImpl(val, curr);
    }
}
```

The refactoring cannot determine automatically the interface type that we want to be returned by the factory method, so it uses the concrete class name of the class being created. A few manual edits are required to make this change to the generated code, but the **Introduce Factory** refactoring did most of the heavy lifting for us. We'll leave this code as-is for now and use the Eclipse search function for final cleanup in the last step of this task.

Repeat this refactoring operation for each of the constructor methods in all of the UBL data type classes. In addition to `AmountImpl`, we also have classes for `MeasureImpl` and several others. The final results of all refactoring operations completed in this design task are displayed using the **Package Explorer** view shown in Figure 11-9.

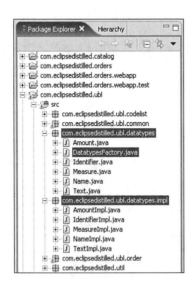

Figure 11-9   Results of our refactoring work.

11.2.5 Search for Class References

We are almost finished, but we need to make a few manual edits to resolve changes that could not be handled automatically by the refactoring operations. Fortunately we can use the powerful search facility within Eclipse to make quick work of this task and to be sure that we don't miss anything.

These manual changes were left by the refactoring operations:

❍ **Extract Interface** cannot determine every case where the original class reference can be replaced by the new interface.

❍ **Introduce Factory** creates factory methods that return instances of the concrete class instead of the interface it implements.

We can resolve both issues by searching for references to each data type class name, reviewing each occurrence of its use, and replacing the class name with the corresponding interface. Select the `MeasureImpl` class in the **Package Explorer** view and press the shortcut keys **Ctrl+Shift+G,** or open the context menu and select **References > Workspace**. The search results are displayed in a **Search** view, as shown in Figure 11-10. This view is opened automatically if it is not already available in the perspective.

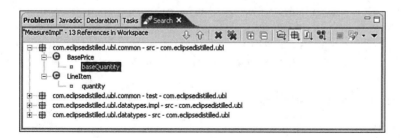

Figure 11-10   Search results for `MeasureImpl` references.

Shortcut: Ctrl+Shift+G: Search for all references to the selected Java element.

By searching the entire workspace, we are assured of finding references in all projects that use the UBL data type classes. All projects were also included in the refactoring operations. The search results show that the `baseQuantity` attribute in the `BasePrice` class and the `quantity` attribute in the `LineItem` class refer to the `MeasureImpl` class. Double-click on each of these lines in the search view to open their respective class editors, where you can replace `MeasureImpl` with `Measure`.

The refactoring operations also leave behind a few unused `import` statements for class implementations such as `AmountImpl` and `MeasureImpl`. The Eclipse **Problems** view displays each unused `import` statement as a warning message. Double-click each warning message to open a Java editor positioned on the offending line. Delete the unused `import` statement and save the file.

11.2.6 Verify and Commit Results

We have finished the refactoring necessary to proceed with the next iteration of development. We did not change the behavior of the UBL library code or any of the other projects that use it, but this restructuring results in a more general design. Alternative implementations of the new interfaces are now possible where the objects are persisted in a database or bound to XML data received by Web Services transactions.

However, before patting ourselves on the back for a job well done, we need to verify that success. Rerun all JUnit test cases and confirm that they all continue to pass. This is an important step that should not be neglected. A failed test may be easy to fix at this point before any new unrelated changes are introduced into the code, or significant problems may cause you to roll back to the repository state we established before starting the refactoring operations.

If everything checks out, commit the refactored code to the repository. Now you can pat yourself on the back for a job well done!

11.3 Catalog of Refactoring Commands

This catalog of refactoring operations is organized into categories equivalent to those in Martin Fowler's book, *Refactoring: Improving the Design of Existing Code*. Only refactoring operations available in Eclipse 3.0.0 are listed. In a few cases, one Eclipse command is listed under multiple categories using more specific names. For example, Eclipse contains only one Rename refactoring command, but the catalog describes it in three parts: Rename Method, Rename Type or Package, and Rename Source Folder or Project. A similar classification split is done for the Move and Inline commands.

11.3.1 Composing Methods

A large part of refactoring work consists of composing methods to package code properly. The refactored code is easier to understand. If many inline comments are required to explain parts of a long method, then this may be a cue to extract separate methods whose names describe their separate purposes.

Extract Method. Turn a code selection into a new method whose name explains the purpose of the method. Replace the selection with a reference to the new method. You can get a valid selection range by using the menu command **Edit > Expand Selection To > Enclosing Method** (or shortcut keys: **Alt+Shift+Up-Arrow**). This refactoring is useful for cleaning up lengthy, cluttered, or overly complicated methods.

Inline Method. Put the method's body into the body of its callers and remove the method. Sometimes a method's body is as clear as its name, or it may perform unnecessary simple delegation.

11.3.2 Moving Features Between Objects

One of the most fundamental, if not *the* fundamental, decision in object design is deciding where to put responsibilities. Use these refactoring operations to correct design mistakes or to reassign responsibilities when an evolving code base would be simpler with different class responsibilities. A design decision that is reasonable and correct one week can become incorrect the next.

Consider moving a field when more methods on another class use the field than methods on the class where it is declared. This usage is often indirect through getter and setter methods. Move methods when classes have too much behavior or when classes are collaborating too much and are too tightly coupled. Methods may need to be moved after moving a field.

Move Field. Move a field declaration from one type to another. Additional refactoring is usually required to resolve broken references to a private field.

Move Method. Create a new method with a similar body in the class it uses most. Either turn the old method into a simple delegation or remove it altogether. An instance method can be moved to new source classes that are used as types of its parameters or types of fields declared in the same class as the method. An error dialog will be shown if these conditions are not satisfied.

Extract Class. Create a new class and move the relevant fields and methods from the old class into the new class. This refactoring is not included in any Eclipse menus, but it can be accomplished via a series of Move Field and Move Method refactorings.

11.3.3 *Organizing Data*

Organize fields, local variables, and constants in a class to make working with its data easier.

Encapsulate Field. Make a field private and provide getter and setter methods. This operation includes an option that changes current field access to use the getter and setter methods.

Extract Local Variable. Create a new variable assigned to the selected expression and replace it with a reference to the new variable. You can get a valid selection range by using the menu command **Edit > Expand Selection To > Enclosing Method** (or shortcut keys: **Alt+Shift+Up-Arrow**).

Extract Constant. Create a static final field from the selected expression and substitute a field reference; optionally rewrite other places where the same expression occurs.

Convert Local Variable to Field. Turn a local variable into a field. If the variable is initialized on creation, then the operation moves the initialization to the new field's declaration or to the class's constructors.

Inline Local Variable or Constant. Replace references to a local variable or static constant with the expression that is assigned to that variable or constant. Optionally remove the variable or constant declaration.

11.3.4 *Making Method Calls Simpler*

These refactoring operations help make object interfaces easier to understand and use. A method's name is a key factor in communicating its purpose and behavior. The simplest refactoring to improve your code's clarity is to rename methods with more descriptive names. A method's parameters, return type, and visibility complete the definition of its full signature. This signature should be as simple as possible without sacrificing relevant information. Good object interfaces show only what they have to and no more.

Rename Method. Change the name of a method. Optionally update all references to this method.

Change Method Signature. Change parameter names, parameter types, parameter order, or thrown exceptions and update all references to the corresponding method. Parameters also can be removed or added, and the method return type or visibility can be changed.

Introduce Parameter. Add a new parameter to a method signature. Select an expression in the method body before starting this refactoring. The containing method is given a new parameter, and the selected expression is copied into the argument list of all the callers.

Introduce Factory. Replace the selected constructor with a factory method. Create a new static factory method in the specified class and replace all uses of the constructor with the new method.

11.3.5 Dealing with Generalization

These refactoring operations help you to manage the inheritance hierarchy of your classes and interfaces. Methods and fields may be moved up or down the hierarchy, new interfaces may be created to represent relevant subsets of behavior, or type references may be generalized to more abstract types.

Push Down. Use this refactoring when behavior on a superclass is relevant only for some of its subclasses. Move a set of methods and fields from a class to its subclasses. This refactoring can be applied to one or more methods and fields declared in the same type. Often used when you are extracting a new subclass.

Pull Up. Eliminate duplicate behavior in two or more subclasses. Move a field or method to a superclass of its declaring class or, in the case of methods, declare the method as abstract in the superclass. This refactoring can be applied to one or more methods, fields, and member types declared in the same type.

Extract Interface. Create a new interface with a set of methods selected from a class and make the selected class implement the new interface. Optionally change references to the class to use the new interface wherever possible.

Generalize Type. Replace a type with one of its supertypes. Select a declaration of a variable, parameter, field, or method return type in the Java editor before starting this refactoring. The refactoring wizard shows the supertype hierarchy for the original type and updates the declaration with the selected supertype.

Use Supertype Where Possible. Replace occurrences of a type with one of its supertypes after identifying all places where this replacement is possible.

11.3.6 Organizing Classes and Packages

Java package naming is an important part of a library's design for reuse and extensibility. Classes within a package should have related responsibility and gain access to package-protected methods. However, as a project grows and evolves, it is inevitable that packages will be split, merged, or renamed to reflect their new purpose. Type names should describe their role and may need to be renamed. All of these changes can have significant impact on code that references these packages and types. The refactoring operations in this section help you reorganize Java packages and types and update their references.

Rename Type or Package. Rename a type or package. Optionally modify all references to the changed element.

Move Package. Move one or more packages (and all of the types they contain) to a new source folder. The underlying operating system folders and files are also moved to the new location.

Move Type. Move one or more types to a new destination package, or move inner classes into a different class.

Rename Source Folder or Project. Rename a source folder or project. This does not affect Java elements directly, but project configuration properties are updated with the new name.

Move Member Type to New File. Create a new Java compilation unit (file with .java extension) for the selected member type and update all references as needed. For non-static member types, a field is added to allow access to the former enclosing instance.

Convert Anonymous Class to Nested. Convert an anonymous inner class to a named member class.

11.4 Distilled

○ Refactoring makes software easier to understand and cheaper to modify, and it prepares a design for the next development iteration, but it does not change the current behavior.

○ The only way to know whether your program's behavior is unchanged by refactoring is to run a complete JUnit test suite both before and after refactoring. Refactoring without unit tests to validate the operations is very risky.

○ Commit all code to a repository before and after refactoring to establish known states for rolling back changes.

○ Several different refactoring operations are often applied in a sequence to accomplish a complex task. For example, extracting a group of interfaces is accompanied by renaming a package, moving types, and introducing factory methods.

○ Preview the results of refactoring operations to omit individual changes or cancel an entire operation that does not accomplish what you expected.

○ Refactoring operations can update references to changed elements and save you a large amount of time compared to performing the same changes manually.

○ A catalog of all refactoring operations available in Eclipse is categorized by common tasks during your refactoring activities.

11.5 References

Fowler, Martin. *Refactoring: Improving the Design of Existing Code*. Reading, MA: Addison Wesley, 1999.

CHAPTER 12

Continuous Integration with Ant

Successful agile development requires that you deliver complete, tested applications at the end of an iteration. An iteration is completed within a few weeks and often integrates the results of several small teams. Integrating one set of changes at a time makes it easy to identify problems and prevents a surprise at the end. The developers and customers working on a team keep a view of the iteration's progress.

It would not be possible to work in this style if integration took several hours or required significant human intervention. It is important to have tools that support a fast, automated build and test cycle. You also need a reasonably complete test suite that verifies successful integration of each new or modified component.

Continuous integration occurs at two points in the development cycle. First, each developer uses Eclipse to keep his or her view of the project's code synchronized with a team repository. The automated project builders within Eclipse assist developers in performing continuous compilation and unit testing of their component. Second, a *build machine* is used to compile and test the application in a clean environment. This should be done at least once per day. Eclipse includes excellent support for writing and running Ant build files that automate the build process.

This continuous integration environment is illustrated in Figure 12-1.

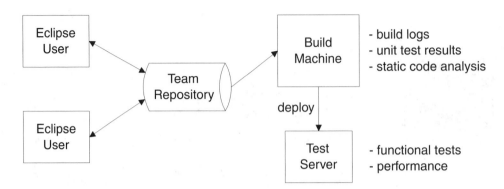

Figure 12-1   Continuous integration with a team repository.

In this chapter, we'll see how to

○ Automate incremental building of each change to your Eclipse projects

○ Customize the build process to include other tools

○ Use Eclipse's Ant editor and **Outline** view with Content Assist and templates similar to the Java editor

○ Configure and run Ant build files within the workbench

12.1 Automatic Incremental Build

Many projects gain the benefits of continuous integration with little or no additional effort beyond project configuration and testing described in Chapter 6, "Java Project Configuration," and Chapter 10, "Continuous Testing with JUnit." When the workspace and projects are configured correctly, continuous integration is automatic and nearly instantaneous. This automatic build includes project dependencies that integrate modules from other teams.

The default Java project builder compiles all code from the source folders into the output folders. The builder runs automatically whenever any source file is updated. If desired, you can disable the automatic build and choose to rebuild projects at your discretion. The workbench **Project** menu is shown in Figure 12-2. If you uncheck the option to **Build Automatically**, then the two other menu items for **Build All** and **Build Project** will be enabled. You can also choose to clean all output from one or all projects and rebuild them from scratch.

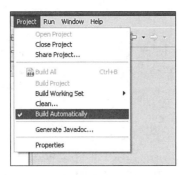

Figure 12-2   Project menu with build options.

It's common to include other steps in a project's build process. For example, you might generate code from database or XML Schemas, or you might generate code from models (see the Eclipse EMF and UML2 technology projects). Our UBL project includes code generated from XML Schemas that represent standard data types and enumeration lists used in electronic commerce. A build process might package JAR archives, generate Javadoc files, and use FTP to deploy an application to a test server.

These other build steps may be performed by Java applications or by running non-Java tools that are executed from the command line. Any external tool can be configured and run from within Eclipse, but it's more common to use Ant build files to run other Java or non-Java tools. Figure 12-3 shows the **External Tools** menu, which is opened by clicking on a toolbar icon. You can configure and run any tool from this menu, including Ant build files within your projects (for your convenience, the first two items shown in this menu are tool names that were run previously in this workspace).

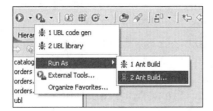

Figure 12-3   Configure and run external tools.

12.2 Customized Build with Ant

We'll take a quick tour through the basic features of Ant and then begin implementing a build file that automates the generation of Java code from XML Schemas.

12.2.1 Introduction to Ant

Ant, part of the Apache open source project, is a Java-based build tool designed to be cross-platform, easy to use, extensible, and scalable. It works equally well in small personal projects or in large, multi-team, distributed development efforts.

Ant's benefits are enabled by three core concepts:

○ Ant build files use a *declarative syntax* to represent build targets, tasks, and dependencies.

○ New tasks may be added that support additional tools or operations, e.g., to invoke the Axis WSDL-to-Java code generator.

○ The build files are written with an *XML format* that helps to provide a flexible and extensible structure. This also allows use of standard XML tools for editing and parsing the build files.

The primary elements in an Ant build file are as follows:

Project. Each build file contains one project. It's not necessary for an Ant project to be equivalent to an Eclipse project; an Ant project represents a logical group of related targets.

Target. An Ant project contains one or more targets that produce the build output, such as a library archive, or that perform interim steps, such as compiling source code or running tests. Dependencies between targets assure that prerequisites are completed before a target is run.

Task. Each target contains tasks that represent its individual operations. Ant includes a long list of built-in tasks for performing operations such as copying files, running the Java compiler, or setting property values. Other tools can contribute new tasks that extend Ant's capabilities.

A skeleton outline of our Ant build file for code generation contains three targets, two of which depend on completion of the `init` target.

```
<project name="UBL data type generation"
         default="wsdl2java" basedir=".">
```

```
<target name="init"
        description="Define folder locations and classpath">
</target>

<target name="wsdl2java" depends="init"
        description="Generate Java from WSDL">
</target>

<target name="clean" depends="init"
        description="Remove build folders">
</target>

</project>
```

For a more detailed explanation of writing Ant build files for large projects and continuous integration, see the Ant Web site, *http://ant.apache.org/*, or the book *Java Development with Ant* (Hatcher and Loughran, 2003).

12.2.2 Build Properties

An Ant project can have a set of *properties* that are used to parameterize aspects of the build file, such as the folders in which source files are located and where output files are written. These properties might be set in the build file using the `property` task, or they might be set outside of Ant and passed via the command line. Properties are global within a build file after they have been declared. If one task assigns a value to a property, another task in the same build file can then use that property.

A property has a name and a value; the name is case-sensitive, and the value is immutable. After a property is declared, its value cannot be changed for the remainder of the build file execution. Please take note of this immutability because it is a common source of confusion for those new to Ant.

The `property` task in an Ant build file assigns a single property by name and value or assigns a set of properties read from a file. This task assigns a single property value:

```
<property name="javacVerbose" value="false" />
```

This task assigns multiple properties read from a file:

```
<property file="build.properties" />
```

Alternatively, use the `location` attribute instead of `value` to set the property to the absolute path of the given file or directory. If the `location` attribute value is an absolute path, it is left unchanged (with / and \ characters converted to the platform's conventions where this build file is running). Otherwise the value is set to an absolute path by expanding the given relative path using the project's base directory.

The project's base directory is always available in the `basedir` property that may be set using an attribute on the `project` element, or it will default to the parent directory of the build file if unspecified. These property values are set using relative path locations:

```
<property name="src.dir" location="src" />
<property name="build.dir" location="build" />
<property name="build.classes.dir"
         location="${build.dir}/classes" />
```

Notice that the third property uses the second property value as its base path. Properties may be used in the value of other task attributes by placing the property name between `${` and `}`. In this example, the `build.classes.dir` property value is set to an absolute path of the `basedir` location appended with "`build`" and then appended with "`/classes`".

Unfortunately, a reference to an undefined property will not be reported during Ant execution—instead, it will be silently ignored. This can lead to confusing results when undefined references are used to construct file paths. You can use the `echo` task to help you debug these situations while running Ant. For example, if you reference the `src.dir` property before it is defined:

```
<echo message="The source directory is: ${src.dir}" />
```

then Ant will leave `${src.dir}` unchanged and the message displayed will be

```
The source directory is: ${src.dir}
```

The immutability of properties can be used to your advantage when generalizing an Ant build file to run with different file locations. In this example, the `junit.jar` property is set as part of the `condition` task, but only when the `available` file is present. If it is present and the property is set, then the `property` task following `condition` will have no effect because the immutable property is already set. When the file is not available and the `condition` fails, then the second `property` task will assign a value:

```
<condition property="junit.jar"
           value="${ant.home}/lib/junit.jar">
    <available file="${ant.home}/lib/junit.jar" />
</condition>
```

```
<property name="junit.jar"
        location="${ant.home}/../org.junit_3.8.1/junit.jar" />
```

12.2.3 Build Tasks

Many tasks are built into the standard Ant library, and other tasks can be added by third-party extensions. The following tasks are used in the Ant build files described in this chapter; see the Ant documentation for a complete list. Most of these tasks also have additional optional attributes.

ant—Run Ant on the supplied build file; this can be used to build subprojects. The ant task is included within a target of an Ant build file whose conditions and sequence determine if and when the subproject build is invoked. In the following example, a build file named javadoc.xml is invoked to prepare Javadoc HTML from the source code.

```
<ant antfile="javadoc.xml" />
```

The Javadoc build tasks could be included in the master build file, but we can leverage an Eclipse wizard via the menu **Project > Generate Javadoc...** to create and maintain a separate javadoc.xml build file.

copy—Copy a file or fileset to a new file or directory. By default, files are only copied if the source file is newer than the destination file, or when the destination file does not exist. However, you can explicitly overwrite files with the overwrite attribute. The following example copies all files from the src.dir that do *not* have the extension .java or .htm*. This pattern is used in a build file to copy resource properties files from the source folder into the build folder.

```
<copy todir="${build.classes.dir}" failonerror="true">
   <fileset dir="${src.dir}"
            excludes="**/*.java, **/package.htm*" />
</copy>
```

A fileset is a group of files. These files can be found in a directory tree starting in a base directory and are matched by patterns taken from a number of pattern sets and selectors. A fileset can appear inside tasks that support this feature.

delete—Delete a single file, a specified directory and all its files and subdirectories, or a set of files specified by one or more `fileset` child elements. When specifying a set of files, empty directories are not removed by default. To remove empty directories, use the `includeEmptyDirs` attribute.

```
<delete dir="${doc.dir}" />
```

echo—Echo a message to Ant's loggers and listeners, which is `System.out` unless overridden. A `level` attribute can be included to filter messages that are logged; this attribute is optional and defaults to `debug`. Possible values are `error`, `warning`, `info`, `verbose`, and `debug`.

```
<echo level="info"
     message="Generating WSDL Java mapping into: ${src.dir}" />
```

jar—Create a JAR file containing the specified set of files. The following example includes all files in the `basedir` attribute location. One or more `fileset` child elements can be nested in the `jar` task that filter the selected files or gather files from several different locations.

```
<jar jarfile="${build.dir}/myProject.jar"
     basedir="${build.classes.dir}" />
```

javac—Compile the specified source file(s). The source directory is recursively scanned for `.java` source files to compile. Only Java files that have no corresponding `.class` file in the destination directory or whose class file is older than the `.java` file will be compiled. In the following example, the `classpath` element refers to a `compile.classpath` property that was set before this task is reached.

```
<javac destdir="${build.classes.dir}"
       failonerror="false"
       debug="on"
       source="1.4"
       target="1.3">
   <classpath refid="compile.classpath" />
   <src path="${src.dir}" />
</javac>
```

junit—Run the JUnit testing framework. The `batchtest` element specifies that all unit test classes within the `${test.classes.dir}` location matching the `*Test.class` pattern are run (e.g., `AmountTest.class` from Chapter 10). The test results are produced as per the `formatter` element specification (XML format in this example) and written to `${test.data.dir}`.

```
<junit printsummary="yes" fork="yes"
       errorProperty="test.failed"
       failureProperty="test.failed">
   <classpath refid="test.classpath" />
   <formatter type="xml" />
   <batchtest todir="${test.data.dir}">
      <fileset dir="${test.classes.dir}"
               includes="**/*Test.class" />
   </batchtest>
</junit>
```

junitreport—Merge the individual XML files generated by the `junit` task and apply a stylesheet to produce an HTML report of the JUnit results.

```
<junitreport todir="${test.data.dir}">
   <fileset dir="${test.data.dir}" includes="TEST-*.xml" />
   <report format="frames" todir="${test.reports.dir}" />
</junitreport>
```

mkdir—Create the specified directory. Also create the parent directories if they don't already exist. This example creates the `classes` directory to hold the results of compiling the source code.

```
<mkdir dir="${build.classes.dir}" />
```

taskdef—Add a task definition to the enclosing project, such that the new task can be used in this project's targets. The `classname` attribute refers to a fully qualified Java class name whose definition contains an Ant task that is written as per the Ant API specifications. In this example, we define a task named `wsdl2java` that is contributed by the Apache Axis library to generate Java source files from WSDL files.

```
<taskdef name="wsdl2java" classname=
            "org.apache.axis.tools.ant.wsdl.Wsdl2javaAntTask">
   <classpath refid="axis.classpath" />
</taskdef>
```

12.2.4 Building the UBL Project

In the remainder of this chapter, we'll use Ant to implement a customized build process that prepares a complete distribution of the UBL component library. Most of our attention is devoted to running the Apache Axis tool that generates Java code from Web Services definitions based on WSDL and XML Schemas. We'll review the following steps required to prepare a complete build:

1. Generate Java code from XML Schemas that define UBL data types and enumerated code lists

2. Run all JUnit tests and generate an HTML report of the test results

3. Generate Javadoc HTML files from the source code

4. Automate the entire project build and test process so that it can be run either inside or outside of Eclipse

Our UBL project contains an additional folder, named `schemas`, which we have not discussed in previous chapters. This folder contains XML Schema files from the UBL standard distribution downloaded from the OASIS Web site. The files are organized as follows:

```
com.eclipsdistilled.ubl
    src
    test
    schemas
        xsd
            codelist
                (several .xsd files)
            common
                (several .xsd files)
        ubl.wsdl
        build.xml
```

In addition to the schemas, we created a `ubl.wsdl` file required to run the Axis code generator. This is not a complete Web Services interface definition for using UBL but rather is simply a small stub that references the XML Schema files relevant to our work. For complete details of this example, download the project from this book's companion Web site at *www.EclipseDistilled.com*. We keep our focus on learning about Eclipse facilities for developing and running Ant build files that automate project building.

12.3 Ant Editor and Outline

Start by implementing the skeleton build file used to generate code from the UBL schemas. In the `com.eclipsedistilled.ubl` project's `schemas` folder, create a new file named `build.xml`. A specialized Ant editor and coordinated **Outline** view will be opened for this file, as shown in Figure 12-4. This editor contains a completed version of the `init` target.

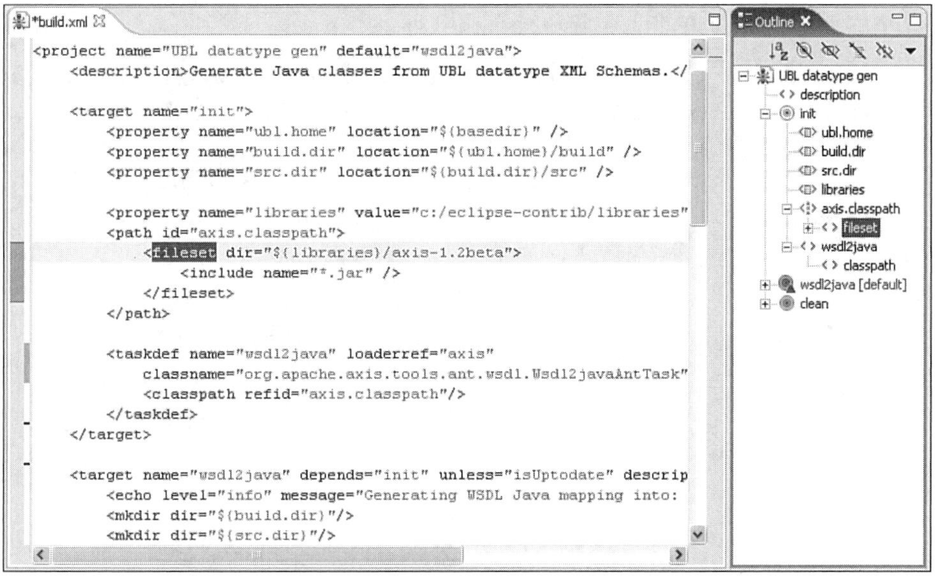

Figure 12-4 Ant editor with **Outline** view of its targets and tasks.

You'll notice a strong parallel between the Ant editor features and those from the Java editor described in Chapter 5, "Rapid Development." The analogous Ant editor features are as follows:

- ❍ **Outline view.** Select any target or task name in the **Outline** view to navigate to its location in the editor.

- ❍ **Hover text.** Position the cursor over an Ant property reference to see its value, over a target reference to see that target's description, or over a `refid` attribute to see the expanded reference value.

- ❍ **Content Assist.** Press **Ctrl+Space** to activate Content Assist that proposes a list of valid attributes within an Ant element or a list of new elements that can be inserted at the cursor location.

○ **Code templates.** The Content Assist proposals include templates that insert predefined code snippets into your build file.

○ **Text formatting.** Format the entire file contents to indent and align the XML structure. Text color highlighting distinguishes elements, attributes, and comments in the editor.

○ **Real-time syntax checking.** Some invalid Ant structures are highlighted as errors in the editor. For example, unmatched XML begin/end tags, missing default targets or missing target dependencies, and incorrect project or target declarations are highlighted.

Type a "t" and press **Ctrl+Space** to activate Content Assist that displays the list of suggestions shown in Figure 12-5. Most of the suggestions are for Ant's XML elements beginning with the letter "t", but this list also contains two templates. You can preview each template's content while scrolling through the list. It is also possible to add, delete, or modify Ant templates in the preferences page **Ant > Editor > Templates.**

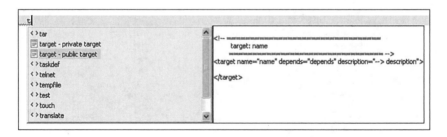

Figure 12-5   Content Assist showing a template for adding a new public target while editing an Ant build file.

Ant is an extensible language, and many third-party tools include Java classes that implement new Ant tasks. The `init` target shown in Figure 12-4 includes a `taskdef` declaration for a new task type named `wsdl2java` and maps it to the Java class implementation contributed by the Apache Axis library. The child elements and attributes allowed by this new task are defined by the Axis implementation and are documented in its user manual.

It's not necessary to name the target `wsdl2java` in our build file, but we used this name because it describes the target's primary purpose: running the `wsdl2java` task. Using the Ant editor, fill in the target as follows:

```
<target name="wsdl2java" depends="init"
        description="Generate Java code for WSDL">
```

```
<echo level="info"
      message="Generate Java mapping into: ${src.dir}" />
<mkdir dir="${src.dir}"/>
<wsdl2java url="${ubl.home}/ubl.wsdl"
           output="${src.dir}"
           deployscope="session"
           serverSide="no"
           skeletonDeploy="no"
           noimports="no"
           verbose="no"
           typeMappingVersion="1.1"
           testcase="no">

<mapping namespace=
       "urn:oasis:names:tc:ubl:CoreComponentTypes:1:0"
     package="com.eclipsedistilled.ubl.datatypes.ccts" />
<mapping namespace=
       "urn:oasis:names:tc:ubl:codelist:CurrencyCode:1:0"
     package="com.eclipsedistilled.ubl.codelist" />

</wsdl2java>
</target>
```

The `wsdl2java` task includes nine attributes, one of which is the output location
where the Java code is generated; we use the Ant property `${src.dir}` that
resolves to `./schemas/build/src` in the current configuration. If we plan to
write several Ant build files that use this new task, then it would be helpful to
add a new Ant editor template named `wsdl2java` that inserts text similar to that
shown here. We could simply replace the `url` and `output` attribute values and
have the template complete the rest.

12.4 Running Ant in Eclipse

You run an Ant build file in Eclipse by selecting it and optionally specifying
which of its targets should be used. If no target is specified, then the default target is run. Any dependencies of the selected targets will be run automatically to
fulfill their prerequisites. Our UBL code generation build file contains three targets, and `wsdl2java` is the default.

There are several ways to run Ant in Eclipse:

❍ Select an Ant build file in the **Package Explorer** view and pick **Run > Ant
Build** from the context menu. This choice runs the targets as specified in
that build file's launch configuration, or the default target is used if no
configuration exists or launch targets were not specified.

❍ Choose **Run > Ant Build...** from the context menu to open a launch configuration dialog where you can specify which targets to run.

○ While editing an Ant build file, open the context menu on a specific target in the **Outline** view and pick **Run > Ant Build**.

○ Open the **Ant** view, add one or more build files, and then double-click on a target that you want to run.

○ After you have run a build file, its name appears in the **External Tools** workbench menu. You can run it again by picking this menu item.

12.4.1 Ant Runtime Configuration

Some Ant tasks require additional configuration before being run. These changes are not needed for our initial build file, but we'll need them before building the entire UBL component library, so let's configure the Ant runtime preferences now. The configuration options shown in Figure 12-6 are located in a workbench preferences page under **Ant > Runtime**.

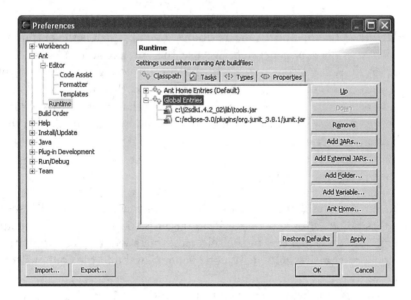

Figure 12-6   Runtime configuration shared by all Ant build files.

○ On the **Classpath** tab, you can add classes required on the classpath when running Ant. These classes define contributed tasks and types or provide classes required by these contributions.

- ○ On the **Tasks** tab, you can add tasks defined in one of the classes on the classpath. The `wsdl2java` task is an example of what can be configured here.

- ○ On the **Types** tab, you can add types defined in one of the classes on the classpath. Built-in Ant types include `description`, `fileset`, and `patternset`. It is possible, although uncommon, to add new types contributed by third-party tools.

- ○ On the **Properties** tab, you can add property names and values that are passed into Ant. These become global property values available in all of your build files.

The **Classpath** entries shown in Figure 12-6 are grouped into two categories. **Ant Home Entries** include JAR files that are available in the Ant home directory, located in the `org.apache.ant_1.6.1` plug-in folder by default. Eclipse includes several JAR files here that contribute additional tasks. The second category, **Global Entries**, is empty by default. We need to add two JAR files here:

- ○ `tools.jar` is required when using the `<javac>` Ant task. This JAR (or others with equivalent classes) includes the Java compiler provided by your Java SDK. This JAR file is not included with Eclipse or with the Java JRE. You must download and install a full Java software development kit, e.g., available for free from Sun or IBM.

- ○ `junit.jar` is required when using the `<junit>` Ant task that runs JUnit tests. This JAR is included with Eclipse in the `org.junit_3.8.1` plug-in folder.

Using these preferences, you can add the Apache Axis JAR files in the **Classpath** tab and then declare the `wsdl2java` task in the **Tasks** tab. Doing so would make this task available in all of your build files without `taskdef` declarations in each project's `init` target. This works very well if you always run the build files within Eclipse, but those tasks would fail when run outside of Eclipse. We declared the `taskdef` within our build file for this reason.

You can also customize the launch configuration of individual build files instead of using the global configuration for all uses of Ant. The dialog shown in Figure 12-7 is displayed when you select the **Run > Ant Build...** menu item for a build file.

The dialog opens with the **Targets** tab displayed. You can select the targets to run and the order in which they are run. You may also add or override global Ant preferences for **Classpath** and **Properties** runtime configuration options. The **Refresh** tab allows you to refresh the workspace or selected resources within a project after the Ant build targets are finished. See Chapter 3, "Managing Your Projects," for a description of refreshing the workspace.

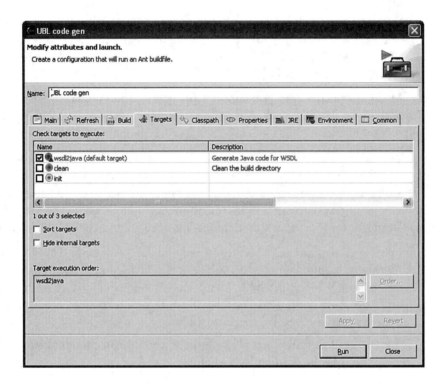

Figure 12-7   Runtime configuration for an individual Ant build file.

You can rerun or modify a build file's runtime configuration by selecting **External Tools...** from the menu shown in Figure 12-3.

12.4.2 Ant View and Console Output

The **Ant** view, shown in Figure 12-8, is the quickest way to select and run targets from several different build files. Position this view in a corner of your Java perspective so that it is easily accessible without taking much space, or add it as a tab in the same space as the **Outline** view.

You can add any number of build files to the **Ant** view and then select the view toolbar command to **Hide Internal Targets**. An internal target in Ant is one without a description attribute, typically used for prerequisite dependencies such as init.

Figure 12-8 **Ant** View showing public targets (and hiding internal targets) in three build files. Double-click a target to run it.

All output written to the console (e.g., System.out and System.err in Java or the <echo> task in Ant) is displayed in the **Console** view when build files are run within the workbench. This view is shown in Figure 12-9 containing output from the wsdl2java target in our UBL code generation build file.

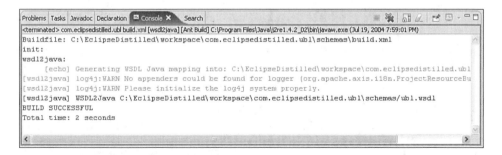

Figure 12-9 **Console** view displaying output from running the wsdl2java target.

12.4.3 Automatic Project Builder

New Java projects are configured by default with a **Java Builder** that automatically compiles Java source files when they are saved. However, this is not always enough to rebuild your project completely when changes are made. Eclipse includes the ability to define new project builders that fill this gap.

Any external tool can be configured and run as a custom project builder, but it's convenient to use Ant build files to coordinate the execution of other Java or non-Java tools.

Follow these steps to create a new project builder:

1. Open the project properties dialog by right-clicking on a project and selecting **Properties**.

2. Choose the **Builders** page. In default configurations, there will be only one builder named **Java Builder**.

3. Press the **New...** button. You will be asked to choose either **Ant Build** or **Program**. Choose Ant Build.

4. The configuration dialog will appear as in Figure 12-10. This is the same runtime configuration used with any Ant build file. You can select the targets to run, modify the classpath, and choose to refresh the workspace when finished. Change the configuration name to "XSD Codelists".

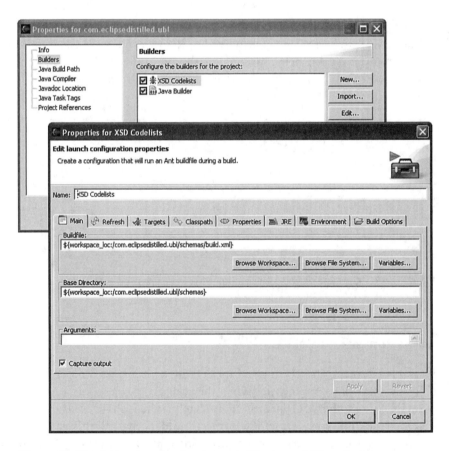

Figure 12-10   Add and configure a custom builder in our UBL project.

5. Fill the **Buildfile** field by pressing its **Browse Workspace...** button and picking the `schemas/build.xml` file.

6. Fill the **Base Directory** field by pressing its **Browse Workspace...** button and picking the `schemas` folder.

7. The **Build Options** tab shown in Figure 12-11 is specific to configuring project builders. We want to run the Axis code generator automatically, so check the option **During Auto Builds**.

8. Specify the working set of relevant resources that will trigger an automatic build. For our UBL project, choose the `./schemas/xsd` folder and the `ubl.wsdl` file.

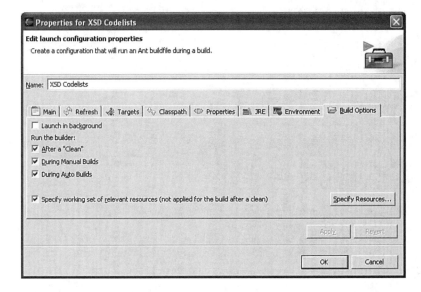

Figure 12-11   Configure the custom builder to run automatically whenever schema resources are modified.

9. In the **Properties** tab shown in Figure 12-12, we need to override one of the property values set in the build file's `init` target. First, uncheck the option to **Use global properties**.

10. Press **Add Property** and enter the name "`src.dir`". Press **Variables** and choose `build_project`. Click **OK**. In the **Value** field, append `/src` to the variable. Click **OK** to save the new property.

11. Finally, click **OK** to save the new builder in your project configuration. Be sure that the **XSD Codelists** builder is listed before the **Java Builder** so that the generated code is automatically compiled after creation.

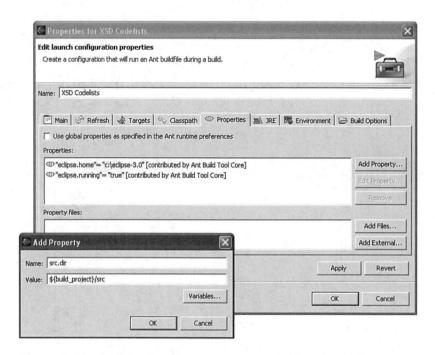

Figure 12-12   Adding and configuring an automatic builder in our UBL project.

Now, whenever the `ubl.wsdl` file or any file within the `./schemas/xsd` folder is modified, new Java code is generated directly into the `com.eclipsedistilled.ubl` project source folder. Then it is immediately compiled.

You can disable this builder temporarily by unselecting the **XSD CodeLists** item on the project's **Builders** page. For example, when you are making a series of changes to the schemas, it would be best to disable the builder and run the build file locally within the `schemas` folder. Code will be generated into the temporary `./schemas/build` folder. When your design is stable, re-enable the builder to resume automatic building into the project's source directory.

For more significant customization of the build process, you can disable the built-in **Java Builder** and replace it completely with your own Ant build file. This custom builder could be used to run alternative Java compilers, C++ compilers, or other tools in projects that use a combination of programming languages and technologies.

12.5 Building and Testing Complete Projects

Now that you've mastered the details of creating, configuring, and running Ant build files, we return to our original goal of continuous integration. As illustrated in Figure 12-1, we need to build the projects automatically on the build machine, as well as within each developer's Eclipse workbench.

Create a `build.xml` file within the `com.eclipsedistilled.ubl` project folder. Ant targets that use the tasks `javac`, `junit`, and `junitreport` are needed for compiling and testing this project's code. These steps are similar to the work already completed for running the Axis code generator.

The build file described in this section can be run within Eclipse as we've already seen, or the same build file can perform a complete build and test while running outside of Eclipse. Most open source Java applications include Ant build files in their distribution, so there are many examples to follow. Also see the references at the end of this chapter for more information on developing with Ant.

This Ant build file project is named `com.eclipsedistilled.ubl`, although it's not necessary for the Ant project to have the same name as the corresponding Eclipse project. The project specifies that the `dist` target is default, so if the build file is run without indicating which target is to be run, then `dist` is used. We declare several properties outside of the targets in this project; they define constants used by several `javac` tasks in this project. These `property` tasks are evaluated before any targets are executed.

```
<project name="com.eclipsedistilled.ubl"
         default="dist" basedir=".">

  <property name="bootclasspath" value="" />
  <property name="javacFailOnError" value="false" />
  <property name="javacDebugInfo" value="yes" />
  <property name="javacVerbose" value="false" />
  <property name="javacSource" value="1.4" />
  <property name="javacTarget" value="1.4" />
  <property name="compilerArg" value="" />
```

The `init` target is a common convention used when writing Ant build files. It defines properties used by other targets in the project and is included as a dependency on those targets.

```
<target name="init">
  <property name="src.dir" location="src" />
  <property name="build.dir" location="build" />
  <property name="build.classes.dir"
            location="${build.dir}/classes" />
```

```
<property name="test.src.dir" location="test" />
<property name="test.dir" location="${build.dir}/test" />
<property name="test.classes.dir"
          location="${test.dir}/classes" />
<property name="test.data.dir"
          location="${test.dir}/data" />
<property name="test.reports.dir"
          location="${test.dir}/reports" />

<property name="dist.dir" location="dist" />
<property name="doc.dir" location="doc" />

<property name="libraries"
          value="c:/eclipse-contrib/libraries" />
<path id="compile.classpath">
  <pathelement path=
          "${libraries}/jakarta-basic/log4j-1.2.8.jar" />
  <fileset dir="${libraries}/axis-1.2beta">
     <include name="*.jar" />
  </fileset>
</path>

<!-- set junit.jar location, conditional on ant.home -->
<condition property="junit.jar"
           value="${ant.home}/lib/junit.jar">
   <available file="${ant.home}/lib/junit.jar" />
</condition>
<property name="junit.jar"
    location="${ant.home}/../org.junit_3.8.1/junit.jar"/>

<path id="test.classpath">
  <path refid="compile.classpath" />
  <pathelement path="${junit.jar}" />
  <pathelement path="${build.classes.dir}" />
  <pathelement path="${test.classes.dir}" />
</path>
</target>
```

The `wsdl2java` target invokes a separate Ant build file to build the subproject. This is the build file that was written previously in this chapter. The Axis code generation tasks could have been included directly in this build file, but we want to maintain independent specifications of the procedure for generating Java from the XML Schemas.

We instruct this target to invoke the build file in the `schemas` directory and to run the `wsdl2java` target found there; because the build file name is not indicated, it uses the default `build.xml` name. When the subproject build file is invoked, we specify that it does not inherit all properties from this master project, and the `src.dir` property is explicitly passed. Because Ant properties are immutable, this `src.dir` property value takes precedence over any `property` task that attempts to set this same property name in the subproject build file.

```
<target name="wsdl2java" depends="init"
        description="Generate Java from WSDL">
  <ant dir="schemas" target="wsdl2java" inheritAll="false">
    <property name="src.dir" value="${src.dir}" />
  </ant>
</target>
```

The next target compiles all Java source files in this project's `src` directory. This target depends on completion of the `wsdl2java` target because it generates source directly into the project's `src` folder, and then this target compiles all source that is generated or written. Compiled class files are written to the `${build.classes.dir}` location that was assigned in the `init` target.

The global properties at the start of this build file are used to parameterize the `javac` compiler execution. When you want to omit debug information from compiled class files while preparing a production build, you can pass the `javaDebugInfo` property a value of "no" from the command line when invoking this build file. Properties are immutable, so that value overrides the property assignment in this build file.

When compilation is finished, all other resource files are copied from the source folder, and then the contents of the `classes` folder are collected into a JAR file named `ubl.jar`.

```
<target name="compile" depends="wsdl2java"
        description="Compile all sources">

  <mkdir dir="${build.classes.dir}" />

  <!-- compile the source code -->
  <javac destdir="${build.classes.dir}"
         failonerror="${javacFailOnError}"
         verbose="${javacVerbose}"
         debug="${javacDebugInfo}"
         bootclasspath="${bootclasspath}"
         source="${javacSource}"
         target="${javacTarget}">
    <compilerarg line="${compilerArg}" />
    <classpath refid="compile.classpath" />
    <src path="${src.dir}" />
  </javac>

  <!-- Copy necessary resources -->
  <copy todir="${build.classes.dir}" failonerror="true">
    <fileset dir="${src.dir}"
             excludes="**/*.java, **/package.htm*" />
```

```
    </copy>

    <!-- Create a distribution JAR -->
    <jar jarfile="${build.dir}/ubl.jar"
         basedir="${build.classes.dir}" />
</target>
```

The `test` target performs several tasks required to run the JUnit test suite in this project. First, all source files are compiled from the `${test.src.dir}` folder; this location was assigned in the `init` target. Then the `junit` task runs all test cases and writes the results in XML files. Those results are then used to prepare an HTML report. If any of the unit tests fail, the entire build file is terminated after this target. See the section entitled "Build Tasks" earlier in this chapter for additional description of the `junit` and `junitreport` tasks.

```
<target name="test" depends="compile"
        description="Compile and run JUnit tests">

    <mkdir dir="${test.classes.dir}" />
    <mkdir dir="${test.data.dir}" />
    <mkdir dir="${test.reports.dir}" />

    <!-- compile the unit test source code -->
    <javac destdir="${test.classes.dir}"
           failonerror="${javacFailOnError}"
           verbose="${javacVerbose}"
           debug="${javacDebugInfo}"
           bootclasspath="${bootclasspath}"
           source="${javacSource}"
           target="${javacTarget}">
      <compilerarg line="${compilerArg}" />
      <classpath refid="test.classpath" />
      <src path="${test.src.dir}" />
    </javac>

    <!-- Copy necessary resources -->
    <copy todir="${build.classes.dir}" failonerror="true">
      <fileset dir="${src.dir}"
               excludes="**/*.java, **/package.htm*" />
    </copy>

    <!-- Run the tests -->
    <junit printsummary="yes" fork="yes"
           errorProperty="test.failed"
           failureProperty="test.failed">
      <classpath refid="test.classpath" />
      <formatter type="xml" />
      <batchtest todir="${test.data.dir}">
        <fileset dir="${test.classes.dir}"
                 includes="**/*Test.class" />
```

```
      </batchtest>
   </junit>

   <junitreport todir="${test.data.dir}">
     <fileset dir="${test.data.dir}" includes="TEST-*.xml"/>
     <report format="frames" todir="${test.reports.dir}" />
   </junitreport>

   <!-- Build fails if any of the unit tests fail -->
   <fail if="test.failed"
         message="JUnit tests failed. Check reports." />
</target>
```

This build file also generates API documentation using Javadoc. The Javadoc tool has many options for customizing its output, such as choosing which Java packages to include, which external referenced packages are included as hyperlinks, and which Javadoc tags are documented. Eclipse makes this configuration easy by supplying a Javadoc wizard. Run it by selecting the workbench menu command **Project > Generate Javadoc...** and filling in the options. Your selections in the wizard are saved to an Ant build file named javadoc.xml.

> **Tip:** Use a small number of consistent names for your build files. Any names other than build.xml must be associated with the **Ant Editor**. In the preference page **Workbench > File Associations**, add **javadoc.xml** and associate it with the **Ant Editor**.

We invoke the generated Ant build file from our master build file in the javadocs target. The javadocs target depends on init where the doc.dir location is assigned. This target assumes that the javadoc.xml file is in the same folder as this Ant build file.

```
<target name="javadocs" depends="init"
        description="Generate Javadoc">
  <mkdir dir="${doc.dir}" />
  <ant antfile="javadoc.xml" />
</target>
```

The last two targets are used to prepare a complete distribution of this project and to clean up after it finishes. The targets named dist and clean are a common convention used in many Ant build files. The requirements for the dist target have not been completed, but it would probably create a ZIP file containing the binary JAR file, the API documentation, and maybe the source files and test results if this is an open source project.

```
<target name="dist" depends="compile,test,javadocs"
        description="Create distribution">
  <!-- TODO: package up the distribution ZIP -->
</target>

<target name="clean" depends="init"
        description="Clean the build, dist, doc folders">
  <delete dir="${build.dir}" />
  <delete dir="${dist.dir}" />
  <delete dir="${doc.dir}" />
</target>

</project>
```

This Ant build file is mostly generic and could be used to build and test other Java projects in your Eclipse workspace. The only non-generic elements are property values in the `init` target that include external libraries in the classpath required to compile the sources.

12.6 Distilled

The results of our work in this chapter are shown in a **Package Explorer** view in Figure 12-13. Three Ant build files were created. When run, these tasks create additional folders within our project, but they can be removed at any time by running the `clean` target in the project's build file.

○ Many projects gain the benefits of continuous integration with little or no additional effort beyond routine Java project configuration. All source files are compiled automatically when they are saved, and complete unit testing is only one click away.

○ Supplementing the default Java builder with Ant build files can often fulfill non-routine build requirements. Ant is a declarative and extensible build tool, and its capabilities are seamlessly integrated with the Eclipse workbench.

○ The Ant build file editor has many features in common with the Java editor, such as a coordinated **Outline** view, hover text tips, Content Assist, templates, and automatic formatting.

○ Workbench preferences for Ant include runtime configuration where additional JAR files may be added to the classpath used to run build files.

Individual build files have their own runtime settings that can override or extend the defaults.

❍ Ant build files may be configured to run automatically whenever project resources are modified. For example, whenever an XML Schema is modified, your project can generate new Java classes and compile those with the manually created sources.

❍ A complete project build file compiles all source files, compiles and runs all JUnit tests, prepares an HTML report of JUnit results, and generates Javadoc API documentation. This build file may be run either within Eclipse or independently on a separate build machine as part of an automated continuous build process.

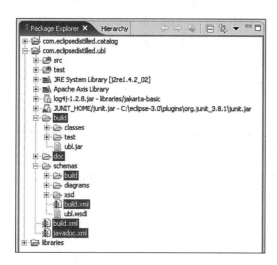

Figure 12-13   Package Explorer view showing three build files in the UBL project. The doc and build folders are created when running Ant.

12.7 Contributions

Many tools are available that analyze code and produce reports of the results. This kind of analysis is often included as part of an automated build file to detect problems and audit compliance with your team's standards and best practices. The PMD tool is available as both an Eclipse plug-in and an Ant task.

PMD is a utility for finding problems in Java code, which it achieves through static analysis—that is, analyzing the source code without running the program.

PMD comes with a number of analysis rules that you can run on your source code, or you can write your own rules to enforce coding practices specific to your organization. For example, if you are doing EJB programming, you could write a PMD rule that would flag any creation of `Thread` or `Socket` objects. PMD scans Java source code and looks for potential problems such as

❍ Empty `try`, `catch`, `finally`, or `switch` blocks

❍ Unused local variables, parameters, and private methods

❍ Empty `if` or `while` statements

❍ Overcomplicated expressions, e.g., unnecessary `if` statements, or `for` loops that could be `while` loops

❍ Classes with high Cyclomatic Complexity measurements

Download an Eclipse plug-in for PMD at: *pmd.sourceforge.net/index.html*

12.8 References

Hatcher, Erik, and Loughran, Steve. *Java Development with Ant*. Greenwich, CT: Manning, 2003.

Massol, Vincent. *JUnit in Action*, Chapter 5 Automating JUnit. Greenwich, CT: Manning, 2004.

Copeland, Tom. *Static Analysis with PMD*. See *www.onjava.com/pub/a/onjava/2003/02/12/static_analysis.html*

CHAPTER 13

Team Ownership with CVS

Team ownership is an essential part of agile development. All source code is available for contribution by any team member, and frequent, short iterations require that code be committed to the repository for continuous integration and testing. Eclipse supports this practice with generalized APIs for team repositories and a complete implementation of those APIs for the open source Concurrent Versions System (CVS).

This chapter explains how to share your projects using CVS team capabilities built into the workbench. Other repository client implementations are available as Eclipse plug-ins that work in a similar way and share common views for repository synchronization and code comparison; see the section entitled "Contributions" at the end of this chapter.

In this chapter, we'll see how to

○ Use best practices for successful code sharing with CVS

○ Add a new repository location and share your projects

○ Check out projects contributed by other team members

○ Synchronize changes between your local workspace and the repository

○ Assign tags and check out versions of a project

13.1 Team Programming with CVS

CVS is one of the most widely used team repositories and is especially well suited for distributed teams using the Internet for connectivity. It is easy to install on a server for small ad-hoc project teams that need to coordinate their development activities, or on a notebook computer for versioning private work. Because CVS is open source and used by many other open source projects—including Eclipse—many developers are already familiar with its use, and good documentation is available at no cost to you.

Team repositories use a client-server architecture for sharing files and coordinating interaction among users. The client side is built into the Eclipse workbench as plug-ins that provide views and preferences to

○ Configure one or more repository locations with protocols and user authentication for secure access

○ Share existing local projects by committing files to the repository

○ Browse repository contents and check out projects for local use

○ Synchronize your workspace contents with the repository by retrieving updates from others, committing your changes, and resolving conflicts

○ Compare the content of a local file with its counterpart in the repository

○ Review a history of revision dates and notes for each file

These tasks are explained in detail for CVS, although most of the activities are similar when using other repositories. We'll review CVS server installation and best practices before proceeding with sharing our product catalog and UBL component library projects.

13.1.1 CVS Server

A CVS server must be accessible by team members that want to share files. However, server connectivity is required only when committing or updating files, so you can still work successfully on a notebook computer with intermittent network access. Your Eclipse workspace contains a copy of all resources checked out from the repository. See the References at the end of this chapter for Web sites where you can download the CVS server and associated documentation.

CVS servers are most widely deployed on Linux, which is the primary platform used when developing CVS itself (*www.cvshome.org*). A CVS client is built into Eclipse and runs on any platform where the Eclipse workbench is available. Most organizations use a Linux CVS server for large projects, but a port to the Windows platform, called CVSNT, is gaining popularity. You can also realize significant benefits by installing a CVS or CVSNT server on your personal computer and versioning private, single-developer projects.

CVS installation and secure configuration on Linux is beyond the scope of this book, but see *Open Source Development with CVS* (Bar & Fogel, 2003) for an excellent guide to its installation and use. Ask your administrator for connection information if CVS is already used in your organization. If you are new to CVS and want to follow along with this chapter while working on the Windows or Mac OS X platforms, a brief introduction to installing CVSNT is included here. The client side of CVS included with Eclipse works the same way, regardless of the operating system where the server is running.

13.1.1.1 CVSNT Server Installation

CVSNT (*www.cvsnt.org*) is not officially supported by Eclipse (the Linux release of CVS from *www.cvshome.org* is supported), but many developers use it and get good results. CVSNT development began as simply a port of CVS 1.10 and then 1.11 to Windows. However, use of "NT" in the name is misleading because CVSNT is now available on Windows, Mac OS X, Solaris, HPUX, and Linux. The description here is based on CVSNT 2.0.51d for Windows.

(As this book was going to press, the Eclipse project announced that CVSNT will officially be supported, beginning with CVSNT version 2.0.58b and Eclipse version 3.1.)

Download and execute the Windows CVSNT setup program to install the server on your computer. It runs as a Windows service and includes an administration utility for starting or stopping the server and configuring its options. As shown in Figure 13-1, you must add a repository location before connecting from Eclipse. The first column is the alias name of the repository as seen by clients. The second column is the actual location of the repository root on the server machine. We chose an alias name that mimics a common convention used for repository locations on Linux servers. The repository root location can be anywhere on your file system; we use C:\cvsroot in this configuration.

More detailed CVSNT installation instructions are available at *www.cvsnt.org/wiki/InstallationTips*.

When using CVSNT with Eclipse, you must also check one option on the **Advanced** tab, as shown in Figure 13-2. The option **Pretend to be a Unix CVS version** allows Eclipse CVS clients to use repository alias names instead of absolute file path locations.

Figure 13-1   Add a new CVSNT repository.

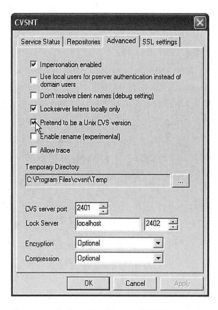

Figure 13-2   Configure CVSNT to work with alias repository names (required by the Eclipse client).

13.1.2 CVS Workflow

CVS uses an *optimistic model* for coordinating work among team members. Any member of the team can make changes to any resource to which he or she has access. Because two team members can commit changes to the same resource, conflicts can occur that must be resolved by the second committer. This system is called optimistic because it is assumed that these conflicts are rare.

The optimistic model works very well for most projects. Conflicts are rare when using good object-oriented design practices because it's unlikely that two developers will modify the same class responsibilities at one time. You will encounter minimal conflicting changes if you follow this workflow while using CVS:

1. **Start fresh.** Before starting work, *update* the resources in your workspace with the latest from the repository.

2. **Run all unit tests.** Run the unit tests and be sure that they all pass. If the system is broken when you start, you'll have more difficulty testing your own changes.

3. **Make changes.** Add, delete, and edit resources in your local workspace. If necessary, write new unit tests that exercise the new behavior. Debug until the new feature is working successfully.

4. **Run all unit tests again.** Run all unit tests again to ensure that none of the changes broke other components that you thought were unrelated.

5. **Synchronize.** When you are ready to commit your work, *synchronize* with the repository. First, examine incoming changes and add them to your local workspace. Resolve conflicts. Rerun unit tests to verify integrity of what you are about to commit. Finally, *commit* your changes.

Many developers synchronize with the repository several times per day, perhaps only to retrieve changes by others without committing work in progress. By doing so, you detect conflicts early in the cycle, and you can either merge changes with your own or discuss mutually agreeable modifications with the other committer.

The significance of unit testing in this workflow underscores the importance of having an automated test suite and adopting a strategy for continuous testing, as explained in Chapter 10, "Continuous Testing with JUnit." A key part of successful team development is each member being committed to the quality of the whole project, not just his or her own lines of code. You run all tests for a module—whether or not you wrote the code or the test—before and after making modifications.

> **Tip:** The golden rule of shared development is: *Don't break the build!* Test the complete integration build with your changes and the latest repository updates *before* committing your changes to the repository.

13.2 Sharing Your Projects

When you join an existing team, it's likely that all of the projects you will work on are already in a repository. Add that repository location to your workspace configuration and check out the relevant projects, or check out all of the projects required to perform an integration build when you test your code.

Alternatively, you may have developed a new project in your private workspace and may now be ready to share it with other team members. This is the case with our product catalog and UBL component library projects. In addition, you can share other projects containing JAR libraries and Eclipse configuration files needed by other members.

13.2.1 Add a Repository Location

A CVS repository location is not a live connection to a server, but a description of the repository location and user authentication for establishing a connection. A connection is opened and maintained only as long as required to complete a single command, such as committing files or retrieving a file's status. This is similar to the way a Web browser connects to an HTTP server when retrieving a new page.

Open the **CVS Repository Exploring** perspective, where you will see the **CVS Repositories** view, as shown in Figure 13-3. Initially there are no locations available, so add a new one for your team's repository. Right-click within the view and select **New > Repository Location...** from the context menu.

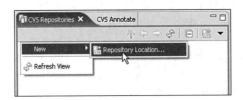

Figure 13-3   Add a new repository location.

In the **Add CVS Repository** wizard, shown in Figure 13-4, enter the host, repository path, and user authentication as provided by your CVS server administrator. If you installed a local CVSNT server, then a `localhost` server will be used. The default `pserver` connection type is probably correct, unless your team uses another authentication protocol such as SSH.

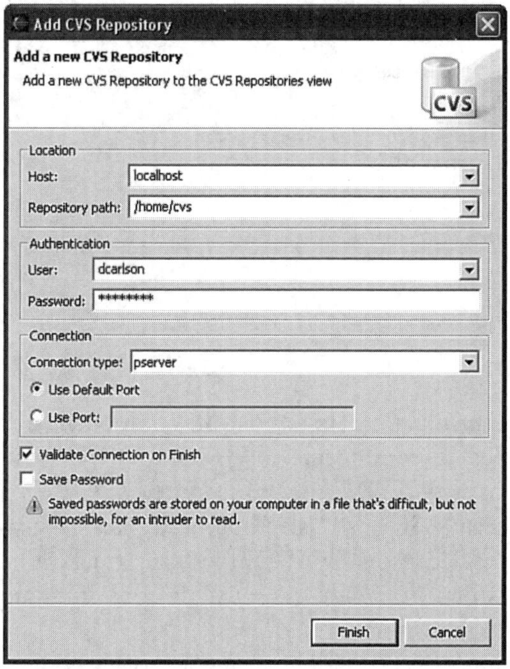

Figure 13-4   Add a new repository location.

Click **Finish** to add this repository location, after which you will see it listed in the **CVS Repositories** view. Right-click on the location and select **Properties** to change the connection parameters at a later time.

The projects required for your work may be stored at more than one repository location. The primary location is usually managed by your organization to hold your team's work. However, it's becoming common to also work with one or more open source projects that are included as a library or component in your application.

You could download the binary or source file distribution for an open source project, as we did when incorporating Apache Axis into our work in Chapter 6, "Java Project Configuration." However, if you are working with the latest revision of an active development stream, then it may be preferable to pull that project's code directly from its CVS repository and synchronize your workspace periodically to review and update changes. You can also create and submit patches for bug fixes and enhancements, even if you are not authorized as a committer to that repository location.

You will use an anonymous user name when connecting to most open source project repositories; this gives you read-only access to the repository contents. To connect to the Apache Jakarta CVS repository (see *jakarta.apache.org/site/cvsindex.html*), use these location parameters:

```
Host:               cvs.apache.org
Repository path:    /home/cvspublic
User:               anoncvs
Password:           anoncvs
Connection type:    pserver
```

13.2.2 Share Projects

Our next task is to share the product catalog and UBL component library projects in a CVS repository. Before committing any files to the repository, you should review the file types in each project. Each file stored in CVS is flagged as either ASCII or Binary (the term ASCII is misleading; it applies to any encoding of text files). This is significant because only ASCII files keep track of line-by-line differences in the revision history. In most cases, any file containing text should be configured as ASCII in the repository.

It's best to set the file content types before sharing a project because you can set global preferences by file extension. If you are sharing a Java project that contains only standard Eclipse configuration files and .java source code, then there is nothing to do; these file extensions are already configured properly. However, our UBL project contains other text files with extensions .xsd and .wsdl that are undefined. Undefined files are stored as Binary content and will not support line-by-line comparison or merging of conflict differences. Configure these file extensions as ASCII before sharing the UBL project.

ASCII Versus Binary: Set the content type by extension on the **Team > File Content** preferences page. After sharing a project with the repository, change this setting for individual files using the context menu **Team > Change ASCII/Binary Property...**.

Now we are ready to share the project. Right-click on the `com.eclipse-distilled.ubl` project in either the **Navigator** view or the **Package Explorer** view and select **Team > Share Project....** On the first page of the wizard shown in Figure 13-5, select the repository location where this project will be stored. The Apache CVS location is listed in this view, but you would not be allowed to share your project here because you are authenticated for read-only access.

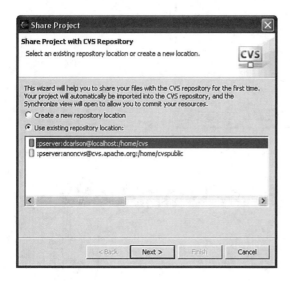

Figure 13-5   Select a repository location where the project will be shared.

We will use the project name as the CVS module name, but you could enter a different module name in Figure 13-6. The CVS module name appears in the **CVS Repositories** view when browsing repository contents. It's not necessary for the Eclipse project name to equal the module name, but this is a convenient common practice. This is also a reason for using qualified project names in your workspace (e.g., `com.eclipsedistilled.ubl` instead of simply `ubl`), which assures unique and descriptive module names when shared in CVS.

Your final step is to select which project resources are committed to the repository. As shown in Figure 13-7, press the **Commit All Changes...** toolbar button, or select one or more resources (files or folders) in the left pane and select **Commit...** from the context menu. If you had chosen an existing repository module when sharing this project, the right pane would be filled with the module's contents, which might duplicate the project contents you are now committing. You could then compare individual files and commit only those that are new.

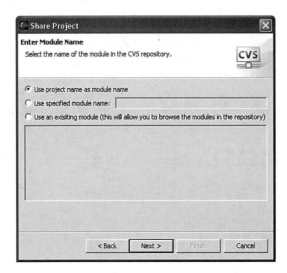

Figure 13-6   Specify the CVS module name.

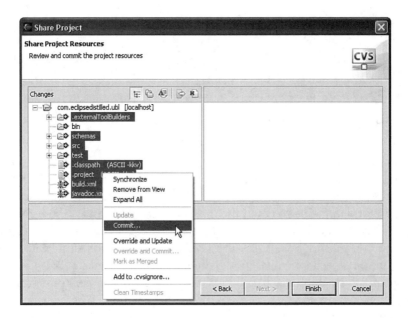

Figure 13-7   Commit selected project resources to the repository.

All of the `bin` folder contents are derived during a project build, so these files are not shared in the repository. When another team member checks out this project, it is built automatically and the `bin` folder is filled. Instead of omitting this folder each time you share or synchronize a project, it is easier to instruct CVS to ignore specified files or folders in your projects. You must make this selection before those files are committed to the repository. Select the `bin` folder in a project and choose **Team > Add to .cvsignore...** from the context menu. You can choose this command while sharing resources in Figure 13-7 or from the **Navigator** or **Package Explorer** views. The resulting dialog is shown in Figure 13-8.

Figure 13-8   Add the `bin` folder name to the list of ignored resources.

When you click **OK**, a file named `.cvsignore` is added to the parent folder containing this resource. It is a simple text file, with each line containing the name or pattern of ignored resources *in that folder*. If you need to ignore resources in other folders, even if those resources have the same name and are in subfolders, each folder must contain its own `.cvsignore` file. You can easily edit the `.cvsignore` file from the **Navigator** view and add, remove, or modify ignored resources.

Alternatively, you can instruct CVS to ignore all resources fitting a specified pattern (e.g., "bin" or "`*.log`") in the entire workspace by adding these patterns to the **Team > Ignored Resources** preferences page. The downside of this approach is that you cannot instruct CVS to *not* ignore a pattern in a special case. For example, you may have a library project where the `bin` folder contains binary files that you do want to save in the repository.

It's helpful to include project configuration files such as `.project`, `.class-path`, and `.cvsignore` when committing Eclipse projects to the repository. By following this approach, new team members check out projects that build successfully in Eclipse without additional configuration. Those new team members are productive in a short time, even when new to Eclipse and before reading Chapter 6 of this book.

You can also export and share Eclipse preferences and other configuration files that span the entire workspace. In the section of Chapter 6 entitled "Create Shared User Libraries," we created a user library that groups together several Apache Axis JAR libraries for quick configuration and reference. To share this definition with other team members, create a new simple project in your workspace (it does not need to be a Java project) named `eclipse-config`. Then export the user library definitions into a file named `EclipseDistilled.userlibraries` and save that file in the new project. This project appears as in Figure 13-9.

Figure 13-9   Create and share a project containing workbench settings.

Share `eclipse-config` to the CVS repository as a new module and notify other team members to check it out along with the Java projects. They can then import the user library definitions from this file.

One more dependency is required before others can build our projects. The Apache Axis libraries and the Jakarta log4j library are located in a separate project named `libraries`. In Chapter 6, we created the following file structure and added a new simple project linked to the `libraries` folder:

```
/eclipse-contrib/
    libraries/
        axis-1.2beta/
        j2ee/
        jarkata-basic/
        jakarta-j2ee/
```

We'll share the `libraries` project to CVS in the same way as the other projects. Other team members simply check out this project into a linked folder at `/eclipse-contrib/libraries`. Any projects that use a relative build path to JAR files in the `libraries` folder, as we did when referring to `log4j-1.2.8.jar` in the `com.eclipsedistilled.catalog` project, will be intact in others' workspaces.

13.2.3 Team Project Sets

It becomes increasingly difficult to get new team members started when the number of projects in your workspace grows. In addition, large repositories may contain dozens or hundreds of modules, and it's difficult for others to find the projects necessary to fulfill all dependencies. This problem is resolved by using a *team project set.*

Select **File > Export... > Team Project Set** from the workbench menu. In the resulting wizard dialog, choose the projects from your workspace that are part of a team project set and save the project set definition to a file named, by default, `projectSet.psf`. Save this file into the `eclipse-config` project created in the previous section and commit it to CVS. Other team members simply check out the `eclipse-config` project and use the project set file to import all other project dependencies in a single step, using the menu **File > Import... > Team Project Set.**

13.2.4 CVS Metadata Files

When you share a project with CVS, additional subfolders and files are added to contain metadata used by CVS operations. These metadata files are not unique to Eclipse; they are also used by other CVS client tools, including the command-line CVS programs available from *www.cvshome.org.* If you perform CVS operations from the command line or from an Ant build file, the metadata file changes will be recognized the next time you synchronize with the repository in Eclipse. Similarly, if you perform CVS operations in Eclipse, the metadata changes will be recognized when using the command-line tool at a later time.

Eclipse views are designed to hide these CVS metadata, so you will not see the files from the **Package Explorer** or the **Navigator**. However, you will see the metadata when viewing files from your operating system. As shown in Figure 13-10, a folder named CVS is added within each folder committed to the CVS repository.

These CVS metadata folders can be a problem if you want to create a ZIP or JAR archive from shared project files. For example, you may want to create a ZIP file of your project source files to share with developers who do not have access to your repository or a JAR file of your bin folder contents. Eclipse includes an export wizard that filters out CVS metadata while creating archives.

Figure 13-10   CVS metadata folders and files as seen from Windows Explorer.

Select **File > Export...** from the workbench menu and then select **Zip file,** **JAR file,** or **File system.** The export wizard displays the page shown in Figure 13-11, and the resulting ZIP file will not include the CVS metadata files.

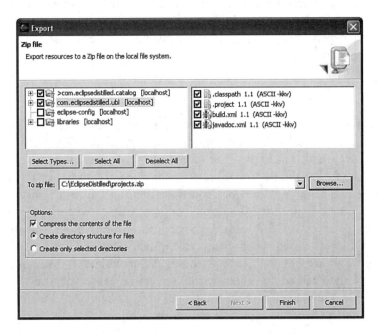

Figure 13-11   Export project files to a ZIP archive without CVS metadata files.

13.3 Check Out Projects from CVS

After you have shared all necessary projects, libraries, and configuration files to a version control repository, other team members can check these out to review, contribute, and test the application. When checking out a module from CVS, you copy all files from a selected branch into a corresponding project in your Eclipse workspace. Eclipse creates the necessary CVS metadata in your project to remember the repository location, branch, and dates used to synchronize changes back to the server.

It's best to work through the remainder of this chapter with another team member. However, you can also use two separate workspaces on your computer that represent two independent views of the repository state. In the following examples, the first user name is dcarlson, and the second user name is mrichards. CVS keeps track of each revision made by these two users. After mrichards checks out the files shared originally by dcarlson, we'll synchronize independent changes made by each user.

> **Tip:** If you'd like to try the examples in this chapter while working alone, create a new workspace on your computer and start two instances of the Eclipse workbench at the same time. One workspace cannot be opened twice, but several instances of Eclipse can be running with different workspaces. If you are using a localhost CVS server, create two user accounts on your computer so that you can differentiate between user logins to CVS.

The second user named mrichards should create a new Eclipse workspace following the directions in Chapters 2 and 3. Start the Eclipse workbench with that workspace, add a repository location, and use the CVS import wizard to populate the projects.

1. Add a repository location in the CVS perspective, as in the previous section entitled "Adding a Repository Location," except the user name is mrichards instead of dcarlson.

2. Select **File > Import...** from the workbench menu and pick **Checkout Projects from CVS** as the import source. The first page of the checkout wizard is shown in Figure 13-12. Choose or create the repository location where your team project is stored.

Figure 13-12 Select the repository where the project is located.

3. The next checkout wizard page shown in Figure 13-13 prompts you to select the module to be checked out from CVS. It's usually best to browse the repository modules for your choice, although another member of your team may have provided the exact module name, in which case the first option can be used.

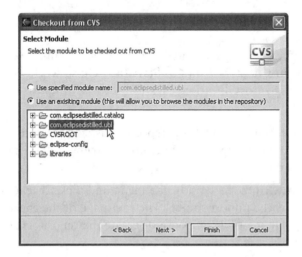

Figure 13-13 Select the CVS module to be checked out.

4. Check out the module as a new project in your workspace having the same name as in CVS, as shown in Figure 13-14. You could specify a project name that is different from the corresponding CVS module, but it's usually best to keep these names the same.

We included the .project file when sharing the projects with CVS. This file contains Eclipse metadata about the project nature (e.g., Java) and configuration details required to build its output. When the project is checked out, the .project file is also retrieved and used to create an identical configuration.

If you check out CVS modules that were not created by Eclipse, or where the .project file was not checked in, then the first option in Figure 13-14 can be used to invoke the **New Project Wizard,** where you specify the kind of project that will contain these files. You can also use the third option to check out the files into a folder of an existing project in your workspace.

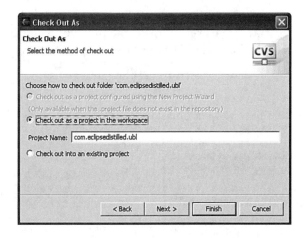

Figure 13-14   Check out as a new project having the same name as in CVS.

1. Select the project location on your computer, as shown in Figure 13-15. The default location is within the workspace folder, although you can assign a different path outside of the workspace. A similar option exists whenever you create a new project.

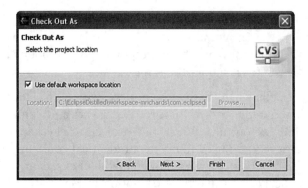

Figure 13-15   Select the project location on your computer; the default location is within the
workspace folder.

Sometimes you want to check out a module representing a particular released version or as of a certain date. Versions in CVS are tagged with a label that captures a snapshot on the tag date. However, most of the time you want the latest revision of each file; this is called the HEAD tag in CVS.

1. Choose the HEAD tag in Figure 13-16 to get the latest revision of each file in our project.

2. Click **Finish** to create a new project and check out the files.

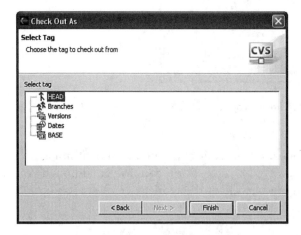

Figure 13-16   Check out the main HEAD tag, sometimes called the "trunk."

There is an alternative approach to selecting which project and version you want to check out from CVS. Expand the HEAD tag for a repository location in the

CVS Repositories view, right-click on a module, and choose **Check Out As...**
from the menu, as shown in Figure 13-17. This opens the wizard directly to
Figure 13-14, and the process continues the same from there. Using the **Check
Out** command is even simpler; it immediately checks out the HEAD tag of the
selected CVS module into a project with the same name.

Figure 13-17   An alternative approach to checking out a project from CVS. Use **Check Out** or
Check Out As... commands from the context menu in **CVS Repositories**.

You will now see `com.eclipsedistilled.ubl` as the only project in your
workspace. Because the `.project` file was included in the files retrieved from the
repository, Eclipse will try to build this Java project immediately after checkout
is complete. However, you will see errors listed in the **Problems** view that are
caused by missing dependencies. This project requires the log4j JAR library and
the Apache Axis user-defined library in its build path.

We shared the `libraries` project in CVS; check it out to get the complete
set of third-party JAR files used by your team. As described in Chapter 6, we also
downloaded source code and Javadoc files for each of these libraries, so this
project contains everything needed to gain maximum benefit from Eclipse navigation and Content Assist features. When new versions of these third-party
libraries are released, one team member downloads and commits the changes to
CVS, and all others synchronize their `libraries` project to receive updates.

If you want to use these JAR libraries in several Eclipse workspaces, then it's
helpful to assign the project path to a physical location that is outside of the
workspace. We set up our original project this way in Chapter 6, where the
`libraries` project is located at `C:\eclipse-contrib\libraries`. You also
have the option of setting a different location when creating a new project while

checking out a CVS module. In Figure 13-15, uncheck the default option and enter `C:\eclipse-contrib\libraries`.

If you've already checked out the `libraries` project for one workspace and now want to reuse it in a second workspace, don't import it from CVS; instead, import the existing project on your computer. Use the workbench menu **File > Import... > Existing Project into Workspace**. One project is now shared by two workspaces.

Finally, check out the `eclipse-config` project from CVS. This project contains the `EclipseDistilled.userlibraries` file used to define the Apache Axis user library. After retrieving it from CVS, use the **Java > Build Path > User Libraries** preference page to import the user library definition into your workspace.

One additional configuration issue may arise if you've made a different choice for the `libraries` project location. As explained in the "Create Shared User Libraries" section of Chapter 6, a user library definition uses absolute file paths for the JARs contained in it. If your JAR file locations are different from the team member who defined the user library, you'll need to edit the `EclipseDistilled.userlibraries` file to modify the paths for your computer.

After completing these steps, the `com.eclipsedistilled.ubl` project has all the required dependencies and will build successfully. You may need to clean the project's output in the workspace to force it to rebuild after finishing the user library configuration—select **Project > Clean...** from the workbench menu. If you knew these dependencies in advance, you could have imported the `libraries` and `eclipse-config` projects before importing the UBL project. Or better yet, you could use a team project set as explained in the "Team Project Sets" section earlier in this chapter.

13.4 Synchronizing with the Repository

The primary reason for using a source control repository is to share and coordinate the simultaneous work of several developers. As explained in the "CVS Workflow" section earlier in this chapter, CVS uses an optimistic model for coordinating work. *Synchronization* is the combined activities of updating, committing, and resolving conflicts between your workspace and the repository. A basic workflow was described for using CVS successfully while minimizing conflicts. The commands built into Eclipse support this workflow and many other variations that might be required for large, complex projects.

These synchronization capabilities are based on CVS client commands, but their realization in a graphical interface that maximizes developer productivity is an especially strong feature of the Eclipse IDE. We'll work through one set of tasks where `mrichards` will synchronize her workspace to update changes committed by `dcarlson` and then will resolve one conflicting change before committing her other work.

First, let's take a look at `mrichard`'s workspace, shown in Figure 13-18. Eclipse includes a general capability for adding *label decorations* to resources in several of its views. The CVS decorations give you information about synchronization status at a glance while working. However, they do not show you the status of repository updates made by others.

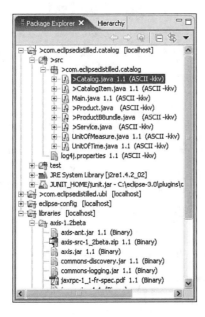

Figure 13-18   CVS label decorations showing added and changed resources.

The CVS decoration icons and labels are summarized as follows:

❍ **Repository host name.** Each project is suffixed with the repository host name where it is shared. The suffix "[localhost]" is shown here.

❍ **Files not shared.** Files that are not shared with the repository (typically new files created and not yet committed) are shown with a "?" overlaid on the file icon. The catalog project contains three such files. Files that are shared have a cylinder-shaped decorator icon.

❍ **Files changed locally.** Files that have been modified since they were last checked out (sometimes referred to as "dirty") are prefixed with ">". To make changes obvious when packages are collapsed, all containing packages, folders, and projects are also prefixed. Two files were modified in this project, in addition to the three new files.

○ **Revision number.** The CVS revision number is appended to each file name.

○ **ASCII vs. Binary.** Each file stored in CVS is flagged as either ASCII or Binary (the term ASCII is misleading; it applies to any encoding of text files). This is significant because only ASCII files keep track of line-by-line differences in the revision history.

You can turn these label decorations on or off using the CVS checkbox on the **Workbench > Label Decorations** preference page. You can also customize the CVS decorations on the **Team > CVS > Label Decorations** preferences page. For example, you can remove the revision number or the ASCII/Binary keyword suffix to reduce clutter in the labels.

> **Tip:** If your project includes text files with extensions such as `.bat`, `.sh`, or `.php`, you must add these extensions as ASCII content types in Eclipse. Make this change on the **Team > File Content** preferences page before committing new resources. Otherwise, these unknown types will be versioned as Binary files, and line-oriented text comparison will not be available.

We've now determined that local changes were made that must be committed to the repository. What we don't know yet is whether other developers have changed files in this project, possibly in conflict with changes made by `mrichards`. Open the context menu for the `com.eclipsedistilled.catalog` project, and you'll see three commands in the submenu under **Team:**

Synchronize with Repository... Open the **Team Synchronizing** perspective with this selection.

Commit... Commit the changed files in this selection to the repository. This command will fail if another developer has committed a conflicting change.

Update... Receive updates to files in this selection. If you also changed one of the updated files, CVS will automatically merge the changes.

Using these **Commit** and **Update** commands can yield unexpected results when conflicting changes exist in the repository. It's generally better to use the **Synchronize with Repository** command and review all incoming and outgoing changes. An alternative approach is to open the **Team Synchronizing** perspective from the workbench toolbar and specifically select the resources to be synchronized.

While in the **Team Synchronizing** perspective, you will find a synchronize command button on both the workbench toolbar and the **Synchronize** view toolbar. The drop-down list on the toolbar button contains a **Synchronize...** command that opens a dialog shown in Figure 13-19. Select the resources that you want to be included in the **Synchronize** view. In this example, we selected the **Workspace** scope that includes all projects. Press **Finish** to refresh the view with this selection.

Figure 13-19   Select the resources or working sets to be synchronized.

The **Team Synchronizing** perspective is shown in Figure 13-20. If any resources within the selected scope contain incoming or outgoing changes, then they are displayed in the **Synchronize** view. A benefit of using the workspace scope is that this view is refreshed automatically to show all shared files in your local workspace that have changed. To synchronize your workspace at any future time, switch to the **Team Synchronizing** perspective and review pending commits. Press the **Synchronize** toolbar button to refresh all remote changes coming from the repository, or select **Synchronize** from the context menu of one project to refresh only those remote changes.

For large projects, the number of incoming and outgoing files can become very large. Use the **Synchronize** view toolbar buttons to switch between four modes that filter displayed resources:

○ **Incoming.** Changes in the repository that you have not yet updated to your workspace.

○ **Outgoing.** Changes in your workspace that you are committing to the repository.

○ **Incoming/Outgoing.** Show incoming and outgoing changes.

○ **Conflict.** Both you and the repository have modifications to the same resource. Conflicts are displayed in all four modes, but this mode displays only conflicts.

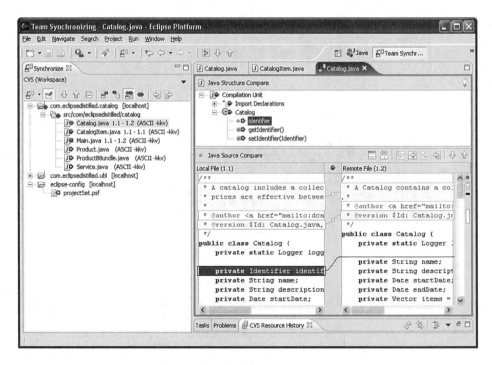

Figure 13-20   Team Synchronizing perspective showing incoming and outgoing changes, plus a **Compare Editor** for one file with conflicts.

Let's zoom in on part of the **Synchronize** view to analyze the icons that display repository status, shown in Figure 13-21. We are reviewing both incoming and outgoing changes. There is one conflicting change on the `Catalog.java` class;

this is shown with a red, double-headed arrow icon. When a conflict occurs, the red conflict icon is propagated up to all containing folders and project. If the project folder is collapsed, you can still see at a glance that one or more of its resources contain a conflict.

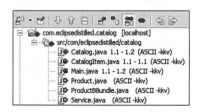

Figure 13-21   Synchronize view icons.

This project contains three new files that must be added to the repository; these are indicated by an arrow icon pointing from left to right and annotated with a "+" symbol. If a file had been deleted, there would be a "-" symbol on the arrow, meaning that it will be removed from the repository. In addition to the conflict, which is both incoming and outgoing, the Main.java file is an incoming change from the repository, indicated by an arrow pointing from right to left, and CatalogItem.java is an outgoing change.

The preferred workflow is as follows: first, examine incoming changes and add them to your local workspace. Then resolve conflicts. Next, rerun unit tests to verify the integrity of what you are about to commit. Finally, commit your changes.

The context menu on selected resources in the **Synchronize** view contains these commands:

> **Update.** All selected incoming and automergable conflicting changes are processed by updating local files with repository content. Conflicts that are not automergable will not be updated.
>
> **Override and Update.** This command operates on conflicts by replacing the local resources with the remote contents. Use this command with caution—use it only on conflicts where you want to throw away your local changes.
>
> **Commit...** All selected outgoing files with no conflicts are committed to the repository.

Override and Commit… This command operates on conflicts by replacing the remote repository resources with the local contents. Use this command with caution—use it only on conflicts where you want to ignore changes made in the repository by another developer.

When files are processed successfully by these commands, they are removed from the view. Files remaining will need manual attention. It is important to understand the difference between three kinds of incoming changes:

- ○ A *non-conflicting change* occurs when a file has been changed remotely but has not been modified locally.

- ○ An *automergable conflicting change* occurs when an ASCII file has been changed both remotely and locally (i.e., it has non-committed local changes) but the changes are on different lines.

- ○ A *non-automergable conflicting change* occurs when one or more of the same lines of an ASCII file or any part of a binary file has been changed both remotely and locally (binary files are never automergable).

When you select **Team > Update** on resources in the **Navigator** or **Package Explorer** views, the contents of the local resources will be updated with incoming changes of all of these three types. For non-conflicting and automergable conflicts, no additional action is required (for automergable conflicts, the changed local resource is moved to a file prefixed with ".#" just in case the automerge wasn't what the user wanted). However, for non-automergable conflicts, the conflicts are either merged into the local resource using special CVS specific markup text (for ASCII files), or the changed local resource is moved to a file prefixed with ".#" (for binary files). This matches the CVS command-line behavior but can be problematic when combined with the Eclipse auto-build mechanism. Also, it is often desirable to know what incoming changes there are before updating any local resources.

For all of these reasons, it's best to use the **Team Synchronizing** perspective for all repository updates. Running the **Update** command from the **Synchronize** view will never apply the CVS automerge operation to overlapping conflicts.

Resolve non-automergable conflicts by merging the remote differences into your local file manually, as follows:

1. Open a **Compare Editor** by double-clicking on the conflicted resource or selecting **Open in Compare Editor** from the context menu. The local workspace file is shown on the left, and the repository file is shown on the right. Examine the differences between the two.

2. In the text area of the editor, copy changes from the repository revision of the file to the local copy of the file. Select a change and use the toolbar button to **Copy Current Change from Right to Left,** or edit the local file manually by cutting and pasting content from the remote file.

3. Save the merged local file by selecting **Save** from the context menu in the left pane.

4. After you have merged all desired changes from the remote file into the local file, choose **Mark as Merged** from the context menu on this file in the **Synchronize** view. This will mark the local file as having been updated and will allow your changes to be committed.

In our `Catalog.java` class, the only conflict is in the class comment text, indicated by a red box around these changes in the **Compare Editor.** Merge these comments following the previous steps and then commit the file to CVS.

Before deciding whether to accept changes from the repository, you may want to review the date, author, and comments about those changes. Select a file in the **Synchronize** view and select **Show in Resource History** from the context menu. The **CVS Resource History** view, shown in Figure 13-22, is opened or refreshed with the selected file. The row starting with a "*" indicates the file revision in your workspace. Here you can see that the class comments were modified and a new property was added. You can enable the **Link with Editor** toolbar button to have the history displayed automatically for the current editor. This allows a quick review of comments while browsing repository updates.

For more detail on CVS synchronization, search the Eclipse online help for the topic "Synchronizing with the repository."

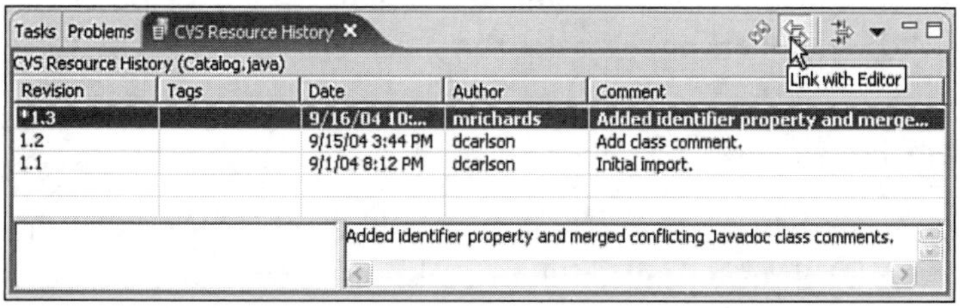

Revision	Tags	Date	Author	Comment
*1.3		9/16/04 10:...	mrichards	Added identifier property and merge...
1.2		9/15/04 3:44 PM	dcarlson	Add class comment.
1.1		9/1/04 8:12 PM	dcarlson	Initial import.

Added identifier property and merged conflicting Javadoc class comments.

Figure 13-22   Resource history in CVS repository.

13.4.1 Keyword Substitution

CVS can substitute some keyword patterns in your files, allowing you to keep revision information automatically up-to-date in your files. These keyword patterns are surrounded by dollar signs in your files. For example

```
/**
 * @version $Id$
 */
```

in a Java file comment expands to the revision identification from CVS:

```
/**
 * @version $Id: Catalog.java,v 1.1 2004/09/02 02:12:21 dcarlson Exp $
 */
```

CVS substitutes this keyword automatically whenever a new revision is committed to the repository. For a detailed explanation of CVS keyword substitution, and especially the alternative kinds of substitution, see page 291 of *Open Source Development with CVS* (Bar & Fogel, 2003).

13.5 Managing Versions

It's often helpful to assign a version to a project or set of related projects at the end of each development iteration and on the release date. This allows anyone to check out the correct revision for each file corresponding to a particular version milestone. They can then rebuild the entire system in that state. In CVS, each file has a revision number that is incremented independently of other files, so you cannot use those numbers as the basis for checking out milestone versions.

13.5.1 Tagging Files

A *CVS version* is marked by a *tag* assigned to all related files on a particular date. A tag assigns a label to the collection of revisions represented by the files in one developer's workspace. Those files should be completely up-to-date with repository changes so that the tag name is attached to the latest tested revisions.

Creating a CVS version does not freeze the tagged files or otherwise prevent you from committing and updating those files in the HEAD stream of the CVS module. In CVS, you can assign any number of version tags to files in the HEAD stream of a module to help you identify related sets of files at project milestone dates.

CVS has strict rules about what constitutes a valid tag name. The rules are that it must start with a letter and contain letters, digits, hyphens ("-"), and underscores ("_"). No spaces, periods, colons, commas, or any other symbols may be used.

Version a project by following these steps:

1. Select one or more projects from the **Navigator** or **Package Explorer** view in your workspace.

2. Select **Team > Tag as Version...** from the context menu.

3. When the **Tag Resources** dialog opens, enter the version name, e.g., "Iteration_2004-06-30".

4. Select the **CVS Repositories** view in the CVS perspective. Expand **Versions** and then one of the projects just versioned. Observe that there is now a version of this project named "Iteration_2004-06-30".

13.5.2 *Checking Out a Version*

Checking out a project version is the same as explained previously, except that now we choose a version tag instead of HEAD—the HEAD label is a special tag in CVS representing the "trunk" of a (possibly) branched revision tree.

To check out a version, start out with an empty workspace and use the file import wizard as before, but expand the **Versions** node in Figure 13-16 and select the version you want to check out. Alternatively, expand the **Versions** in the **CVS Repositories** view, shown in Figure 13-17, and select a project listed under the desired version. In most cases you'll want to check out all of the projects listed under that version in the repository to get a consistent configuration.

When you check out files representing a version, you cannot commit changes back to the HEAD stream. This is because other changes may have been made after the version tag was assigned. Instead, you must create a *branch* for changes to a version, or you must work with files checked out from the HEAD stream. If you do modify a file checked out from a version and attempt to commit it without creating a branch, you will receive a general CVS error message. Unfortunately, Eclipse does not return a message explaining why this is not allowed, and it does not prevent you from attempting the commit action.

13.5.3 Branching and Merging

Creating and working with a *branch* is similar to working with versions, except that changes committed to a branch remain independent of the HEAD (i.e., the "trunk") until they are merged back in. In fact, the HEAD is a special kind of main branch, and branches can split off of other branches at multiple levels.

Why would you want to use branches? Creating a branch and committing resources to that branch is useful in situations where you want to isolate a set of changes, but you still want to manage and share those changes in the source control repository. For example

○ Adding bug-fix changes to an old product version while the next release is under active development in the HEAD. Later, these bug fixes may need to be merged back in to the next release. This way you don't need to make duplicate changes in both the HEAD and bug-fix branch.

○ You may need to prototype a significant design change in a branch but only merge it back into the HEAD if the redesign is successful.

If we wanted to prototype the use of JAXB specifications instead of Apache Axis (which implements JAX-RPC) for generating Java classes from UBL schemas, we can create a branch as shown in Figure 13-23. Open this dialog by selecting all affected projects in your workspace and picking **Team > Branch...** from the context menu. When creating a branch, you must specify an existing version tag or create a new version at the same time. A branch always starts from a version tag in the repository.

Other developers can check out a branch from the repository in the same way they check out a version. Figures 13-16 and 13-17 contain a list of **Branches** immediately above the list of **Versions**. Changes made to files checked out from a branch are committed back to that branch in CVS, not to the HEAD.

You should consult other CVS documentation and user guides if you need to work with CVS branches. In particular, it's important to have a deeper understanding of best practices for branching and merging to be prepared for complexities that may arise. A good introduction to CVS branching in Eclipse is available online: *Branching with Eclipse and CVS* (Glezen, 2003).

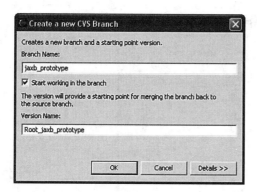

Figure 13-23   Create a new branch for selected projects in your workspace.

13.6 Creating and Applying Patches

A *patch* is a plain text file that contains differences between project files and the last revision checked out from the repository. These differences are not complete files (except in the case of new files), but only incremental add or delete notations for lines modified in the files. Patch files are not unique to Eclipse; they are available in most CVS clients and servers. However, the workbench support in Eclipse makes patches very easy to create and apply.

Patches allow developers to share work without storing it in a repository. This is helpful when you want to contribute to a project that is shared through a repository but do not have write access to the repository. You may have privileges for writing to the repository but don't have access while traveling. In this situation, you can create a patch and either email it to a developer who does have write access or attach it to a bug in the bug reporting system, depending on the process defined by the project. A developer who does have write access can then apply the patch to the project and commit the changes.

To create a patch, select the resource that contains modifications and choose **Team > Create Patch....** The dialog shown in Figure 13-24 is opened, where you choose how to save the patch and, on the next page, whether to recurse into subfolders or to include new files in the patch.

Although you can create a patch from any folder or individual file, it is easiest to select the project itself because the patch must be applied to the same resource from which it is generated. The patch should also be applied to the same file revisions that it is generated on, so steps should be taken to ensure that the patch is applied to the same resource line-up (the easiest way to do this is to create the patch on top of a version).

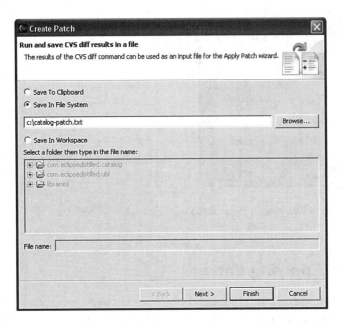

Figure 13-24   Create a patch from changes to files in your workspace.

To apply a patch, select the resource from which the patch was generated and choose **Team > Apply Patch....** The **Resource Patcher** wizard will open and indicate whether the patch can be successfully applied to files in your workspace. You can then choose which patches you want to apply by checking or unchecking them in the wizard. For more details on how patches are applied to files and ways to correct problems, search the Eclipse online help for "Working with patches."

13.7 Distilled

○ Eclipse includes a generic team API for supporting the client side of source control repositories. A complete CVS client is included, and other vendors have written Eclipse plug-ins for their repositories.

○ CVS uses an optimistic model for coordinating work among team members. This works best when following a workflow where you stay current with CVS updates and synchronize frequently to resolve conflicts as they occur.

○ Add CVS repository locations and browse available modules using the **CVS Repository Exploring** perspective.

○ When you share projects, include the configuration files, such as `.project` and `.classpath,` so that other team members check out a complete Eclipse project definition.

○ Also share third-party libraries and global workspace preference settings in CVS so that new team members can check out all required dependencies.

○ Synchronization is the combined activity of updating, committing, and resolving conflicts between your workspace and the repository. The **Team Synchronizing** perspective is provided to support all of these activities.

○ The **Compare Editor** allows you to review all incoming and outgoing changes and is essential for merging conflicts.

○ A project version is created by assigning a CVS version tag to a set of files in the repository. You can later check out all related files having the same tag.

○ Creating a branch tag is similar to creating a version, with the added capability of merging changes from the branch back into the main HEAD (i.e., the "trunk") at a later time.

○ Use CVS patches to exchange project differences with others when the CVS server is not available or when you do not have commit privileges.

13.8 Contributions

See the Team Repository Providers section of the Eclipse Community Projects Web page for a list of repository client plug-ins. Both open source and commercial contributions are available for most common source control tools, although not always with features as complete as those for CVS.

○ See *www.eclipse.org/community/index.html*

13.9 References

Bar, Moshe, and Fogel, Karl. *Open Source Development with CVS, 3rd Edition.* Scottsdale, AZ: Paraglyph Press, 2003. Available for free download in HTML and PDF formats at *cvsbook.red-bean.com/*

Concurrent Versions System (CVS) Web site, *www.cvshome.org/*

CVS for the Windows NT platform, *www.cvsnt.org*

Cederqvist, Per. *Version Management with CVS. www.cvshome.org/docs/manual*

CVS User's Guide, *www.loria.fr/~molli/cvs/doc/cvs_toc.html*

Glezen, Paul. *Branching with Eclipse and CVS.* IBM, 2003. *www.eclipse.org/articles/Article-CVS-branching/eclipse_branch.html*

Vesperman, Jennifer. *Essential CVS.* O'Reilly, 2003.

CHAPTER 14

Coding Standards

Assuring the quality of your team's development requires more than passing unit and integration tests successfully; it includes the full lifecycle of your software's maintenance and perception by its customers or users. The following objective guides the development of the Eclipse project:

> As with any product being built by a team, there are various areas where standards, conventions, and other guidelines can play a role in helping to ensure that the resulting product presents to developers and customers as a unified whole rather than as a loose collection of parts worked on by a variety of individuals each with their own styles and ways of working. *(from* Eclipse Standards, Conventions, and Guidelines*)*

The Eclipse project guidelines are stated in three parts:

Naming Conventions. How to name packages, classes, methods, variables, and constants.

Coding Conventions. Consistent practices for declarations, statements, indentation, whitespace, and other programming practices that influence the ability to understand, reuse, and debug source code.

Javadoc Comments. How to write documentation comments, which are especially important for public APIs.

Sun Microsystems's *Code Conventions for the Java Programming Language* document is often cited as a sound basis for software development. The Eclipse project, Apache Jakarta project, and many private corporate development teams base their Java guidelines on Sun's code conventions. Additional constraints are often added that provide more specific guidelines or extend the conventions into specifications such as J2EE. However, changes to the conventions are not arbitrary.

The Eclipse conventions "deviate only in places where our needs differ from Sun's; when we do deviate, we explain why."

Why have code conventions? Code conventions are important to programmers for a number of reasons:

- ○ 80% of the lifetime cost of a piece of software goes to maintenance.
- ○ Hardly any software is maintained for its whole life by the original author.
- ○ Code conventions improve the quality and readability of the software, allowing engineers to understand new code more quickly and thoroughly.

In this chapter, we'll see how to

- ○ Configure and use built-in Eclipse features for Java code formatting, templates, spell checker, and compiler warnings
- ○ Install and configure the Checkstyle plug-in to audit compliance with coding standards
- ○ Automate Checkstyle to run as part of Ant build files

14.1 Coding Java with Style

The readability of source code is especially important when following agile development practices that emphasize community ownership. In addition, readability is essential for open source projects such as Eclipse and Apache where the source code is delivered as a fundamental part of the documentation and provides examples for use and best practices.

But coding standards are about much more than a nice readable format. Following best practices can lead to higher-quality code with fewer bugs, and when there are bugs, they're easier to find and fix.

Several features are built into the Eclipse standard distribution that support or enhance adherence to your team's coding standards. These features increase developer productivity by reducing effort required to use the coding conventions.

- ○ **Code formatter.** Format a selection of source lines or Java files to follow a configured set of formatter rules.
- ○ **Code templates.** Configure comment text and code statements added to generated code.
- ○ **Spell checker.** Check the spelling of comments in your Java source files.
- ○ **Compiler warnings and errors.** Configure the Java compiler to produce warnings or errors for common problems beyond the usual syntax errors.

14.1.1 *Code Formatter*

Eclipse includes an extensive set of formatting rules for Java source code that are based on Sun Microsystems's *Code Conventions for the Java Programming Language*. The default formatting rules are built into the workbench, but you can copy and customize these for your team's conventions. Review or change the formatter on the **Java > Code Style > Code Formatter** preference page, as shown in Figure 14-1.

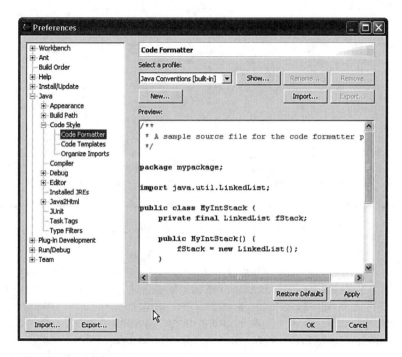

Figure 14-1 Setting Java code formatter preferences.

To customize the formatter, press the **New...** button and enter a name for your profile, such as "Eclipse Distilled". Choose a category of formatting rules where you can change rules related to a particular syntactic element and review its impact on sample code. For example, select the **White Space** category in Figure 14-2 and change the **Function Invocations** to insert a space before opening parenthesis. After making this modification, the sample code will change from `bar(x, y)` to `bar (x, y)`.

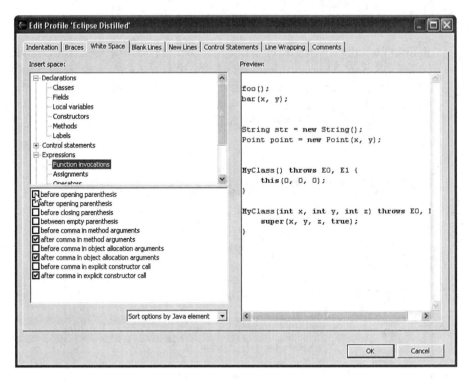

Figure 14-2   Edit Java code formatter preferences for **White Space**.

You can apply the formatter rules to a selection of lines in the current Java editor, for example to format one method copied from a code suggestion in a newsgroup message. Select the source lines and press **Ctrl+Shift+F**, or select **Source > Format** from the editor context menu. Invoking this command from the editor while no lines are selected will format the entire source file.

You can also format all code in every file of a package or project selected in the **Package Explorer** view. Select the desired packages and pick **Source > Format** from the context menu (no shortcut keys are assigned to the format command when invoked from the **Package Explorer**, most likely to avoid mistakenly formatting large amounts of code).

> **Shortcut: Ctrl+Shift+F:** Format the selected lines in the current Java editor, or format all lines if there is no selection. You can also invoke this command via the editor context menu **Source > Format**.

Because the code formatter rules must be applied consistently across team members, you should export your profile to a configuration file and check it into CVS. We created the `eclipse-config` project in Chapter 13, "Team Ownership with CVS," to hold these kinds of configuration files. After creating our customized formatter rules, the profile name in Figure 14-1 will display as "Eclipse Distilled" instead of "Java Conventions [built-in]". The **Export...** button will be enabled; press it and save the profile to `JavaFormatterProfile.xml` or a similar file name. Then commit it to CVS and notify other team members to synchronize this project and **Import...** the profile as their Java code formatter rules.

14.1.2 Code Style and Templates

Support for coding standards begins before formatting the resulting code. The Java preferences include two additional settings for **Code Templates** and **Code Style** of variable names. We'll review these settings by implementing support for two subprojects of Apache Jakarta.

The Turbine subproject (see the References at the end of this chapter) includes this coding standard: "When writing Javadocs for variables, try to keep the comment on just one line."

```
/** Documentation of this variable */
private int myVariable;
```

You can make this coding standard the default on comments generated for fields by modifying the **Fields** entry on the **Java > Code Style > Code Templates** preference page, as shown in Figure 14-3. Modify the default comment pattern to this:

```
/** Comment for <code>${field}</code> */
```

Insert a Javadoc comment by clicking on a field declaration in the Java editor and pressing **Alt+Shift+J** or by selecting **Source > Add Javadoc Comment** from the editor context menu. Generating a Javadoc comment for the field `name` gives the following result:

```
/** Comment for <code>name</code> */
private String name;
```

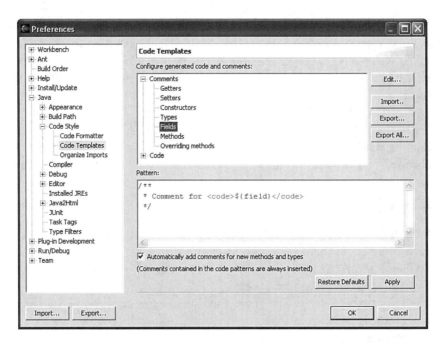

Figure 14-3   Modify a **Code Template** for comments generated on field declarations to satisfy the Jakarta Turbine subproject standard.

Shortcut: Alt+Shift+J: Insert a Javadoc comment for the declaration contained by the current cursor position: a class, field, or method. You can also invoke this command via the editor context menu **Source > Add Javadoc Comment**.

The Cactus subproject of Apache Jakarta includes the following two coding standards (*jakarta.apache.org/cactus/participating/coding_conventions.html*):

"Method parameters should be prefixed by the (for differentiating them from inner variables)."

```
public void someMethod(String theClassName)
{
    String className; // inner variable
}
```

"Class variables should not have any prefix and must be referenced using the this object."

```
public class SomeClass
{
```

```
    private String someString;
    public void someMethod()
    {
        logger.debug("Value = " + this.someString);
    }
}
```

Configure these coding standards on the **Java > Code Style** preference page, as shown in Figure 14-4. Edit the **Parameters Prefix list** to include "the" and then check the option to **Qualify all generated field accesses with 'this.'**

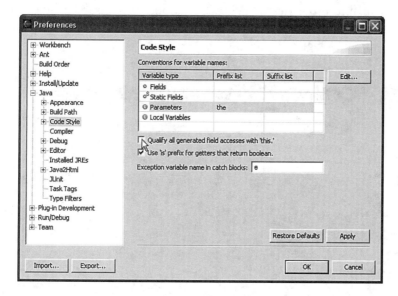

Figure 14-4 Modify two **Code Style** options to satisfy the Jakarta Cactus standards.

Using the same name field created previously, open the Java editor context menu and select **Source > Generate Getters and Setters....** The following two methods are generated in compliance with the Jakarta Cactus subproject standards.

```
/**
 * @return Returns the name.
 */
public String getName() {
    return this.name;
}
/**
 * @param theName The name to set.
 */
```

```
public void setName(String theName) {
    this.name = theName;
}
```

14.1.3 Spell Checker

For most of us, the availability of an automated spell checker is a welcome sight! A spelling option is built into the Java editor for checking the comments in your code. It's only available for Java source files, but it may be generalized for other file types in future releases of Eclipse. This option is disabled by default; you enable it and configure the dictionary in the **Java > Editor > Spelling** preference page, as shown in Figure 14-5.

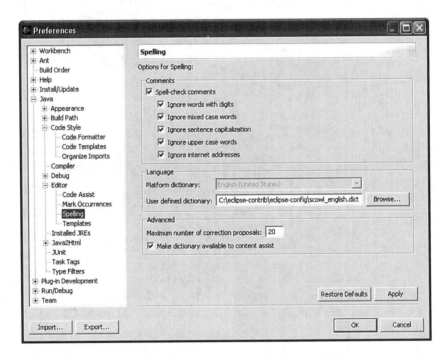

Figure 14-5   Configure the spell checker with a user-defined dictionary.

Three changes were made to this configuration:

1. Check **Spell-check comments** to enable this option.

2. Check **Make the dictionary available to content assist** to help you fix spelling errors.

3. Enter the location for a **User defined dictionary**.

The last change requires some explanation. Through the Eclipse 3.0.1 release, no default dictionary is included in the SDK download. The project members are searching for an open source dictionary contribution, and it probably will be available in a later release. For now, you can download the SCOWL dictionary word lists (see the References section at the end of this chapter) and add that dictionary to your workbench.

SCOWL is distributed as a set of word files divided into major categories for English, American, British, and Canadian words, and subsets within each of these. For most uses, you need to concatenate and sort several files into one dictionary. An easy way to do this is by using the following Linux command to concatenate all American and English words (or another set of word files appropriate to your region and language):

```
cat american-* english-* | sort > scowl_english.dict
```

If you don't have access to a Linux computer, use the open source Cygwin tools (*www.cygwin.com*) for a Linux-like environment on Windows, or with a bit more effort, you could obtain a similar result using a spreadsheet tool to concatenate and sort the word lists.

As you can see in Figure 14-5, we saved this dictionary file to

```
C:\eclipse-contrib\eclipse-config\scowl_english.dict
```

Recall from Chapter 13 that we created the `eclipse-config` project to hold workbench configuration files that are shared among team members. We created the project using a linked location within `C:\eclipse-contrib\`, which is the same folder that contains our `libraries` project. Add your dictionary to the team repository along with other files in `eclipse-config`. Before committing this dictionary file to CVS, be sure to add "dict" as an ASCII file type in the **Team > File Content** preference page. Configuring the dictionary as an ASCII file in CVS allows most conflicts caused by simultaneous edits to be resolved on a line-by-line basis and merged automatically.

All team members can share this same dictionary file and add project-specific words as needed. Each time you synchronize the `eclipse-config` project with CVS, you'll get the latest team dictionary.

Use Content Assist in Java comments to get assistance similar to that with Java coding. Press **Ctrl+Space** while the cursor is within or at the end of a word in a comment to obtain a list of suggestions. Content Assist is shown in Figure 14-6 with corrections for the misspelled word "colection."

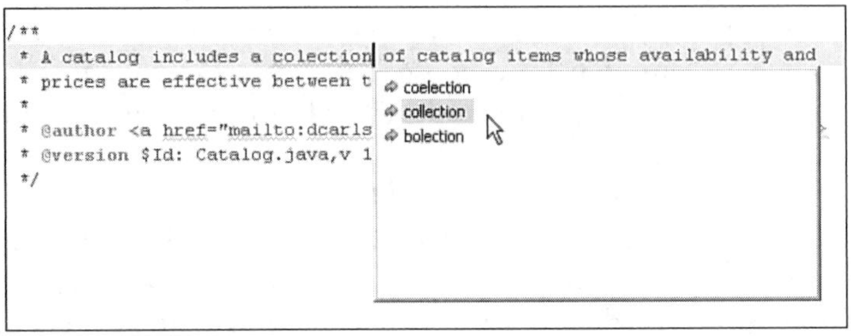

```
/**
 * A catalog includes a colection of catalog items whose availability and
 * prices are effective between t
 *                                  coelection
 *                                  collection
 * @author <a href="mailto:dcarls  bolection
 * @version $Id: Catalog.java,v 1
 */
```

Figure 14-6   Content Assist in Javadoc comment text.

This dictionary file is sufficient for most words in our project comments, with the exception of a few HTML markup keywords used in Javadoc. In Figure 14-6, the words "href," "mailto," and "dcarlson" are shown as spelling errors. Add these words to your dictionary by editing the text file and inserting the words at the correct sort position. Then commit it to CVS for your team.

14.1.4 Compiler Warnings and Errors

The Java compiler used in the Eclipse platform provides support for incremental parsing and validation while editing. It also includes many tests that go beyond basic compilation, and it issues warnings or errors about code usage. You can configure each compiler settings to **Ignore, Warning,** or **Error.**

The compiler settings for **Unused Code** are shown in Figure 14-7. Your team may choose more stringent criteria by issuing warnings for several problems that are ignored by default. For example, unused or unread private members should generate a compiler warning when present in the final release of your project.

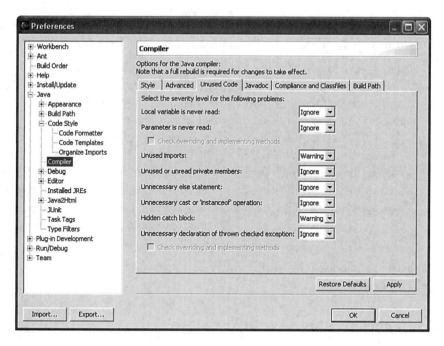

Figure 14-7 Set compiler warnings and errors for unused code.

14.2 Auditing Compliance

When auditing compliance with coding standards, you must ensure that style guidelines such as indentation and whitespace are followed. The code formatter in Eclipse helps satisfy these requirements. But compliance also requires that certain elements are present in your code, such as Javadoc comments for each class, field, and method. In addition, element names must follow stipulated patterns, such as class names beginning with an uppercase letter and method names beginning with a lowercase letter.

The code formatter provided in Eclipse only goes so far; you can't format what doesn't exist in the code. The formatter does not warn you about missing or extra elements in your code. That's the role of a style checker utility.

Discussing compliance with programming standards is often an uncomfortable topic for developers. It sounds a bit like Big Brother watching over your shoulder. However, following the conventions set by your team has a direct, positive impact on the outcome. The Eclipse project guidelines describe the importance of Javadoc comments in the code:

> *The specifications for the Eclipse platform APIs are captured in the form of Javadoc comments on API packages, interfaces and classes, methods and constructors, and fields. The Javadoc tool (running the standard doclet) extracts these specifications and formats them into browsable form (HTML web pages) which become the reference section of the documentation set describing the Eclipse platform to ISVs. As a consequence, the bar is significantly higher for API Javadoc than for non-API.* Sun's Requirements for Writing Java API Specifications *deals with required semantic content of documentation comments for API specifications for the Java platform. All Eclipse project APIs should follow these conventions. (from* Eclipse Standards, Conventions, and Guidelines*)*

We'll use the Checkstyle open source plug-in to audit compliance with our team's Java coding standards.

14.2.1 Configuring the Checkstyle Plug-in

Checkstyle was developed independently of Eclipse as a general-purpose style checker utility for Java. Another contributor built the Eclipse plug-in that adds UI support for setting preferences within your workbench and running Checkstyle automatically when your source files are modified. See the Contributions section later in this chapter for credits and download URLs.

The Checkstyle plug-in is distributed as a ZIP archive containing the plug-in folder, but it does not define an Eclipse feature for use with the workbench update facility. Follow the guidelines in the section "Installing Plug-ins Without Features" in Chapter 9, "Updating the Eclipse IDE," for installing plug-ins without features. After installing Checkstyle and restarting your workbench, the **Checkstyle** preferences page shown in Figure 14-8 will be available for configuring its rules.

Checkstyle includes a large set of style rules based on Sun's Java coding conventions, plus additional rules related to J2EE patterns. Over 200 style rules are defined, and it is extensible so that you can write new rules based on the Checkstyle parser and pattern matching logic. You can edit the built-in checks in the preference configuration, but it's better to clone these rules into your team's configuration.

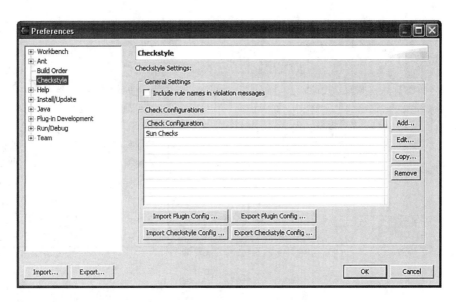

Figure 14-8   Customize your Checkstyle configuration.

Select the Sun Checks configuration and press the **Copy...** button to clone the default rules. A style rule editor is opened, as shown in Figure 14-9, where you should rename the configuration to your team's configuration, e.g., "Eclipse Distilled Checks."

The rules are classified into 14 categories. Not all of the available rules are activated in each category; press the **Add Rule** button to see a complete list of rules for the current category tab. Deleting a rule does not remove its definition—doing so only disables it in the current configuration. In Figure 14-9, we are editing the **Magic Number** rule in the **Coding Problems** category.

Each rule displays a description of its rationale. The **Magic Number** rule is described as "Checks that there are no *magic numbers*, where a magic number is a numeric literal that is not defined as a constant." Rules may include additional configuration properties that are unique for each rule type, such as which numeric literals to ignore and which data types to include. The idea of this rule is that numeric literals have semantic meaning that should be made explicit by a static constant name; not doing so leads to coding problems and bugs that are difficult to diagnose.

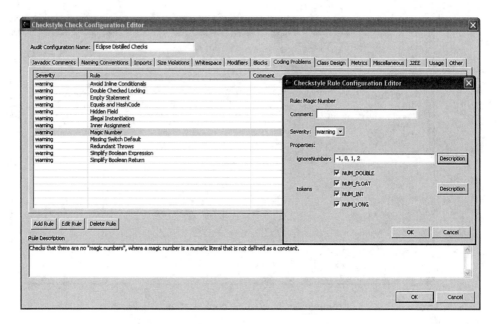

Figure 14-9   Edit Checkstyle rules in your configuration.

Press **Export Plugin Config...** and save the configuration in our `eclipse-config` project to share it with your team members via CVS. Other members use **Import Plugin Config...** to load it or to reload changes when your team's rules are updated. Note that different buttons are labeled as **Export/Import Checkstyle Config....** Use these commands to save or load configuration files used by the Checkstyle engine separate from the Eclipse UI, for example in Ant build files as explained in the section "Automating Checkstyle with Ant" later in this chapter. The plug-in developers expect to merge these two formats in a future release; currently, some plug-in specific information is lost when exporting via the second approach.

14.2.2 Running Checkstyle Rules

Installing and configuring the Checkstyle plug-in does not cause it to check your projects. Each project that you want checked must define one or more **File Sets** that specify which files are checked and which **Check Configuration** to use on those files. You may use several different configurations that tighten or relax particular rules for packages of code, instead of applying one policy uniformly across all code. We'll see a reason for this in the following example.

Activate checking using a project's **Checkstyle** property page, opened by selecting **Properties** from that project's context menu in the **Package Explorer**. Add a new **File Set,** as shown in Figure 14-10. A **File Set** defines a collection of source files and the **Check Configuration** used to audit them. The set is selected by either including or excluding files using regular expression filters. The expression tests each file's fully qualified name within a project, starting with the src folder. In this example, we've selected all Java source files within the datatypes package and its descendents by using this regular expression:

```
.*datatypes.*java$
```

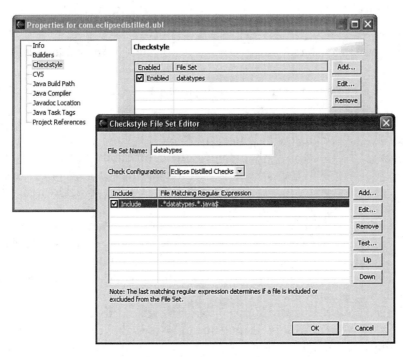

Figure 14-10 Add a Checkstyle file set to a project's configuration. This determines which files are checked by which configuration.

After a **File Set** has been defined, Checkstyle will run and audit its files. Violations are reported in the **Problems** view, as shown in Figure 14-11. Checkstyle will check source files each time a file is modified or when the Checkstyle configuration changes.

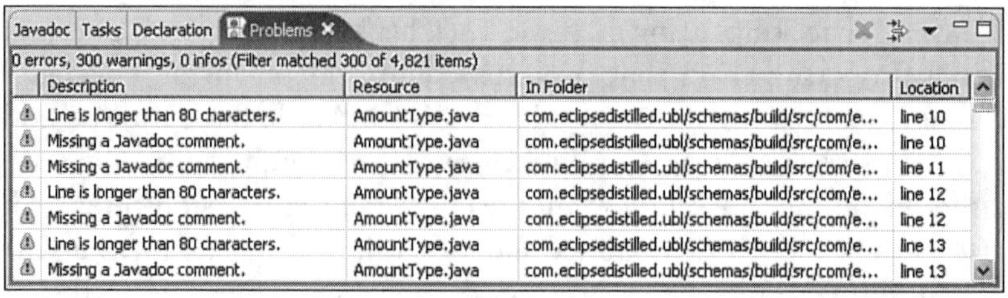

Figure 14-11   Problems displayed by Checkstyle.

We received 4,821 warnings about the code in these files! It appears that all of the warnings are for code generated by Apache Axis from the UBL schemas (see Chapter 12). A quick review shows that many violations are caused by

o Lines longer than 80 characters (true for most of the method declarations in this code).

o Javadoc missing on all field declarations.

o Javadoc missing on about half of the methods.

Return to the preferences in Figures 14-8 and 14-9 and create a new configuration named "Axis Checks" that removes these three audit rules. Modify the project **File Set** to use this configuration; saving the project properties causes Checkstyle to rerun. Now our warning count is down to 3,414 items. It looks like we're not out of the woods yet.

Another Checkstyle rule requires all method parameters to be `final`, with the rationale that code should never modify parameter values and the `final` modifier causes the compiler to enforce this rule. Although this is a reasonable rule, it is usually violated in practice. Reconfiguring our rules once more reduced the warning count to 3,008 items.

There are a few more simple violations related to use of whitespace, but we're getting down to several fundamental issues about the code structure generated by Axis. Maybe it's time to start a discussion thread on the Apache Axis developer's mail list.

Before we leave this topic there are several additional points to cover about Checkstyle configuration. When you activate Checkstyle in a project by defining **File Sets**, a new file named `.checkstyle` is added to the project. You won't see it in the **Package Explorer** view because all files beginning with "." are filtered out; it does appear in the **Navigator**. This file should be committed to the repository so that all team members share the same style rules.

The Checkstyle plug-in also adds a new entry to the project's **Builders** property page, as shown in Figure 14-12. This custom builder is implemented in the
plug-in's Java code and causes the checker to run on all relevant **File Sets** when
one of their files is modified.

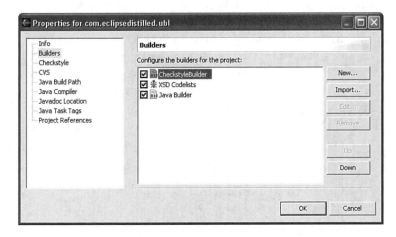

Figure 14-12   Project builder inserted by the Checkstyle plug-in. Uncheck this builder to
temporarily disable Checkstyle from running in auto-build mode.

There are several ways that you can control when and where Checkstyle is
run on each project:

○ Open the **Filters** for the **Problems** view and enable/disable the **Checkstyle
   Marker** (use of this view filter is described in Chapter 4, "Customizing
   Your Workbench"; the Checkstyle plug-in adds a custom marker type).
   Hiding these markers allows you to more easily review other problems in
   your code.

○ Enable or disable a file set in a project's Checkstyle properties page, as
   shown in Figure 14-10.

○ Divide a project's source files into two or more file sets that can be
   enabled or disabled independently to audit specific parts of your code
   during development. For example, use this technique to isolate code
   generated by Axis and to customize the rules applied to that file set.

○ Disable the auto-builder when not using Checkstyle rules on a project.

14.2.3 Automating Checkstyle with Ant

In Chapter 12, "Continuous Integration with Ant," we examined an Ant build file that could be used to run a complete project build inside or outside of Eclipse. That build file included execution of JUnit and creation of an HTML report presenting the unit test results. We'll follow a similar approach by running Checkstyle as an additional target in the same Ant build file. The Checkstyle JAR includes the custom Ant task used in this build file.

Add the following Ant target, named `checkstyle`, to the project build file we created in Chapter 12. No other changes are required; this target depends only on the `init` target that sets up several properties with directory locations. The `checkstyle` target selects all Java files in the project's `src` folder, runs Checkstyle using the default `sun_checks.xml` rules, produces an audit report in XML format, and finally transforms the XML data into an HTML report using an XSLT script.

```
<target name="checkstyle" depends="init"
        description="Run Checkstyle">
  <property name="checkstyle.reports.dir"
            location="${test.dir}/reports/checkstyle" />
  <delete dir="${checkstyle.reports.dir}" />
  <mkdir dir="${checkstyle.reports.dir}" />

  <property name="checkstyle-config"
    value="c:/eclipse-contrib/eclipse-config/checkstyle" />
  <property name="plugins"
    value="c:/eclipse-contrib/tools-plugins/eclipse/plugins"/>
  <property name="checkstyle"
    value=
"${plugins}/com.atlassw.tools.eclipse.checkstyle_3.4.1.0" />

  <taskdef name="checkstyle" classname=
             "com.puppycrawl.tools.checkstyle.CheckStyleTask"
           classpath="${checkstyle}/checkstyle-all-3.4.jar"/>

  <checkstyle config="${checkstyle-config}/sun_checks.xml"
              failureProperty="checkstyle.failure"
              failOnViolation="false">
    <formatter type="xml"
               tofile="${checkstyle.reports.dir}/report.xml" />
    <fileset dir="src" includes="**/*.java" />
  </checkstyle>

  <style in="${checkstyle.reports.dir}/report.xml"
     out="${checkstyle.reports.dir}/report.html"
     style="${checkstyle-config}/xslt/checkstyle-frames.xsl"/>

</target>
```

The HTML report of audit results for the `Party.java` class is shown in Figure 14-13. When a full project build is run using Ant, the results include HTML reports of both JUnit tests and the Checkstyle audit. By including these evaluations in the build archive, you keep a complete record of the project's status at that point in time.

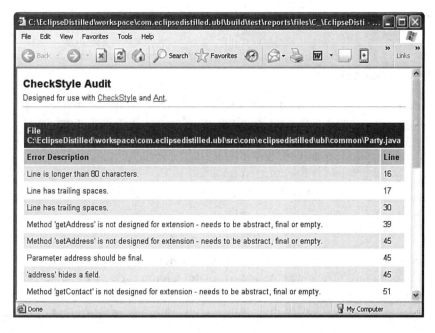

Figure 14-13 HTML report produced by the Checkstyle Ant task.

14.3 Distilled

○ Coding standards are important for collaboration among members of your agile development team and for the long-term maintenance of your software. These standards include conventions for naming, coding style, and Javadoc comments.

○ Eclipse includes built-in facilities that reduce the burden of compliance with these standards. A code formatter applies style rules, code templates insert Javadoc comments per your guidelines, and a spell checker catches comment typos. The Java compiler goes beyond syntax checking to warn you about unused code.

○ Share your formatter rules, code templates, and spell checker dictionary in the team repository to keep all team members coordinated.

○ Use the Checkstyle plug-in (or another similar contribution) to audit your code for compliance with the standards. Automate the style audit as part of a complete Ant build file.

14.4 Contributions

14.4.1 Checkstyle

Checkstyle is an open source tool written by Oliver Burn to help ensure that your Java code adheres to a set of coding standards. Checkstyle does this by inspecting your Java source code and pointing out items that deviate from a defined set of coding rules. It is available at *checkstyle.sourceforge.net/*.

David Schneider has written an open source plug-in to integrate Checkstyle with Eclipse. It is available at *eclipse-cs.sourceforge.net/*.

14.4.2 PMD Analysis Tool

The PMD tool is an open source tool that defines analysis rules that find problems in Java code; it was reviewed in the Chapter 12 "Contributions" section. There is significant overlap between the features of PMD and Checkstyle. Both perform static analysis of Java source code, but they use different approaches for extending the tools with new analysis rules.

The Eclipse plug-in for PMD is available at *pmd.sourceforge.net/index.html*.

14.4.3 Instantiations CodePro Advisor

CodePro Advisor is a commercial third-party Eclipse plug-in that offers these features:

Code Audit. Dynamic, extensible tools that detect, report, and QuickFix repair deviations or non-compliance with predefined coding standards, style, and conventions.

Dependency Analyzer. Automated tools that analyze and visually depict the dependencies between projects packages and types.

Code Metrics. Automated tools that measure and report on key indicators in a body of Java source code.

> **Javadoc Repair.** Automated dynamic tools that analyze, report, and suggest corrections for Javadoc within a body of source code.

CodePro Advisor is available at *www.instantiations.com/codepro/advisor.htm.*

14.5 References

Apache Jakarta Project, *Source Repositories.* See *jakarta.apache.org/site/source.html*

Eclipse Foundation. *Standards, Conventions and Guidelines.* See *dev.eclipse.org/*

Sun Microsystems. *Code Conventions for the Java Programming Language.* 1999. See *java.sun.com/docs/codeconv/*

Sun Microsystems. *Requirements for Writing Java API Specifications.* 2003. See *java.sun.com/products/jdk/javadoc/writingapispecs/*

Sun Microsystems. *How to Write Doc Comments for Javadoc.* 2003. See *java.sun.com/products/jdk/javadoc/writingdoccomments/*

SCOWL (Spell Checker Oriented Word Lists) is a collection of word lists split up in various sizes, and other categories, intended to be suitable for use in spell checkers. See *wordlist.sourceforge.net/*

Index

X-Z

informIT

YOUR GUIDE TO IT REFERENCE

Articles

Keep your edge with thousands of free articles, in-depth features, interviews, and IT reference recommendations – all written by experts you know and trust.

Online Books

Answers in an instant from **InformIT Online Book's** 600+ fully searchable on line books. For a limited time, you can get your first 14 days **free**.

POWERED BY
Safari
TECH BOOKS ONLINE®

Catalog

Review online sample chapters, author biographies and customer rankings and choose exactly the right book from a selection of over 5,000 titles.